MUSIC FOR A KING

MUSIC FOR A KING

George Herbert's Style and the Metrical Psalms

COBURN FREER

THE JOHNS HOPKINS UNIVERSITY PRESS
Baltimore and London

Copyright © 1972 by The Johns Hopkins University Press
All rights reserved
Manufactured in the United States of America

The Johns Hopkins University Press, Baltimore, Maryland 21218
The Johns Hopkins University Press Ltd., London

Library of Congress Catalog Card Number 76-179136
ISBN 0-8018-1290-9

To Mona

Contents

Preface

This will be brief, since the purpose and main assumptions of this book have proved broad enough to require elaboration in an introductory chapter. Here I would stress one point: in this book I have tried simply to study the affinities in form and matter between the versified translations of the Psalms and George Herbert's lyrics. I have not attempted to write a formal history of a genre in English poetry, much less an account of its influence. My reading of Herbert does recognize the historical dimension of his poems; but I have not made that dimension the only significant one in the determination of poetic meaning or poetic value.

In reading Herbert's poetry by way of the metrical psalms that precede it, one has to undertake the trip through Chaos itself, the rise of an English meter, the "new" poetry, the poetry of *discordia concors* and the poetry of formal meditation. Intelligent specialized studies appear on these topics each year; thanks to them I realize (now even more fully than when I began thinking about the subject) the nature of the risks my argument is running. There are, therefore, certain aspects of the subject that I have not treated at all, for example, the common musical elements of *The Temple* and the Psalms, or the thematic interconnections between *The Temple* and the Book of Common Prayer and the different texts of the Psalms, or the varied linguistic properties of stanza forms. In electing not to treat these and related subjects, I have made a tacit bargain with the reader; for I have not attempted to force all the poems of *The Temple* into my thesis, nor have I claimed that I have here the best and only reading of Herbert, the critical equivalent of Volpone's *oglio del Scoto*. The reading I propose, however, could be applied to more poems than are discussed here; rather than multiply examples needlessly, it seemed better in this space to stress a few central poems as models or representatives.

What virtues this book may possess could never have found expression without the work of other readers of Herbert, especially F. E. Hutchinson, Rosemond Tuve, Louis Martz, Joseph Summers, Robert Ellrodt, and Arnold Stein. More immediately, I am grateful for the good counsel and help I received during the composition and revision of the book. From the first, Arnold Stein has been unfailingly generous with his help, with his learning, encouragement, and good humor. Entering later, but such another, has been my colleague Walter King, always willing to prune my prose and share his wide reading. For these two in particular I hope the book can indicate some of my gratitude. Ben Drake shared photocopies and made literally dozens of comments, fruitful even in disagreement; E. L. Epstein suggested several corrections in detail in my comments on Sidney; E. G. W. Bill, Librarian of Lambeth Palace, answered questions on psalters; and Douglas Mills, Technical Services Director of the University of Montana Library, located and obtained numerous microfilms not in the library's regular holdings.

Portions of Chapter 2 on Sir Philip Sidney and the Countess of Pembroke have appeared, in somewhat different form, in *Language and Style* and *Style* respectively. I am obliged to the editors of these journals for permission to reprint. For quotations from other copyrighted material I have been granted permission by the following: the Clarendon Press, Oxford, for George Herbert's *Works*, revised edition (1945), edited by F. E. Hutchinson, for John Donne's *Divine Poems* (1952), edited by Helen Gardner, for Sir Philip Sidney's *Poems* (1962), edited by William A. Ringler, Jr., for *The Spectator* (1965), edited by Donald F. Bond, and for Surrey's *Poems* (1964), edited by Emrys Jones; Doubleday and Company for *The Psalms of Sir Philip Sidney and the Countess of Pembroke* (1963), edited by J. C. A. Rathmell; Alfred A. Knopf, Inc., for Wallace Stevens's *Collected Poems*, copyright 1954 by Wallace Stevens; Harvard University Press and Routledge and Kegan Paul, Ltd., for *Sir Thomas Wyatt: The Collected Poems* (1950), edited by Kenneth Muir. Special thanks are due to Dr.

E. B. Juel-Jensen for permission to quote from his text of the Countess of Pembroke's poem "To the Angell Spirit of Sir Philip Sidney."

I wish to thank also the Dean of Arts and Sciences and the Dean's Advisory Board of the University of Montana for a summer fellowship to work on the book and the University of Montana Foundation for the funds necessary to have the manuscript typed and copies prepared. I am especially grateful to the editors and staff of The Johns Hopkins University Press, who made many valuable suggestions.

My greatest and happiest debt is to my wife, whose good taste and general knowledge were helpful in countless ways, and it is to her that I dedicate the book.

Short Titles of Editions
and Frequently Cited Critical Works

Addison, *Spectator*   Joseph Addison, *The Spectator*, ed. Donald F. Bond, 5 vols. (Oxford: The Clarendon Press, 1965).

Augustine, *Expositions*   St. Augustine, *Expositions on the Book of Psalms*, ed. A. Cleveland Coxe, Vol. 8 in Nicene and Post-Nicene Fathers of the Christian Church (Grand Rapids, Mich.: Eerdmans, 1956).

Donne, *Divine Poems*   John Donne, *Divine Poems*, ed. Helen Gardner (Oxford: The Clarendon Press, 1952).

Dryden, *Poems*   John Dryden, *Poems*, ed. Bonamy Dobrée (London: Everyman's Library, 1966).

Ellrodt, *L'Inspiration*   Robert Ellrodt, *L'Inspiration Personelle et l'Espirit du Temps chez les Poètes Métaphysiques Anglais*, 3 vols. (Paris: José Corti, 1960).

Herbert, *Life and Works*   George Herbert, *Life and Works*, ed. G. H. Palmer, 2d ed., 3 vols. (Boston: Houghton Mifflin, 1915).

Herbert, *Works*   ———, *Works*, ed. F. E. Hutchinson, 2d ed. (Oxford: The Clarendon Press, 1945).

Martz, *Poetry of Meditation*   Louis L. Martz, *The Poetry of Meditation*, 2d ed. New Haven: Yale University Press, 1962).

Old Version   Thomas Sternhold, John Hopkins, W. Whittingham and Others, *The Whole Booke of Davids Psalmes* (London: John Daye, 1582).

Pembroke, *Psalms*   Sir Philip Sidney and the Countess of Pembroke, *Psalms*, ed. J. C. A. Rathmell (New York: Anchor Books, 1963).

Puttenham, *Arte of English Poesie* The *Arte of English Poesie*, ed. Gladys Doidge Willcock and Alice Walker (Cambridge: Cambridge University Press, 1936).

Rathmell, *The Psalms* J. C. A. Rathmell, *The Psalms of Sir Philip Sidney and the Countess of Pembroke* (New York: Anchor Books, 1963).

Sidney, *Poems* Sir Philip Sidney, *Poems*, ed. William A. Ringler, Jr. (Oxford: The Clarendon Press, 1962).

Smith, *Elizabethan Critical Essays* G. Gregory Smith, ed., *Elizabethan Critical Essays*, 2 vols. (Oxford: The Clarendon Press, 1904).

Stein, *George Herbert's Lyrics* Arnold Stein, *George Herbert's Lyrics* (Baltimore: The Johns Hopkins Press, 1968).

Summers, *George Herbert* Joseph Summers, *George Herbert* (Cambridge: Harvard University Press, 1954).

Surrey, *Poems* Henry Howard, Earl of Surrey, *Poems*, ed. Emrys Jones (Oxford: The Clarendon Press, 1964).

Tuve, *A Reading of George Herbert* Rosemond Tuve, *A Reading of George Herbert* (Chicago: University of Chicago Press, 1952).

Walton, *Lives* Izaak Walton, *Lives*, ed. George Saintsbury (London: Oxford University Press, 1927).

Wither, *Preparation to the Psalter* George Wither, *A Preparation to the Psalter* (London: Nicholas Okes, 1619).

Wither, *Psalmes* ————, *The Psalmes of David translated into Lyrick-Verse* (The Netherlands: Gerrits van Breughel, 1632).

Wyatt, *Collected Poems* Sir Thomas Wyatt, *Collected Poems*, ed. Kenneth Muir (Cambridge: Harvard University Press, 1950).

In the text, "Psalms" refers to the Book of Psalms itself, as distinguished from metrical "psalm" translations.

ABBREVIATIONS OF PERIODICALS

EIC   *Essays in Criticism*
ELH   *English Literary History*
HLQ   *Huntington Library Quarterly*
JWCI   *Journal of the Warburg and Courtauld Institutes*
KR   *Kenyon Review*
MP   *Modern Philology*
N & Q   *Notes and Queries*
PMLA   *Publications of the Modern Language Association*
RES   *Review of English Studies*
SEL   *Studies in English Literature*
SP   *Studies in Philology*
SRen   *Studies in the Renaissance*

MUSIC FOR A KING

ONE

Introduction

I. HERBERT AND THE PSALTER:
METHOD AND EXPERIENCE

George Herbert's character and poetry are full of extreme contrasts, which some of his contemporaries misunderstood: Barnabas Oley, for example, said that he had "heard sober men censure [Herbert] as a man who did not manage his brave parts to his best advantage and preferment, but lost himself *in an humble way*."[1] To the modern reader, Oley's remark is apt to seem unintentionally ironic, for time and again Herbert seems to have *found* himself in a humble way, both in spite of his obvious sophistication and because of it. His humble ways and brave parts are essentially united, and one source of Herbert's greatness as a poet is the complete transparency between his brilliance and his humility. But as this reasoning also implies, one side of Herbert's brilliance is not likely to be understood without reference to his homely and familiar materials.

In this study I hope to illuminate *The Temple* by seeing its relation to some of the popular religious verse with which Herbert would have been familiar. In the sixteenth and seventeenth centuries, metrical psalms were one of the most popular genres in English and European poetry and were central to services in nearly all Reformed churches. In Europe the translation of the Book of Psalms into

---

[1] Quoted by F. E. Hutchinson, ed., *Works of George Herbert*, 2d ed. (Oxford: Clarendon Press, 1945), p. xxxii.

vernacular poetry was as widespread as the practice of formal meditation in poetry, and the two were frequently combined; in England,
metrical versions of the psalter were printed in more editions than
any other poems between 1550 and 1650. A poet and parson like
Herbert, who recommended metrical psalms to his parish, who sang
metrical psalms and could write perhaps the best single English
psalm of his age, invites a reading within the context of psalmody.

Most Herbert criticism has not referred to the popular background
of Herbert's poetry, for as Barnabas Oley's remark indicates, it is not
always easy to see the connections between George Herbert the practical country parson and George Herbert the Cambridge Orator.
Rather than face the paradoxes in the man and the poetry, many
readers in the past often found it easier to fabricate a flat Herbert
who was a steeply pious versifier. This was the way Herbert's Augustan
critics saw him: Dryden's and Addison's derogatory comments about
Herbert's shaped poems reveal an insufficient reading of *The Temple*
(as if Herbert wrote nothing but shaped poems).[2] They also reveal a
lack of sympathy for the complex devotional life of the previous
century, with its typical emphasis (quite strong in "The Altar" and
"Easter-wings") upon the process of consciousness in individual worship. Similarly, although nineteenth-century poets such as Coleridge
found much to praise in Herbert,[3] their attitude was not universal,
and in canvassing the multitude of old padded and embossed family
anthologies that are donated to any university library, one can find
repeated pronouncements upon Herbert which deplore his poetic
"artificiality" but assent to his faith with a civil leer. Ultimately, the
attitude that Herbert's faith was firmer than his craft is not far from
the thinking of a late Victorian like George Herbert Palmer. In spite
of his great love of Herbert, Palmer still had (as we shall see later)
some rather tightly preconceived ideas about Herbert's poetic and its
relation to his thought.

Recent Herbert scholarship has corrected the old view that the
poet's faith was "essentially childlike" and purchased at the expense

[2] See *MacFlecknoe* (1682), in Dryden, *Poems*, ed. Bonamy Dobrée (London: Everyman's Library, 1966), ll. 203–10, and Addison, *Spectator* (May 7, 1711), ed. Donald
F. Bond (Oxford: Oxford University Press, 1965), I, 247.

[3] On this issue, see the thorough discussion by Joseph Duncan in *The Revival
of Metaphysical Poetry* (Minneapolis: University of Minnesota Press, 1959), and also
Roberta Florence Brinkley, *Coleridge on the Seventeenth Century* (Durham, N. C.:
Duke University Press, 1955), esp. pp. 533–40.

of his style. But it has not dealt with the humble part of Herbert's poetic materials. William Empson's early studies in the 1930s established—where there was a need to establish—the precision of Herbert's thought, and Rosemond Tuve's *A Reading of George Herbert* (1952) defined with great energy one historical context of Herbert's complexity.[4] In 1954 the work of Joseph Summers and Louis Martz opened a multitude of new approaches to Herbert, and since then studies in Herbert have been as varied as they have been responsive: Rosemond Tuve examined Herbert's conception of *caritas*, and Rosalie Colie has traced his idea of the *logos*; Mary Ellen Rickey has described his stylistic growth, and Fredson Bowers has studied his sequential imagery.[5] On a grander scale, Robert Ellrodt has explored Herbert's attitudes toward consciousness and sacrament, and Arnold Stein has retrieved a whole background of Christian plain style.[6] Even the sketchiest review of Herbert criticism reveals an extraordinary variety of methods and ambitions. Yet it is no distortion to say that from Barnabas Oley to the present there has been little consideration of the common and popular materials in Herbert's life and poetic.

Previous Herbert criticism has thoroughly defined one question that must still be asked: How exactly *did* Herbert find himself in a humble way? This problem can be restated in two forms, one referring to Herbert's character and the other to his poetic (although as I have said before, the two are inseparable). Let us first take Herbert's character and offer some trial problems. Does Herbert's self-deprecation ever fit a comment that Dr. Johnson made one night at Reynolds'?

[4] Empson's first study of Herbert appeared in *Seven Types of Ambiguity* (London: Chatto & Windus, 1930), and along with the work of R. W. Stallman and Cleanth Brooks, set Miss Tuve to work on *A Reading of George Herbert* (Chicago: University of Chicago Press, 1952). Empson has another word in "George Herbert and Miss Tuve," *KR*, 2 (Autumn 1950): 735–38; and René Wellek has some relevant comments in "Literary Theory, Criticism, and History," in *English Studies Today*, ed. G. A. Bonnard, 2d ser. (Berne: Francke, 1961), pp. 53–65. The recent 3d ed. of *Seven Types* (New York: New Directions, n.d.) has an unrepentant prefatory note.

[5] Summers, *George Herbert* (Cambridge: Harvard University Press, 1954); Martz, *Poetry of Meditation*, 2d ed. (New Haven: Yale University Press, 1962); Tuve, "George Herbert and *Caritas*," *JWCI*, 22 (1959): 303–31; Colie, *Paradoxia Epidemica* (Princeton: Princeton University Press, 1966); Rickey, *Utmost Art* (Lexington: University of Kentucky Press, 1966); Bowers, "Herbert's Sequential Imagery: 'The Temper,'" *MP*, 59 (February 1962): 202–13.

[6] Ellrodt, *L'Inspiration Personnelle et l'Esprit du Temps chez les Poètes Métaphysiques Anglais* (Paris: José Corti, 1960), vol. 1, bk. 2; Stein, *George Herbert's Lyrics* (Baltimore: The Johns Hopkins Press, 1968).

"All censure of a man's self is oblique praise. It is in order to shew how much he can spare. It has all the invidiousness of self-praise, and the reproach of falsehood."[7] And yet if facile self-censure can be seen as an obstacle to the achievement of humility, cannot also the steady fight against self-censure? A readiness for great pitched battles does not guarantee success in border skirmishes. This may be illustrated by recalling Izaak Walton's familiar description of Herbert on his death-bed, saying that *The Temple* was "a picture of the many spiritual Conflicts that have passed betwixt God and my Soul, before I could subject mine to the will of *Jesus my Master*: in whose service I have now found perfect freedom."[8] Are these conflicts restricted, however, to those poems that announce conflict as their subject? Or, as in the Book of Psalms, can the difficulty of free subjection appear even in poems of praise? We must ask questions of this sort if we wish to understand Herbert's "perfect freedom" and the humility by which he achieved it.

On the side of Herbert's poetic, there is no lack of commentary which contrasts Herbert to Donne.[9] But the differences between Herbert's poetic and Donne's are, in their present evaluation, ulti-mately unhelpful. It is plain, for example, that much in Donne's metric cannot account for Herbert's subtle modulations, just as Her-bert's stanzaic diversity, while resembling Donne's in its apparent impulse, goes beyond anything that Donne practiced himself. Simi-larly, the conceits that preoccupied a generation of Donne scholars we now recognize (thanks to Ellrodt) as quite different from the con-ceits in Herbert, in spite of occasional resemblances.[10]

It is logically self-evident that satisfying conclusions about Herbert's poetic cannot be drawn solely on the basis of its differences from Donne's. However, there are other, more practical ways to describe

[7] James Boswell, *Life of Johnson*, ed. R. W. Chapman (Oxford: Oxford Univer-sity Press, 1963), p. 972.

[8] Walton, *Lives*, ed. George Saintsbury (London: Oxford University Press, 1927), p. 314.

[9] The studies range—to hit only some high spots—from T. S. Eliot's seminal essays on the metaphysical poets and Andrew Marvell (*Selected Essays* [New York: Harcourt Brace, 1950]) and his British Council essay *George Herbert*, no. 152 in Writers and Their Work (London: Longmans, 1962), to George Williamson's *The Donne Tradition* (Cambridge: Harvard University Press, 1930), to Rosemond Tuve's *Elizabethan and Metaphysical Imagery* (Chicago: University of Chicago Press, 1947), to A. Alvarez, *The School of Donne* (London: Chatto and Windus, 1961).

[10] Ellrodt, *L'Inspiration*, 1:305–56.

Herbert's poetic. Miss Rickey, for example, has attempted to describe the stylistic maturation of Herbert's poetry by comparing the two manuscripts of *The Temple*. Stein, working from a very different direction, has studied classical and patristic theories of style in order to clarify Herbert's poems about poetry and, by extension, the whole of *The Temple*. A third method is the one I attempt in this book: by studying Herbert's relation to one of the broadest currents of Renaissance verse, I hope to show the role of humility in Herbert's religious thought and poetic. In spite of our historical hindsight, we sometimes forget that English religious lyrics before Herbert comprise a larger body than the divine poems of John Donne; there are wide currents in it which do not appear with any strength in Donne's poetry, but which do appear in Herbert's poetry, and which would have been familiar to Herbert in his daily life as a country parson. One of these currents is psalm translation in verse.

Metrical psalms are an appropriate genre to bring to the study of Herbert, first because *The Temple* so frequently resembles a book of metrical psalms in form and content and, second, because of Herbert's great interest in music as a recreation and above all as a source of metaphor.[11] Although Herbert himself did little straight scriptural translation, it was an attraction for most major Renaissance poets at some time in their careers. Psalmody in particular is by no means only an English phenomenon: the vogue for it passed from the neo-Latin poets of Italy and France to the poets of northern Europe from whom, in turn, most of the English psalmodists took their bearings. Psalm translation flourished in all European vernaculars during the sixteenth and seventeenth centuries, but nowhere more than in France, where as a genre it was perhaps even more influential than its counterpart in England. Terence Cave has recently shown how the Psalms—as subjects for both paraphrases and meditations—engaged one major French poet after another: Baïf, Desportes, d'Aubigné, Sponde, La Ceppède, and Malherbe, to name only a few.[12]

Yet in spite of their great contemporary popularity, the metrical psalms have rarely been employed in study of the poetry around them. Several years ago, in her important history of divine poetry and

---

[11] The fullest treatment of music in Herbert remains that by Summers, *George Herbert*, chap. 8.

[12] Cave, *Devotional Poetry in France c. 1570–1613* (Cambridge: Cambridge University Press, 1969). Martz's *Poetry of Meditation* is of course basic to this study.

drama in the sixteenth century, Lily B. Campbell set out "to trace the movement in the sixteenth century which resulted in the poetry of Donne and Herbert and Milton and those others who praised God in nobler words and sounder rhythms."[13] But even with an invitation so attractive, there has been no extended attempt to relate this mass of popular religious poetry to a single English poet, although any member of the Church of England, poetically inclined or not, would have been singing versified psalms in large and often daily doses. Indeed, the modern student of Renaissance poetry has little opportunity to read metrical psalms. To my knowledge, there are no reprints or selections in print as I am writing; and only one current textbook contains even a modest selection of metrical psalms.[14]

The reasons for the neglect of this route into Herbert's poetry are clear. Most metrical psalms are, quite frankly, miserable verse. Their badness is extraordinary, in some cases even legendary, and few of us read any more bad poetry than we have to. This attitude is so deeply a part of our natures that over the centuries critics have evolved only the crudest sort of vocabulary with which to discuss bad verse and have never given the subject much extended study, either historically or theoretically. From Plato through the Italian theorists to Sidney, by

---

[13] Campbell, *Divine Poetry and Drama in Sixteenth-Century England* (Cambridge: Cambridge University Press, 1959), p. 3. Of course the connections between the metrical psalms and devotional poetry had been suggested long before. Some of these suggestions I shall discuss later, but here it would be appropriate to mention the pioneering study by Philipp von Rohr-Sauer, *English Metrical Psalms from 1600 to 1660* (Freiburg: Poppen and Ortmann, 1938). Although von Rohr-Sauer accepted as Herbert's the seven dubious psalms in Playford, he still observed (in commenting upon Herbert's version of the Twenty-third Psalm) that in this poem Herbert is oriented toward church psalmody and "is undoubtedly under the influence of Sternhold and Hopkins" (p. 90). F. P. Wilson, in *Elizabethan and Jacobean* (Oxford: Clarendon Press, 1945), has some helpful comments on metrical psalms in general, and Joseph Hall's in particular, as they are related to devotional poetry (pp. 65 ff.), but essentially his perspective is not different from Lily B. Campbell's. John Thompson, in *The Founding of English Meter* (New York: Columbia University Press, 1961), makes a comment that is of some interest for the present study: "It remains uncertain whether popular verse like Sternhold's and Hopkins's Psalms was an influence on . . . more literary verse or whether it was another symptom" (p. 36; cf. p. 65). I shall be arguing that Herbert's use of popular psalm materials is in some measure parodistic, as Rosemond Tuve employed the term in her essay "Sacred 'Parody' of Love Poetry, and Herbert," *SRen*, 8 (1961): 249–90. This essay has, on the side, many provocative insights into Renaissance psalmody.

[14] *The Renaissance in England*, ed. Hyder Rollins and Herschel Baker (New York: D. C. Heath, 1954).

"bad verse" is usually meant verse that corrupts the soul or leads the reader into vicious or unnatural thoughts and actions. "Bad poetry" in the sense of the mundane or insipid does not come up as a topic; by the nature of his sensibilities the critic avoids such poetry. But there is something anomalous in the traditional rejection of inept or clumsy verse, for from antiquity to the present, few intelligent critics have failed to allow the inspired poet to violate grammar and logic, transpose accents, and generally misbehave at his desk. In his verse this messiness can be ignored: as Horace says, "when a poem is brilliant, I will not take offence at a few blemishes due to carelessness or human nature's lack of foresight."[15] Boccaccio, however, can even go so far as to admit that for the uninitiated, good poems may seem to be only "nonsense in sonorous verse,"[16] and between Horace and Boccaccio lie most critical arguments on the constructive uses of ineptitude. It would be strictly tangential, however, to offer a restatement of these arguments, for to my knowledge no classical or Renaissance critic went so far as to consider where the good poet might have found models for bathos.[17]

Critics who have studied ineptitude directly, on the other hand, have rarely considered bad poetry to be anything but a dead end in itself, just as a critic like Boccaccio considers good poetry to be *sui generis* (at least for the properly initiated reader). One reason for these narrow categories may be the dominance of traditional ideas of decorum. Demetrius, for example, who is, before Pope, perhaps the fullest cataloguer of technical mediocrity, usually describes badness as a comic mixture of styles or the use of a style inappropriate to the subject. In his third book he does go so far as to recognize a kind of absolute bad, which is marked by labored thought and "betrays a character that lacks taste and breeding";[18] but he treats the topic

[15] *The Art of Poetry*, trans. H. Rushton Fairclough, Loeb Classical Library (London: Heinemann, 1926), ll. 351–53. I have given a few terms more literal rendering.

[16] *Boccaccio on Poetry*, trans. Charles G. Osgood (Princeton: Princeton University Press, 1930), p. 76.

[17] C. S. Lewis, whose general knowledge of these matters one is inclined to trust, has said (in *The Abolition of Man* [New York: Macmillan, 1947], p. 23) that as a subject in itself bad poetry had received no substantial examination prior to I. A. Richards's *Practical Criticism* (London: K. Paul, 1929). The reader will see in the next chapter how great my debt is to Richards and the tools he first provided.

[18] *On Style*, trans. W. Rhys Roberts, Loeb Classical Library (Cambridge: Harvard University Press, 1932), bk. 3, sec. 171. All of the third book is relevant.

quickly and moves on to a study of euphony. True, Demetrius did not intend to offer a comprehensive description of badness in style, but one wonders if the idea of decorum alone could ever account fully for the operations of literary bad taste. In the study of poetic incompetence there is perhaps a *sine qua non* which may lie in the nature of the language the poet uses. A deeper source of badness than mere violation of decorum may be violation of basic patterns in the language itself, at its lexical, syntactic, and rhythmic roots, although considerations of this sort rarely enter the traditional discussions. These violations would necessarily be different for every language, and in special cases, as in the sixteenth-century development of English prosody, the violations could permeate the serious work of a whole generation, as it was viewed in retrospect after the turn of the century.

Now whether Herbert actually saw any particular metrical versions of the psalter is for me a matter of less interest than the larger critical problem: does a knowledge of the metrical psalms enlarge our understanding of Herbert's thought and lyric mastery? I have tried to keep this problem constantly in mind, for even if one could prove that Herbert owned and annotated several metrical psalters, one still would have proved nothing about *The Temple*. The critic's task is different from the biographer's. For that reason, I would stress that the metrical psalms offer helpful guides for reading a poet like Herbert who is concerned with religious praise and lament, expressed simultaneously through technical brilliance and homeliness. Further, the matter of the Book of Psalms, which remains relatively constant throughout all the versified translations, can provide for Herbert as for any devotional poet a way of sounding the height of his joy and the depth of his sorrow. And the joy and sorrow, as Herbert reveals them, cannot be separated from the craft of poetry. In reading *The Temple* it is possible to see apparent borrowings and striking parallels with the psalter; but simply to point out these resemblances has seemed to me of less interest than the matters I have just described. My primary interest is in using the metrical psalms to understand whole poems, whole sorrows and joys.

Critical use of the psalter, without specific biographic support, has seemed finally nothing to apologize for, no more than we apologize for bringing to the study of Marvell a virtual library of Hermetic philosophy or (to take a more lurid example) for providing students of Spenser with numerological codebooks. We know that Herbert liked "big books in divinity" and made "clamorous and greedy bookish requests" for money from Sir John Danvers,[19] and here Ellrodt and Stein have gone before us, tracing with great insight the influence of Calvin, Augustine, and others upon Herbert's literary theory. But surely this coin has another side: Herbert read small books, too, like the Psalms, and these might have influenced him as strongly as the Fathers of the Church. To rephrase my opening statement: perhaps by studying some of the humbler stuff in Herbert's life, we can understand something of his own humility, as a religious man, an introspective man, and a poet.

As a strictly secondary line of justification we should note the specific biographical or historical evidence that associates the metrical psalms with Herbert. We have his one attempt in the genre, as well as seven psalms dubiously ascribed to him, but no explicit comment within the poetry.[20] However, the dubious ascriptions themselves are evidence of a sort: to John Playford at least, Herbert seemed to have been the kind of poet who might have written metrical psalms. The burning of Herbert's literary remains in the Civil War eliminated a second place where we might verify his interest in metrical psalms, but on the biographical level in general there does exist other primary evidence of perhaps higher quality.

In 1626 Herbert was instituted by proxy at Lincoln Cathedral into "the canonry and prebend of Leighton Ecclesia founded in the said cathedral church," and one of the duties of the Cathedral chapter was the daily recitation of the Book of Psalms. Herbert himself was responsible for the recitation of two Psalms, the Thirty-first and Thirty-second, the Latin titles of which were carved over his choir stall in the Cathedral.[21] Even more important than this obligation was Herbert's liberal use of the Psalms in daily worship. We could hardly

[19] Letter to Sir John Danvers, 1618, in Herbert, *Works*, p. 367; see also the 1617 letter to Danvers, p. 364. In his will, Herbert mentions that he has "St. Augustines workes" (p. 382). On the influence of Augustine, Heather Asals has done an especially good study: "The Voice of George Herbert's 'The Church,'" *ELH*, 36 (1969): 511–28.

[20] The psalms and the evidence for their ascription to Herbert are discussed by Hutchinson in Herbert, *Works*, pp. 554–55.

[21] The documents of institution are quoted in *ibid.*, p. xxxi. Herbert's responsibility for the two Psalms is noted by Marchette Chute, *Two Gentle Men* (New York: Dutton, 1959), p. 100. There is a good picture of these stalls, with their psalm titles clearly visible, in John Harris's and Jill Lever's *Illustrated Glossary of Architecture: 850–1830* (New York: C. N. Potter, 1966), pl. 94. Together, incidentally, the two psalm titles give the sense of Herbert's "posie," "Less than the least of all God's mercies."

overestimate the influence of the Psalms on Herbert's poetry, if Walton is accurate in his account of Herbert's church calendar:

> [Herbert] instructed his congregation for the use of the Psalms and Hymns appointed to be daily sung or said in the Church-service . . . . he proceeded to inform them why they were so often, and some of them daily, to be repeated in our Church-service; namely the Psalms every month, because they be an historical and thankful repetition of mercies past, and such a composition of prayers and praises, as ought to be repeated often, and publicly; for which such sacrifice God is honoured and well-pleased.[22]

Herbert himself advised the country parson to inquire if his parishioners were in the habit of singing psalms at their work, and this advice is especially significant, for Herbert could not be advocating other than the common psalm with its firm and simple meter.[23] In *The Temple* there is also one reference to psalm-singing in the church, and it too implies the use of the common psalm, as distinguished from elegant psalms such as those by Sidney: "The church with psalms must shout,/No doore can keep them out"[24] ("Antiphon," 9–10).

There is much secondary evidence which suggests that Herbert would have taken a particular interest in the metrical psalms. If we think of Donne as Herbert's sometime poetic and spiritual mentor we should recall that the Psalms were Donne's favorite book of the Bible. A veritable connoisseur of Psalms, Donne had read all the major translations, and compared his fondness for the Book to Augustine's (with whose enthusiasm Herbert himself may have been familiar).[25] We may also consider the possible influence upon Herbert of the metrical psalter written jointly by Sir Philip Sidney and his sister Mary Herbert, the Countess of Pembroke. The connection has been suggested before; as Louis Martz has said, "Sidney's translation of the Psalms represents, I believe, the closest approximation to the poetry

22 Walton, *Lives*, p. 296.

23 Chap. 14, "The Parson in Circuit," in Herbert, *Works*, p. 248.

24 Unless otherwise stated, all quotations are from F. E. Hutchinson's edition of Herbert's *Works*. Line numbers appear after the text of poems, page numbers after quotation from the prose and editorial commentary.

25 See Evelyn M. Simpson's Introduction to her edition of *John Donne's Sermons on the Psalms and Gospels* (Berkeley: University of California Press, 1963), pp. 4 ff.

of *The Temple* that can be found anywhere in preceding English poetry."[26]

There are three reasons why Herbert probably knew the Sidney psalter. First, we know from the testimony of Ben Jonson that the psalter circulated widely; it has survived in fourteen different manuscripts.[27] Second, the psalter has a greater range of forms than any previous collection of English lyrics, and Sidney's and his sister's attempt to suit form to meaning distinctly resembles Herbert's in *The Temple*. Third, the strong family ties between the Sidneys and the Herberts might have given Herbert the opportunity at least to see the psalter;[28] in fact, Herbert's social interchange with the Sidneys, the proximity of Bemerton to Wilton, and the wide circulation of the psalter in manuscript form suggest that Herbert had more than just a casual acquaintance with it.

It is curious that although there have been several suggestions regarding Herbert's familiarity with the Sidney psalter, there has been virtually no comment upon Herbert's relation to another metrical psalter which has an equally plausible claim to our consideration. This is the Sternhold and Hopkins Old Version. No records have survived concerning the psalters in use at Herbert's chapel at Bemerton, or in his curate's church at Fulston St. Peter, but since the Old Version was a uniform singing psalter for the Church of England we may be fairly certain that Herbert used it. (The Prayer Book psalter was of course the Great Bible translation.) The Old Version had gone through over two hundred editions by 1633, the year of Herbert's death; no contemporary psalter even began to approach it in popularity. It is quite likely that Herbert used this psalter. The rustic nature of the Bemerton parish would suggest that the more artfully versified psalms, such as those by the Sidneys, would have gratified neither Herbert's congregation nor his own urge to minister to it. Further, the Bemerton parish was particularly involved in psalm-singing, in spite of its evi-

[26] Martz, *Poetry of Meditation*, p. 273. See also Summers, *George Herbert*, p. 148; John Hollander, *The Untuning of the Sky* (Princeton: Princeton University Press, 1961), pp. 293–94, n. 93; Alicia Ostriker, "Song and Speech in the Metrics of George Herbert," *PMLA*, 80 (March 1965): 62–68.

[27] The manuscripts are described in J. C. A. Rathmell's edition of *The Psalms of Sir Philip Sidney and the Countess of Pembroke* (New York: Anchor Books, 1963), pp. xxvi ff.

[28] Chute (*Two Gentle Men*) has traced in detail Herbert's family relationships and connections with Wilton.

dent illiteracy (as suggested by parts of *The Country Parson*).[29] In *The Temple* itself there is ample suggestion that Herbert would have taken an interest in even the "flat and poor, lamely worded and unhandsomely rhimed" Old Version, as Henry King described it.[30] "The Elixir" offers a useful Christian justification:

> All may of thee partake:
> Nothing can be so mean,
> Which with his tincture (for thy sake)
> Will not grow bright and clean.
>
> (13–16)

Or as Thomas Sternhold puts it: "And though ye were as black as pots,/Your hue shall passe the dove" (Ps. 68:13).[31] In "The Church-Porch" Herbert characteristically views the craftsman's problem of using low materials: "The cunning workman never doth refuse/ The meanest tool, that he may chance to use" (353–54). The transformation is, after all, no less than an analogue to that which the psalmist repeatedly attributes to God (the translator here is John Hopkins):

> Thou mad'st a spring with streams to rise
> From rocke both hard and hie:
> And eke thy hand hath made likewise
> Deepe rivers to be drie.
>
> (Ps. 74:16)

[29] See the amusing glimpses of this in *The Country Parson*, chaps. 6 and 7. Carl Bridenbaugh records some similar incidents in *Vexed and Troubled Englishmen* (New York: Oxford University Press, 1968), pp. 284–85.

[30] Quoted by Margaret Boddy, "Milton's Translation of Psalms 80–88," *MP*, 54 (August 1966): 1.

[31] My text is that of Thomas Sternhold, John Hopkins, W. Whittingham, and Others, *The Whole Booke of Davids Psalmes* (London: John Daye, 1582). Psalm and verse numbers appear in the text. This psalter, because of its great number of editions, exists in an almost infinite number of variant readings; therefore I have chosen to use the single edition most accessible to scholarly readers, that on University Microfilms reel no. 275 (Early English Books, 1475–1640). Variants of course occur for numerous reasons, but I have noticed that as the psalter was printed and reprinted throughout the seventeenth century, its peculiar word choices and violent images were replaced by more decorous terms. So far as I have been able to determine, most of these changes enter between 1640 and 1698, when the Old Version was finally replaced by the psalter of Tate and Brady. Description of these changes would make an interesting study in the development of English poetic taste.

It is so easy to find parallels of this sort between *The Temple* and the Old Version that for now there is little reason to quote more. The essential point so far is Herbert's acceptance of poetic home-liness and his equal emphasis upon rigor in poetic method. Walton's anecdote about Herbert's first sermon shows Herbert's fusion of intel-lect and plainness, his past as the Cambridge Orator and his future as a parson and poet who would not be reluctant to use "the meanest tools":

> [Herbert] . . . deliver'd his Sermon after a most florid manner; both with great learning and eloquence. But at the close of this Sermon, told them, *That should not be his constant way of Preaching; for since Almighty God does not intend to lead men to heaven by hard Questions, he would not therefore fill their heads with unnecessary Notions; but that for their sakes, his language and his expressions should be more plain and practical in his future Sermons.*[32]

As usual Walton gives us good theater, but even if we allow for some dramatic lighting in his account, the contrast itself seems a true one, for it appears again in *The Country Parson*, this time with a seriousness so high as to transcend the question of a mere psalter's influence:

> [the County Parson] holds the Rule, that Nothing is little in God's service: If it once have the honor of that Name, it grows great instantly. Wherefore neither disdaineth he to enter into the poorest Cottage, though he even creep into it, and though it never smell so lothsomly. For both God is there also, and those for whom God dyed: and so much the rather doth he so, as his accesse to the poor is more comfortable, then to the rich; and in regard of himself, it is the more humiliation (p. 249).

In short, there are obvious pressures within Herbert—doctrinal pressures, literary and critical pressures, and the obligations of his humanity—that would have predisposed him to an interest in versi-fied psalms, the crude popular ones included. Showing this is very different, however, from showing the ambience of the psalms in which Herbert and his contemporaries lived; and unless we have some acquaintance with the history of the metrical psalm we are not likely

[32] Walton, *Lives*, p. 295.

to believe that it might actually have been a sufficient object for Herbert's attention as a parson and poet.

Preliminary to the argument of the book, therefore, is a brief history of the genre; to this, and some of its implications, I devote the remainder of the Introduction. The rise of the metrical psalm has been documented in several brief accounts, the best of these being those by Lily B. Campbell and Hallett Smith.[33] Their studies are valuable introductions to the topic, but I have found it necessary to expand and clarify several of their points and add some fresh material. For this reason it has seemed wiser to offer an account of my own rather than a long list of modifications to the pioneering studies in the field. There are also problems of historical analysis that can only be treated after the reader has been reminded of authors, editions, and dates.

II. A CENTURY OF PSALMS

Psalm translation into verse is one small part of the Reformation practice of making sacred texts available to the laity. Like so much else in our culture it has little history before Luther. The springs of psalmody are social rather than literary, and thus translation of the Psalms into modern English verse may be said to have begun in the 1540s, after Luther had made his first exemplary translations in 1524.[34] Although Thomas Brampton had made a paraphrase of the Seven Penitential Psalms in 1414, there were no other translations in the vernacular for over a hundred years and no gathering literary momentum that would in itself account for the rapid growth in popularity of the metrical psalm. And it was unusually popular. If we open the *Short Title Catalogue* and count all the metrical versions

---

[33] Campbell, *Divine Poetry and Drama*, pt. 1, chaps. 4, 5, and 6; Smith, "English Metrical Psalms in the Sixteenth Century and Their Literary Significance," *HLQ*, 9 (1946) : 249–71. John Julian's *Dictionary of Hymnology*, rev. ed. (London: J. Murray, 1915; reprint—New York: Dover, 1957) remains a good handbook.

[34] In all, Luther translated seven psalms in addition to composing original hymns and hymns based on scriptural paraphrases. There were also a few vernacular hymns that preceded the advent of the metrical psalm; the most familiar of these was the "Primer" of Henry VIII (1545), which was organized upon the lines of the offices. The vogue for psalm translation generally redirected efforts such as this.

of the psalter printed before 1640, we find three hundred twenty editions in England alone (Scottish psalmody is altogether another matter). But figures of this sort are not an adequate measure of the popularity of the metrical psalm, for not every translator was brilliant or dogged enough to translate all one hundred and fifty Psalms: many poets would print only a selected dozen or so in a larger miscellany or append one or two to a prose work as a benediction.[35] Considering the number of complete psalters against this background of selections, inserts in prose, and the many extant manuscript psalters, we have to conclude that the metrical psalm was as much a movement as a genre.

The proliferation of metrical psalms began with two translations wholly opposite in form and intention. Working independently, the first two English psalmodists, Miles Coverdale and Sir Thomas Wyatt, arrived at strikingly different solutions to their task; they are almost prototypes of two kinds of psalm and psalmodist. Credit for writing the first sixteenth-century psalms in verse is usually given to one or the other, although it appears to me that first place would have go to Coverdale's *Goostly Psalmes and Spiritualle Songs* (*ante* 1538). The *Goostly Psalmes* exist only in a unique copy at Queen's College, Oxford, and it is not likely that they had the great influence of Wyatt's psalms. Their own literary qualities do conform, however, to those of most popular later psalms. First, they were derived from European Protestant models, principally the translations of Luther. Second, the verse is quite simple in technique. Coverdale uses stanzas of four, seven, nine, ten, and thirteen lines, all rhymed *a b a b*, with an occasional couplet or triplet concluding the psalm; musical notes are printed with every first stanza. The scansion is similarly plain: although Hallett Smith remarks that it is "bewildering,"[36] it is actually quite simple if one follows the prick song. Coverdale imitates the plain song of the German chorale in his use of one note per syllable, and if the reader attends to elided and expanded syllables, Coverdale's scansion seems not so much versification as words-for-music.[37] Consider his Psalm 129:

---

[35] An example would be Queen Elizabeth's translation of Psalm 14 at the end of *A Godly Meditation of the Christian Soul* (1548).

[36] Smith, "English Metrical Psalms," p. 261.

[37] The distinction has been nicely framed by V. C. Clinton-Baddeley in *Words for Music* (Cambridge: Cambridge University Press, 1941).

Out of the depe crye I to the
O lorde lorde heare my callynge.
O let thyne eares enclyned be
To the voyce of my complaynynge.
If thou (lorde) wylt deale with stratenesse,
To mark all that is done amysse,
Lord who may abyde that rekenynge.[38]

The apparent thud of line four disappears when *complaynynge* takes its intended four syllables, *com-pla-yn-ynge*, each receiving a whole note. This kind of catch-as-catch-can prosody is employed by many later psalmodists, perhaps more successfully because their tunes are generally simpler. But verse technique appears to interest Coverdale less than the production of a working psalter, and he willingly admits that he has subjugated most of the poetry to the realities of congregational performance. As he says in his verse preface "To the boke,"

Be not ashamed I warande the
Though thou be rude in song and ryme
Thou shalt to youth some occasion be
In godly sportes to passe theyr tyme.[39]

These lines indicate the connection between verse technique and the missionary purpose of the Coverdale psalter. Most Church psalmodists from Coverdale to Wither considered themselves to be in direct competition with popular song. In the Preface to the *Goostly Psalmes*, "Miles Coverdale to the Christen Reader," Coverdale exclaims

. . . wolde God that oure mynstrels had none other thynge to playe upon, nether oure carters & plow men other thynge to whistle upon, save Psalmes, hymnes, and soch godly songes as David is occupied with all . . . . I nede not rehearce what euell ensamples of ydelness, corrupte talkyng (and all soch vyces as folowe the same) are geuen to yonge people thorowe . . . unchristen songes. Alas the worlde is all to full of vicious and euell lyvers already. It is no nede to cast oyle in ye fyre.[40]

[38] Coverdale, *Goostly Psalmes*, sig. M 1v-r.
[39] *Ibid.*, sig. * 1 r.
[40] *Ibid.*, sig. * 3 v.

As Lily B. Campbell has shown, sentiments of this sort are by no means peculiar to Coverdale. Not as crude as it may seem to be at first, Coverdale's justification forestalls objection to the clumsy rhymes and meters of the verse.

Wyatt's psalms differ from Coverdale's in nearly every respect. All they would seem to have in common is propinquity in time; Wyatt wrote his psalms—his last poems—in 1541. Unlike Coverdale's, these translations circulated in several manuscripts and enjoyed a substantial popularity after their publication in 1549, seven years after Wyatt's death. The most pervasive contrast between Wyatt and Coverdale is in the matter of sources: Coverdale translates after the lyric model of Luther, Wyatt translates the Seven Penitential Psalms after the prose of the divine Aretino. (There is also one additional psalm, the Thirty-seventh.) Wyatt's selection of the Psalms is significant in itself: here is King David repentant that "his hete, his lust and plesur" at the sight of Bathsheba has made him send Uriah to the battlefront, and the *persona* of David, with all his "stormy syghes," might easily be taken for the lover in much of Wyatt's amatory verse.[41] A second major difference involves verse form. Wyatt uses *terza rima* for the psalms and has added connecting prologues in *ottava rima,* a device which produces not only a narrative line but also a poem that would be nearly impossible to sing. These qualities may not entirely disqualify Wyatt's psalms as *song,* but no doubt the thought of a congregation singing his psalms would have horrified Wyatt, much as Yeats once was shocked by hearing "The Lake Isle of Innisfree" sung, in a stadium, by ten thousand Boy Scouts. Finally, in contrast to Coverdale's public moral intention, any moral purpose Wyatt's psalms may have is probably personal: it is likely that Wyatt wrote his Penitential Psalms shortly before Bishop Bonner publicly accused Wyatt of "abominable and vicious living" among the nuns at Barcelona, a charge that Wyatt did not categorically deny.[42]

Somewhat later than Coverdale's and Wyatt's psalms are Surrey's

[41] Hallett Smith, in "English Metrical Psalms," p. 262, has noted and discussed this theme of the *de remedia amoris.*

[42] See Wyatt, *Collected Poems,* ed. Kenneth Muir (Cambridge: Harvard University Press, 1950), pp. xv-xvi, for the relevant portions of Wyatt's letter to the Privy Council. On the dating of Wyatt's psalms, Muir has argued persuasively for 1541 (*Life and Letters of Sir Thomas Wyatt* [Liverpool: Liverpool University Press, 1963], p. 256 and n. 7). He stands by this date in his recent edition of Wyatt (see p. 52, n. 3), though he also cites arguments for an earlier date.

four very free translations (ca. 1546–47). Frederick Morgan Padelford considered that there was "unequivocal evidence, quite aside from
internal evidence, that the Psalms were translated during Surrey's
final imprisonment," and later editors have agreed.[43] Even though
Surrey did not translate the same psalms as Wyatt, his translations
clearly owe something to him, though just what is uncertain. It has been
maintained that for several years Surrey had by him a copy of Wyatt's
psalms; but even though it is possible to find parallels between these
two versions there are no word-for-word echoes, and no similarities
that cannot be explained by the fact that both poets occasionally gloss
difficult passages by using the prose paraphrases of Joannes Campensis.[44] Formally, Surrey's psalms differ from Wyatt's by their use
of Poulter's measure, which has some obvious affinities with the
Common Meter that was to dominate psalm translation. Surrey's
psalms were not as well known as Wyatt's, however, and probably
were not instrumental in the creation of a taste for the religious use
of ballad meter.

In late 1548 or early 1549 Thomas Sternhold published nineteen
metrical psalms under the title *Certayne psalmes chosen out of the
psalter of David and drawen into English metre.* Although this collection was the start of the highly influential Old Version, I shall
defer comment on it until later, for it did not reach its final form
until 1562. It seems to be at this time, about mid-century, that the
metrical psalm began to establish itself as a legitimate genre, for in
the fifties new versions began to appear with some regularity. In 1549
Wyatt's psalms were published, as was the Puritan Robert Crowley's
Psalter of David newely translated, the first complete metrical psalter
in English. Also in this year appeared John Wedderburn's *Gude and
Holy Ballatis;* chiefly of interest in the development of Scottish
hymnody, Wedderburn's many translations from German versions of
the Psalms demonstrate the continuing influence of Lutheranism.

The next ten years of English psalmody show some rear-guard sup-
porting action, chiefly as a result of the 1549 Act of Uniformity which

---

[43] *Poems of Henry Howard, Earl of Surrey,* ed. Frederick Morgan Padelford,
University of Washington Publications in Language and Literature, vol. 5, rev. ed.
(Seattle, 1928), p. 228; Surrey, *Poems,* ed. Emrys Jones (Oxford: Clarendon Press,
1964), pp. 153, 158.

[44] On the Wyatt-Surrey parallel, see H. A. Mason, "Wyatt and the Psalms-II,"
TLS, Feb. 27, 1953, p. 160; on the influence of Campensis, "Wyatt and the Psalms-
I," *TLS,* Feb. 20, 1953, p. 144.

provided for psalm-singing in the churches. William Hunnis published his first selection of psalms in 1550, and in 1551 the third edition of Sternhold's psalter appeared. Sternhold himself had died in 1549, by that date having completed eighteen more psalms, and to these John Hopkins, apparently a clergyman and schoolmaster, had added seven of his own, making a total of forty-four. Typical of the minor versions appearing at this time are those by John Bale (in his *An expostulation or complaynt against the blasphemys of a franticke papyst of Hamshyre,* 1551–52) and Crowley's friend Francis Seager (*Certayne psalmes* . . ., 1553). In 1556 an enlarged Sternhold-Hopkins psalter appeared. Published in Geneva because of the Marian persecutions, this version now had fifty-one psalms, including seven new translations by Whittingham.[45]

In 1562 all this industrious enterprise, the work of what might be called the second-generation psalmodists, was crowned by the publication of the complete Sternhold-Hopkins psalter. In its final form, the Old Version contained the work of twelve different poets, including Thomas Norton, that "forward and busy Calvinist,"[46] as Anthony à Wood called him, and William Kethe. Yet in spite of this multiple authorship, the Sternhold-Hopkins psalter is remarkably uniform in style, and the whole work is both literally and figuratively a product of its age. Most of these psalms are written in Common Meter, well-established before the psalmodists and about to be a mainstay of much Elizabethan verse: the ballad stanza, consisting of two "fourteeners," each broken after the fourth foot to yield a quatrain of alternating four- and three-stress lines. (Most frequently—109 times out of 150—two of these quatrains were run together to form one eight-line Double Common Meter stanza.) Rhyming in the quatrains is usually *a b a b,* although the *b*-lines are sometimes unrhymed, revealing the stanza's descent from two heptameter lines. The music printed with many editions of the Old Version shows that the musical basis of the poetry is—like that of Coverdale's *Goostly Psalmes*—still the plain song of one syllable per note. From the standpoint of prosody, the lines are almost perfectly iambic, with virtually no metrical substitutions or displacements. Some lines require rather strenuous elision or expansion

---

[45] In all editions, each psalm is prefixed by the translator's initials. Some psalters contain more than one translation for each psalm.

[46] *Athenae Oxoniensis,* 2d ed. (London: R. Knaplock, D. Midwinter, and J. Tonson, 1721), 1: 77.

of syllables, but the pressure of as many as several hundred voices could be counted on to flatten any irregularities. Syllabic regularity is of course necessary for congregational singing, but its appearance at this particular time in English literary history had an influence that far exceeded the bounds of church song. It is no exaggeration to say, as does Hallett Smith, that the Sternhold-Hopkins psalter was "of significance in the great change in the mid-sixteenth century from somewhat loose, syllabic versification, Skeltonics, and degenerated accentual alliterative poetry to the prevailing Elizabethan iambic manner first prominent in *Tottel's Miscellany*."[47] In fact, the Old Version became so thoroughly identified by its stanza and meter that the whole psalter was frequently referred to as the "Old Metre."[48]

None of these observations make any statement as to the quality of the craftsmanship in the psalter, and on this matter opinion was divided, at least between the educated and the uneducated. Certainly the collection was popular with the folk and had been so even prior to its completion. Bishop John Jewel, writing in 1560, reported that "You may now sometimes see at Paul's Cross after the service, six thousand persons old and young of both sexes, all singing together and praising God."[49] The bishop had vested interests, however, and less partisan critics have always ridiculed the Old Version. Thomas Fuller claimed that "sometimes they make the Maker of the tongue to speak little better than barbarism, and have in many verses such poor rhyme that two hammers on a smith's anvil would make better music."[50] The Old Version psalms were often derided as "Geneva jigs" (a term sometimes applied to psalms in general), but probably the harshest criticism came from the poets. As Donne had asked in his poem "Upon the translation of the Psalms by Sir Philip Sidney, and the Countesse of Pembroke his Sister," "shall our Church, unto our Spouse and King/ More hoarse, more harsh than any other, sing?"[51]

[47] Smith, "English Metrical Psalms," p. 254.

[48] For example, George Wither, in *The Schollers Purgatory* (London: The Honest Stationers, [1625?]), p. 38: "Some I know will be obstinate in defence of their oulde Meeter." The usage is still current in the time of Addison; see n. 59 in this chapter.

[49] Quoted by Rathmell, *The Psalms*, p. xiii. In his *General History of Music*, originally published between 1776 and 1789, Charles Burney had said that the Old Version psalms were "roared like orgies" in the streets (New York: Harcourt Brace, 1935), 2: 50.

[50] Quoted in Smith, "English Metrical Psalms," p. 250.

[51] Donne, *Divine Poems*, ed. Helen Gardner (Oxford: Clarendon Press, 1962), ll. 43–44.

Criticism of the Sternhold and Hopkins psalter became a common way to introduce a new translation of the Psalms. Thus Falkland, or Lucius Cary, in verses "To my Noble Frend, Mr. George Sandys, upon his excellent Paraphrase on the Psalms" (1636), magnanimously grants that the Old Version's

> Eloquence, that though it were abus'd
> Could not but be (though not Allow'd) excus'd,
> Ioin'd to a Worke so chose, that though ill-done,
> So Pious an Attempt Praise could not shun.[52]

In other lines upon Sandys' *Paraphrase upon Divine Poems* (1638), Sidney Godolphin remarks complacently, in apparent reference to the Old Version: "Humane Language only can restore/ What human Language had impair'd before."[53] George Wither sums up the charges against the Old Version by claiming that

> no man of understanding can sing many of those psalmes, but with trouble to his devotion. And I dare undertake to demonstrate, that they are not onely full of absurdityes, soeloscismes, improprieties, non-sense, and impertinent circumlocutions (to more than twice the length of their originalles in some places) but that there are in them many expressions also, quite beside, if not quite contrary, to the meaning of the text. Which I would not thus openly have declared, but that even schoole boys perceive it . . . [the Old Version] has given the papist, the Atheist, and the Libertyne occasion to skoffe at our christian exercises, and troubles the devotion of many a religious man, who being desirous to sing with his understanding in the congregations, doth often (before he is aware) loose the sence of the Prophet: yea, and sometimes fall upon direct nonsense, among those many impertinent circumlocutions and independencies which he is (for Rhymes sake) compelled to wander through in that Translation.[54]

More often the Old Version was attacked simply because it was bad song. The opinions of some poets have been noted, but that of the greatest authority has not. Several times in his plays, Shakespeare has characters allude to metrical psalms, usually in the context of poor music and killjoy stuffiness. The references most often imply a jibe at psalters like the Old Version. When Falstaff laments his robbery on

[52] *A paraphrase upon the psalms of David* (London: A. Hebb, 1636), p. xi.
[53] *A paraphrase upon the divine poems* (London: A. Hebb, 1638), p. vii.
[54] Wither, *Schollers Purgatory*, pp. 37–38.

the highway near Gadshill, he says that if good manhood is not forgot, "then am I a shotten herring. There live not three good men unhanged in England, and one of them is fat, and grows old. God the while! A bad world, I say. I would I were a weaver, I could sing psalms or anything" (*1 Henry IV*, II.iv. 43–47). Falstaff's benign alter ego Sir Toby Belch has a similar, low opinion of the song and the character of the psalm-singer: "Shall we make the welkin dance indeed? Shall we rouse the night owl in a catch that will draw three souls out of one weaver?" (*Twelfth Night*, II.iii.59–61). In each case, the joke is directed at the low church psalms sung by the European refugees who comprised the larger part of England's weavers.

As bad music the Old Version remained a joke well into the next century. Edward Phillips, Milton's nephew, describes the "woful noise" of someone singing, "Like a crack'd saints' bell jarring in the steeple,/ Tom Sternhold's wretched prick-song for the people."[55] The following lines, "Spoken *Extempore* to a County Clerk, after hearing him sing Psalms," are dubiously ascribed to the Earl of Rochester, but whoever wrote them was setting down a received idea:

> Sternhold and Hopkins had great Qualms,
> When they translated *David's Psalms*,
> 　　To make the heart full glad:
> But had it been poor David's fate
> To hear thee Sing, and them Translate,
> 　　By ——! twould have made him Mad.[56]

But for other poets, simple scorn is never enough. Both Dryden and Pope found it possible to praise the Old Version, but in jangling contexts that made an effective attack on the psalter's very claim to poetry. The end of the *Religio Laici* is at once harsh and ingenious:

> this unpolish'd, rugged Verse I chose;
> As fittest for Discourse, and nearest prose:
> For while from *Sacred Truth* I do not swerve,
> *Tom Sternhold's* or *Tom Sha——ll's Rhimes* will serve.[57]

55 Quoted by Rowland E. Prothero, *The Psalms in Human Life* (New York: Everyman's Library, [1903?]), p. 113.

56 John Wilmot, Earl of Rochester, *Poems*, ed. Vivian de Sola Pinto (Cambridge: Harvard University Press, 1953), p. 148.

57 Dryden, *Poems*, ll. 453–56.

Pope's comments on the Old Version, in his Epistle "To Augustus," contain not only some good literary criticism but also some close description of psalm-singing in the rural parish church. The picture fills in the outline we found in Herbert's writings:

> Hopkins and Sternhold glad the heart with Psalms:
> The Boys and Girls whom charity maintains,
> Implore your help in these pathetic strains:
> How could Devotion touch the country pews,
> Unless the Gods bestowed a proper Muse?
> Verse cheers their leisure, Verse assists their work,
> Verse prays for Peace, or sings down Pope and Turk.
> The silenced preacher yields to potent strain,
> And feels that grace his prayer besought in vain;
> The blessing thrills through all the laboring throng,
> And Heaven is won by Violence of Song.[58]

Since the psalter of Tate and Brady had officially replaced the Old Version in 1689, Pope's lines also suggest how thoroughly Sternhold and Hopkins must have saturated the rural English mind. But even the urbane Addison could joke in 1711 about the "Eke and Aye, which are frequent in the Metre of *Hopkins* and *Sternhold*,"[59] thus suggesting that the tenacity of the Old Version was more than a country matter. At any rate, as the laughter goes on, it should not be surprising that the pious song-collectors of the nineteenth century virtually ignored the Old Version psalms. One looks in vain for them in popular anthologies of hymns; even a substantial historical work such as *Hymns Ancient and Modern* (printed, reprinted twice, and revised, in 1861, 1875, 1904, and 1909) gives Sternhold and Hopkins only brief notice.[60]

Perhaps because it was so perfectly offensive to most poets, the completed Old Version seems to have stimulated the production of more metrical psalms, many of which had the formal variety that Sternhold and Hopkins lacked. In 1564 the Scottish Psalter appeared, with a great assortment of stanza forms, although subsequent revision soon

---

[58] "Epistle to Augustus," ll. 230–40, in Pope, *Poems*, ed. John Butt (New Haven: Yale University Press, 1963), pp. 643–44.

[59] Addison, *Spectator* (October 25, 1711), 2: 305.

[60] Ed. Sir Henry Williams Baker (London: George Bull, 1909), p. 301.

ironed the collection into uniformity. The psalter of Archbishop
Matthew Parker, published about 1567, was a good indicator of the
variety entering the English psalm at this time. Printed with music in
four parts by Thomas Tallis, the Parker psalter relies heavily upon
Common Meter, although there are several more elaborate stanzas,
such as a six-line stanza consisting of an alternately rhymed quatrain
followed by a couplet that acts as a refrain. It is doubtful whether the
book could have had any wide influence, for it appears to have been
little known in its time and copies of it are extremely rare.

By this time, the metrical psalm was well enough furnished to enter
the seventies and eighties in a state of luxuriance. To this period
belong the fragmentary efforts of George Gascoigne and William
Byrd,[61] as well as more substantial pieces such as William Hunnis's
*Seven sobs of a sorrowful soule for sinne. comprehending those seven
psalmes of the Princelie Prophet David, commonly called poeniten-
tial* . . . (1583). Even the lushness of the abbreviated title suggests the
sort of sophistication now entering psalm translation; and the ten
editions that the book achieved by 1629 show that there was definitely
a modish trade in metrical psalms. But if by now versified Scripture
had deepened its base, it had also broadened it. From the fifties into
the seventies and eighties, metrical paraphrase seems to have reached
the proportions of a fad. This may be the only way to explain such
metered curiosities as Christopher Tye's twelve chapters of *The actes
of the apostles translated into Englyshe metre* . . . (1553) or Hunnis's
work of 1578, the *Hyve full of hunnye: contayning the first booke of
Moses called Genesis. Turned into English meetre* (in fourteen books);
or John Marbecke's version of the books of Samuel, entitled *The holie
historie of king David* (1579), apparently in order to capitalize upon
the psalm market; or "most foul, strange, and unnatural," an anonymous metrical version of nearly all the Old Testament, including
even the genealogies (1569). These works should probably be considered a sign of health rather than decay. As long as an art form can
afford the luxury of organized idiocy, genuinely fresh work in that
art seems to flower. Blocking off exits always frees the innovator, at
least from pointless innovation. In the case of versified Scripture, a

[61] Gascoigne, *A hundredth sundrie flowers, bound up in one small posie* (London:
H. Bynneman, 1573); Byrd, *Psalms, sonets, and songs of sadnes and pietie* (London:
T. East, 1588).

work such as the metrical *Moses* suggests (to the modern reader, anyway) that technical innovations in the verse might have been more productive than the old process of versified translation simply applied to other books of the Bible besides the Psalms.

The historical proof of this observation may be seen in possibly the greatest work of English psalmody, the psalms of Sir Philip Sidney and his sister, the Countess of Pembroke. The dating of the whole Sidney psalter is uncertain, but Sidney's share (the first forty-three) must have been completed before he left for the Netherlands in the fall of 1585, and William Ringler has proposed that the Countess completed her translations by 1599.[62] The "Sydnean Psalms," as Donne called them, were well known to the chief literary figures of the turn of the century, and in his edition of the psalter (already cited), Rathmell has recorded the enthusiastic comments of such poets as Fulke Greville, Samuel Daniel, Ben Jonson, John Donne, and others. In all, there seems no reason to doubt that the Sidney psalter was highly respected by the best poets of the time.

These psalms are unlike their English predecessors in a number of ways. The collection as a whole has a formal variety unlike that of any previous collection of English poetry, secular or otherwise. Among the hundred and fifty psalms, only two pairs have identical stanza patterns. The purpose behind this variety I shall discuss later; first I should like to trace its origin. To begin we must go back to the French translations of Clément Marot (1495?–1544), a source to which earlier English psalmodists had not gone. In 1533 Marot, chiefly a writer of secular lyrics, had translated Psalm Six, placing it at the end of *Le Miroir de treschrestienne Princesse Marguerite de France, Royne de Navarre*. By 1539 Marot had translated at least thirteen other Psalms, and in 1542 published *Trente Pseulmes de David, mis en francoys par Clement Marot, valet de chambre du Roy*. Set to the tunes of contemporary French love songs, Marot's psalms were a great success in the French court. Indeed, something of the atmosphere of Marot's psalms seems to be caught in the Sidney psalms and *The Temple*, something to do with the idea of devotion as a joyful game. Miss Campbell has already quoted from the following well-documented and reliable account, but I cannot help quoting it again:

[62] Sidney, *Poems*, ed. William A. Ringler, Jr. (Oxford: Clarendon Press, 1962), p. 501.

No one delighted in the *sanctes chansonettes* [Marot's term for his psalms] more passionately than the Dauphin, afterwards Henry II. He sang them himself, set them to music, and surrounded himself with musicians who accompanied his voice on the viol or the lute. To win his favor, the gentlemen of the Court begged him to choose for each a psalm. Courtiers adopted their special psalms, just as they adopted their special arms, mottoes, or liveries. Henry, as yet without an heir, sang to his own music Ps. cxxviii, which promises to the God-fearing man a wife "as the fruitful vine," and children "like the olive branches." Catherine de Medicis, then a childless wife, repeated Ps. vi. ("O Lord, rebuke me not in thine indignation"). Anthony, King of Navarre, chose Ps. xliii. ("Give sentence with me, O God"). Diane de Poitiers sang the *De Profundis* to the tune of a dance. In after years, when Catherine had borne her husband two children, Henry carolled Ps. xlii. ("Like as the hart desireth water-brooks") as he hunted the stag in the Forest of Fountainbleau, riding by the side of Diane, for the motto of whose portrait as a huntress he chose the first verse of his favorite psalm.[63]

I do not wish to imply that our sober English poets behaved like these fugitives from *Love's Labour's Lost*; but it is remarkable that Sidney in his psalms—Mary Herbert only rarely in hers—and Herbert in *The Temple* often capture a similar sense of the *fête galante*, in which the religious joy of many psalms is caught in a manner appropriate to David himself (or his *persona*, as the case may be). In his *Defence*, Sidney states that those who "hath the Holy Ghost in due holy reverence" will respect the Psalms and other divine poetry, which "must be used, by whosoever will follow S. James his counsell, in singing Psalmes when they are merry."[64] Certainly this element of joyful religious play, though present in the use of Marot's psalms, is lacking in most English psalms and contemporary accounts of their performance.

Calvin had seen Marot's psalms during his exile at Strasbourg and had published several along with his own versions in the 1539 *Aulcuns Pseaumes et mys en chant*. Thus when Marot's *Trente Pseulmes* were promptly condemned by the Sorbonne after their publication, it was appropriate that Marot should flee to Geneva. His journey led

63 Margaret Walker Freer, *The Life of Marguerite d'Angoulême, Queen of Navarre, Duchesse d'Alençon and De Berry* (Cleveland: Burrows, 1895), p. 278.

64 In G. Gregory Smith, ed., *Elizabethan Critical Essays* (Oxford: Clarendon Press, 1904), 1: 158.

to a strange but productive literary relationship. Calvin, the great champion of congregational singing, needed a psalter; but he had definite stipulations concerning the double emphasis of ear and mind:

> It is fully evident that unless voice and song, if interposed in prayer, spring from deep feeling of heart, neither has any value or profit in the least with God. But they arouse his wrath against us if they come only from the tip of the lips and from the throat, seeing that this is to abuse his most holy name and to hold his majesty in derision . . . . If the singing be tempered to that gravity which is fitting in the sight of God and the angels, it lends dignity and grace to sacred actions and has the greatest value in kindling our hearts to a true zeal and an eagerness to pray. Yet we should be very careful that our ears be not more attentive to the melody than our minds to the spiritual meaning of the words . . . when this moderation is maintained, it is without any doubt a most holy and salutary practice. On the other hand, such songs as have been composed only for sweetness and delight of the ear are unbecoming to the majesty of the church and cannot but displease God in the highest degree.[65]

All of this may explain why Calvin had laughed—the one and only time, some say—when he first heard Marot's psalms sung to popular French tunes.[66] Notwithstanding his scruples, Calvin commissioned the obviously accomplished poet to complete a psalter for his congregation, and Marot accordingly published versions of the psalter in 1542 and 1543, adding twenty more psalms to his former total. When Marot died suddenly in 1544, the work was carried on by Théodore de Bèze, who had a somewhat less inspired style but still continued to vary stanza patterns to suit the individual Psalms. In 1562 the whole psalter finally appeared, and it was quite likely seen by Sidney in his European travels in the seventies. In any case, the existing manuscript drafts of his and the Countess's psalms show that they were both familiar with the Marot-Bèze psalter.[67]

---

[65] *Institutes of the Christian Religion*, ed. John T. McNeill and trans. Ford Lewis Battles, Library of Christian Classics, vols. 20, 21 (Philadelphia: Westminster Press, 1960), 21: 894–96.

[66] Noted in Albert Schweitzer's *J. S. Bach*, trans. Ernest Neumann (New York: Macmillan, 1949), 1: 20.

[67] Ringler describes in great detail (Sidney, *Poems*, pp. 500–516) the making of the Sidney psalter, the specific parallels with the French psalter, and the revisions made in Sidney's text by his sister.

The mixture of the profane lyric and the holy Psalm which amused
Calvin was to yield several happy results, for Sidney as well as Marot.
First, the metrical psalm could now have some of the prosodic flexibility and surprise of the popular catch. By the use of stanzaic variety
if nothing else, a poet could now avoid the monotony of the Sternhold
and Hopkins Common Meter, with its never-changing medial breaks
and three-beat lines padded out for the rhymes' sake. Much of Marot's
variety also came from his use of what has now come to be called
rhyme counterpoint. This is from the start of his Psalm 27:

> Las, en ta fureur aigue
>   Ne m'argue,
> De mon faict, Dieu toutpuissant:
> Ton ardeur un peu retire:
>   N'en ton rire
> Ne me puniz languissant.[68]

Variation in stanza pattern may not automatically insure variation
in tone, but at least it makes it easier to obtain. Sidney does appear
to have been seeking some variety in tone, but whether he achieved
it by his stanzas alone is difficult to say. It is clear, though, that by
exploiting Marot's use of techniques such as rhyme counterpoint
Sidney was able to achieve effects which were striking to his contemporaries, who were more used to psalms with ruthlessly regular meters
and rhymes. Donne remarks, in praising the Sidney psalms, that

> I must not rejoyce as I would doe
> When I behold that these Psalmes are become
> So well attyr'd abroad, so ill at home,
> So well in Chambers, in thy Church so ill,
> As I can scarce call that reform'd untill
> This be reformed.[69]

As it is doubtful that Donne is referring to Lutheran psalmody—
the play on "reform'd" makes this clear—his reference to the Psalms
"well attyr'd abroad" seems to point to the French psalter. Thus the

---

[68] Marot, *Oeuvres complètes* (Paris: Rapilly, 1824), 3: 260.
[69] "Upon the Translation," ll. 36–44, in Donne, *Divine Poems.*

"attyr" of the Sternhold and Hopkins Old Version is related to its ill song (which could not conceivably be derived from the *matter* of the Psalms themselves). Donne is indirectly alluding to the most conspicuous feature of the Sidney psalter, the technical variety of its verse. As the title page of the Penshurst MS of the psalter points out, these psalms are "translated into divers and sundry kinds of verse, more rare, and excellent, for the method and varietie than ever yet hath bene don in English."[70] The qualifier "in English" is significant.

However, few English translators after Sidney and Mary Herbert show any awareness of either the French or the Sidney psalters. The Sidney psalter may have been highly respected by other poets, but it inspired few imitations. The Sternhold and Hopkins psalter was by now so firmly established with the folk that changes in it would not have been well received, and congregations were not loathe to make known their preferences in such matters.[71] And by this time, many poets seem to have developed quite definite critical ideas as to the proper nature of psalm verse. (The technical influence of Hebrew poetry has been ably discussed by other critics and is a matter distinct from consideration of the metrical psalm as a genre with its own critical theory.)[72] Generally there was critical agreement about the proper form of versified psalms. Most critics adopted one of two stances, the earlier of which was to claim that for religious subjects the long line was more appropriate than the short. Thus Gascoigne, restricting short lines and stanzas to use in secular lyrics, advises the poet that "the long verse of twelve or fourtene sillables, although it be now adayes used in all Theames, yet in my judgement it would serve best for Psalmes and Himpnes."[73] Perhaps for reasons of this sort, when George Puttenham discusses the Psalms in English he mentions only Sternhold by name.[74]

The alternative to this attitude toward the long line is to say, as does Sir John Harington in his *Brief Apology*, that "the learnedest divines do affirme [the Psalms] to be verse and find that they are in

---

[70] There is a facsimile of the title page in Rathmell, *The Psalms*, p. xxxiii.

[71] See Bridenbaugh, *Vexed and Troubled Englishmen*, pp. 350–53.

[72] Israel Baroway, "The Accentual Theory of Hebrew Prosody," *ELH*, 17 (1950): 115–35.

[73] *Certayne Notes of Instruction* . . . , in Smith, *Elizabethan Critical Essays*, 1: 57.

[74] Puttenham, *The Arte of English Poesie*, ed. Gladys Doidge Willcock and Alice Walker (Cambridge: Cambridge University Press, 1936), pp. 16–17, 60.

meeter, though the rules of the Hebrew they agree not on."[75] Probably the most familiar statement of this position is Sidney's comment that the Psalter of David "is fully written in meeter, as all learned Hebricians agree, although the rules be not yet fully found."[76] This view is more honest historically than Gascoigne's (insofar as his view contains any view of history at all), and it allows some technical variety in verse forms by implicitly condoning experimentation. If we are to judge by the history of psalm translation in English, however, this second view was not the prevailing one. Even though the "lost" metrical rules of the Hebrew psalms might have given a poet like Sidney a blank check in his own translations, most poets were content to go on drawing out the same old amounts. What is probable is that by the time of Herbert's death in 1633, no poet besides Herbert had systematically followed up the leads offered by the Sidney collection. One would like to have seen Edmund Spenser's lost version of the Penitential Psalms, which Ponsonby listed among the "Pamphlets looselie scattered abroad";[77] but it is doubtful that it would have rivalled the Sidneys' version in formal variety.

Collections by notable poets continued to appear after the turn of the century and included those by Henry Dod (1603); Bishop Joseph Hall, who translated the first ten psalms in his *Some few of David's Psalms Metaphrazed in Metre* (1607); John Davies of Hereford, who transcribed the Countess of Pembroke's psalms, and then translated his own *Seven Penitential Psalms* in 1612; and Sir Edwin Sandys, whose *Sacred Hymns, consisting of fifty select psalms of David and others* . . . (1615) are rarely mentioned but are not entirely without merit. To this period also belong Phineas Fletcher's paraphrases, which were later printed (appropriately enough) with *The Purple Island* (1633). All of these versions are written in the now traditional Common Meter, although the combinations of stanzas and rhymes show some individual variation. In 1620 Dod reissued his version, adding translations of Canticles, but evidently this second edition was not offered in response to popular demand, and the translation was so wretched that copies of it were publicly burned.[78] Francis Bacon's small version (1625) is of

[75] In Smith, *Elizabethan Critical Essays*, 2: 207.

[76] *Ibid.*, 1: 155.

[77] In "The Printer to the Gentle Reader," in *Complaints*, in Spenser, *Poetical Works*, ed. J. C. Smith and E. de Selincourt (London: Oxford University Press, 1912), p. 470.

[78] See Wither, *Schollers Purgatory*, p. 33.

more than ordinary interest because it is dedicated to Herbert, who had helped Bacon translate *The Advancement of Learning* into Latin; but the verse is tedious and exasperating, and it does not appear to have influenced Herbert. (Signs of *The Advancement*, on the other hand, may be evident in such a poem as "Vanitie" [I].) Other minor psalters of some interest at this time include King James's psalter (1631) and an anonymous psalter setting out the French tunes in English words (1632).

The last significant psalter before Herbert's death in 1633 was that by George Wither, *The Psalmes of David translated into Lyrick-Verse* (1632). Wither had prepared himself for the writing of this collection by issuing four previous books of and about psalms and hymns. His first, *A Preparation to the Psalter* (1619), is an important discussion of psalm translation, but suffers somewhat from Wither's constant drift toward polemic. Much of the *Preparation* consists of a defense of the Psalms as poetry and in translation, and most of the arguments are simply the old ones reheated. Wither is interested in the rhetorical figures of the Psalms, and this interest leads him to an important observation which, if he had followed it through, might have led him into the Marot-Sidney "school" of psalmody: at one point he states that the different forms of the Psalms do not arise "out of any speciall affectation of variety; but with an intent to sute the matter of each Psalme . . . to such Numbers as might most aptly expresse it."[79] After studying David's use of metaphor and "ornament," he asks, "But why doe I stand thus upon particulars, when the whole Booke is full of elegancies? yea, as I sayd before every Psalme has its proper loveliness."[80] He also seems to disapprove of those who "have in scorne tearmed the French Psalter *Geneva Jiggs*, and *Beza's Ballets*."[81] But in spite of these observations, Wither is not concerned, as were Marot and Sidney, with metric or stanzaic variation to express the particularity of each Psalm, and thus his own exemplary translations in this volume are confined to alternately rhymed pentameter lines.

The following year, 1620, Wither published his *Exercises upon the Firste Psalme*, chiefly a detailed "Exposition" of the Psalm with little technical commentary on the verse, and in 1623 the *Hymns and Songs of the Church*. Although this volume contained no psalm transla-

---

[79] Wither, *A Preparation to the Psalter* (London: Nicholas Okes, 1619), p. 16.
[80] *Ibid.*, p. 75.
[81] *Ibid.*, p. 8.

tions, Wither had hoped it would eventually replace the Sternhold-Hopkins psalter and had obtained a patent directly from the king which authorized the placing of the Wither hymnal at the end of every copy of the psalter. The Company of Stationers resisted this patent as an usurpation, and thus Wither's book became a weapon in a familiar struggle. The Stationers finally won a prison term for Wither, and in his leisure he wrote *The Schollers Purgatory* (1624), which makes a justification of his patent, a defense of his hymns and psalms, and an attack on the established psalter. For its plain bad temper, the *Purgatory* makes better reading than the *Preparation to the Psalter*, and in it Wither states more openly the poet-translator's immediate problems:

> If it be well weighed, how full of short sentences, and suddaine breakings off, those scriptures are; how frequently, these Particles, *FOR, BUT* & such lik, (which are graceful in the Originall Text) will seem to obscure the dependancy of Sense in the English phrase, if the power of their signification be not heedfully observed in those places: How harsh the musicke will be, if the chiefe Pauses be not carefully reduced unto the same place in the lyne throughout the whole Hymne, which they have in the first Stanza; how many differences must be observed between Lyricke-Verse and that which is composed for reading only: Howe the Translater is tyed, not to make choice of those fashion Stanzaes, which are easiest, to expres the matter in, but to keep that with which he first began: how he is bound, not only to the sence, (according to the liberty used in other Translations) but to the very words, or words of the same power with those used in our allowed Interpretations: Lastly, how precise he must be, when he is forced to expresse any sentence by circumlocution, to labor stil to retayne a relish of the holy phrase in his expressions: I say, if all these circumstances be well considered, (and how difficult they make it to close up every Stanza with a period, or some such point that the voice may decently pause there,) I am parswaded a worke of this nature could not have been persisted in, to this conclusion, by a man having so many weaknesses, and discouragements as I have had; unless the Almighty had beene with mee.[82]

Here and in his translations, Wither picks up and exaggerates the bitterness and self-righteousness of some of the Psalms; the rhetorical turn into self-pity seems designed to head off criticism of the poetry.

[82] Wither, *Schollers Purgatory*, pp. 36–37.

Unfortunately Wither has little concern for what we would regard as the doggerel qualities of popular psalmody. Indeed, when he defends his own hymns, he suggests that they too have those qualities; quoting his critics at length—always a risky tactic—Wither says that they

> object (forsooth) that they are not worthy to be annexed with their Psalmes in meeter, in respect of that insufficiency which they have discovered in my expressions. For so harsh and improper do my lynes appeare to these juditious censurers, and their chaplins; that some compare them to DOD the silke-mans late ridiculous translation of the Psalmes, which was by authority worthily condemned to the fire. Some Tearme them in scorne, WITHERS SONNETS; and some, among them, the better to expresse what opinion they have of their pious use, are pleased to promise that they will procure the roaring Ballett singer with one legg, to sing and sell them about the citie . . . .[83]

Wither's 1632 psalter is the last major translation before Herbert's death, but we need not speculate about whether Herbert had time to read, digest, and be influenced by it.[84] Although Wither had paid a good deal of attention to previous psalters and the task before him, his final product is not very different from its predecessors. The book is mentioned in most standard literary histories, but its reputation seems to be based on Wither's stature in other genres, slight as it is. But the modern reader may suspect that if Wither's psalms were poured onto all the others they would soak in without leaving a trace. One reason for this is that in spite of his criticism of Sternhold and Hopkins, he has, he says in his "Preface to the Reader,"

> confined my selfe to such kinds of Verse as I found in the old Psalmebook; fitting them in such manner, that every Psalme in this Booke may be sung to some Tune formerly in use, either in the single, or in one of the double Translation [that is, single or double Common Meter].[85]

[83] *Ibid.*, p. 33.

[84] In this context it is interesting that when Playford collected what he assumed were Herbert's seven psalm translations, he did not mention Wither's psalms, although he did mention other translators besides Herbert. See Herbert, *Works*, p. 554.

[85] Wither, *The Psalms of David translated into Lyrick-Verse* (The Netherlands: Cornelis Gerrits van Breughel, 1632), p. xi. The place of the psalms in Wither's poetic development has been traced by Charles Hensley in *The Later Career of George Wither* (The Hague: Mouton, 1969), though with little comment on the literary qualities of Wither's translation.

There may seem to be some fundamental confusion on Wither's part between music and poetry; but if we consider what he says here, along with what he is trying to say in *The Schollers Purgatory*, we may find instead of confusion a fairly clear distinction. In his psalms Wither has written, to use again V. C. Clinton-Baddeley's term, words-for-music rather than poetry that can be set to music. For example, the rhythms of Wither's psalms rely to a great extent on the notes of the given tunes, and this practice naturally involves the necessary suppression of poetic rhythms that are too subtle for the setting. This simplicity may make his psalms more of a commercial success, but it also explains why they are so slightly differentiated stylistically from those of Sternhold and Hopkins. The old tunes have committed Wither to the same stanza forms, and to the same rhythmic patterns and phrasal movements. And as long as his verse is "fitted" to the old tunes, it runs the risk of receiving the same criticism. It may well be that Wither's psalms not only could but should be sung by the roaring ballad singer with one leg. The fine but definite distinction between poetry for music and music for poetry is blurred in Wither's criticism and verse, though clear in *The Temple*.

After Wither, the metrical psalm goes on to attract such poets as George Sandys, Henry King, Milton, and others, but their psalms are outside the historical limits of this study. They are also outside its critical limits, for they have a distinct distance from performance which may point to the coming Restoration split between poetry and music, as described in the studies of John Hollander and Wilfred Mellers.[86] This continuing development of the metrical psalm, until its supersession in the eighteenth century by the hymns of the Wesleys and others, is another subject in itself. Examining the progress of the genre as a whole could reveal most fully how the metrical psalm differs from the secular and devotional poetry that is contemporary with it; but, again, there is neither the need nor the space for this study at the moment. There are other ways of approaching that problem, and now that we have some historical data, we might look directly

---

[86] In n. 26 I have already cited Hollander's *The Untuning of the Sky*; Wilfred Mellers, in *Harmonious Meeting* (London: Dennis Dobson, 1965), takes a very different perspective on some of the same material: his approach has shaped my thinking considerably. There is a valuable study of primary material in Gretchen Ludke Finney's *Musical Backgrounds for English Literature: 1580–1660* (New Brunswick, N.J.: Rutgers University Press, 1961).

at some of the essential religious and psychological qualities of the Psalms themselves.

III. INFORMING PATTERNS

There are four elements that all metrical psalms share and in which they differ from other verse composed at the time and often by the same author:

1) They dramatize a common psychological and spiritual pattern or present a descriptive analogue to that pattern.

2) They reveal that the translators' motives have much in common with those of later devotional poets.

3) They involve, for their translators, a conflict between translation and impulse, and this conflict has a bearing on religious problems.

4) They present models for the use of poetic failure as a metaphor for spiritual failure.

Psychological and Spiritual Pattern

Metrical psalms differ from most verse of the sixteenth and early seventeenth centuries in one essential way: they are based upon the subject matter of the Book of Psalms. The Hebrew Psalms present in one collection a range of structures and tones which would be difficult to isolate conveniently in any other grouping of "Drab" verse. Literary form and structure in the Psalms are a relatively recent topic of study among Old Testament scholars; only since the foundation work of Hermann Gunkel in the 1920s has the subject been freed from the exclusive interests of historical and philological critics.[87] (Prior to Gunkel, most critical study in the Psalms appears to have centered upon the search for historical incidents that could account for the composition of individual Psalms.) At the present time, most literary criticism of the Psalms is occupied either with tracing out the generic

---

[87] Gunkel, *The Psalms: A Form-Critical Introduction*, trans. Thomas M. Horner (Philadelphia: Fortress Press, 1967); originally published in the 2d ed. of *Die Religion in Geschichte und Gegenwart* (1927–31). W.O.E. Oesterly's *The Psalms* (London: Society for the Preservation of Christian Knowledge, 1955) is a helpful general guide that includes a review of criticism; Harvey H. Guthrie, Jr., has made an informal study, *Israel's Sacred Songs* (New York: Seabury Press, 1966).

distinctions within the psalter, as laid out by Gunkel, or relating the
psalter more fully to the cultic use of song in worship services and
legal transactions. There is no need to comment on this work; instead
I would like to point to one principal theme which runs throughout
the psalter and then relate this theme to seventeenth-century devotional poetry.

Although the Psalms contain different songs of praise, thanksgiving,
confession, lament, and vengeance, most of them have one dominant
rhetorical pattern, one which in many ways resembles the familiar
mythic pattern of strength developing out of weakness. Rebirth may
not be a precise term for the process, but it does connote some of the
necessary sense of revitalizing strength growing out of human failures
in the present. One of the distinctive ironies of the Psalms is that the
strength the psalmist typically asks for is one which grows out of his
present predicament. He does not seek merely to escape his misery:
an easy course like this would be a sacrilege and an abdication.
Though he may suffer some lacerating disease or humiliation, he still
asks for greater consciousness of it, in order to go through and beyond
it, to a recognition of God as a force stronger than evil. As Psalm 90
asks, "Make us glad according to the days wherein thou has afflicted
us, and the years wherein we have seen evil." The verse immediately
after this (the sixteenth) then sets up the really dense paradoxes in
this point of view: "Let thy work appear unto thy servants, and thy
glory unto their children." The inclusiveness of this vision is what I
wish to stress here, its insistence that the present time, for all its
perturbations and limitations, provides the principal access to transcendent knowledge.

Similarly, the divine power that most excites the psalmist's praise
is that which continually renews itself in the present: the last six
Psalms, for example, show in one unbroken sequence how God perpetually moves from one act to another within man's life. Or for a
fuller example of this spiritual renewal within the present, we might
take the many times the Psalms refer to God's power to inspire fertil-
ity (as in Psalm 115). Throughout all the Psalms of praise, God's
grace is shown actively transforming all things weakest and lowest into
things strongest and highest: in the typically dry wit of the psalmist's
metonymy, "He beautifies the meek" (Psalm 149). In these Psalms
virtually all creation takes a participatory role in making what was
once hostile friendly, what was once empty overflowing. There is no

more penetrating description of this process in the Psalms than Christopher Smart's "Song to David": here all animals, people, and instruments of art spontaneously reveal the transpiring of grace, within the bounds of earthly time.

The theme of regeneration itself is, again, hardly peculiar to the Psalms; what they do stress, with especial energy, is the link between the "eternal return" and the misery of the present. The likelihood of the return is affirmed (as in Psalm 69) by the vigor of the lament. Yet by virtue of the very fullness of the Psalms, and the inclusiveness of the repeated themes, the plain symbolic pattern is rarely enunciated flatly, although its assumptions are present everywhere and particularly inform the psalmist's attitudes toward human limitations and potential power. There is no need here for a full-scale demonstration of the theme in the psalter, and it would be pointless to rehearse matters that will soon appear in specific poems by Herbert; but we might look at one Psalm which is at once typical in its strength-weakness structure and yet does not immediately reveal it. (Here as elsewhere—unless otherwise noted—I shall be using as my text the Authorized or King James version of the psalter.)

On the literal level, in Psalm 35 the speaker, or David, points out the threats to him from wicked people and incites God against them. These enemies are not specifically identified, nor is there any reason for David to do so, in order to achieve his poetic purpose; I shall refer to these enemies with the italic *them*. The speaker's attitude toward *them* develops in three stages and is linked with his attitude toward God. In fact, the Psalm is divided into three approximately equal parts, the end of each being marked by a verse in which the speaker praises God (verses 9, 18, and 28).

In the first section, the speaker's attitude appears to verge on paranoia. He asks God to attack *them* simply because they oppose him. Besides, he is poor and needy. The exposition of this limited and egocentric attitude shades off quickly into that of the second section, which begins in self-justification ("But as for me, when they were sick, my clothing was sackcloth" [13]) but offers little specific description of *their* iniquities beyond the fact that *they* rejoice in his adversity and hypocritically mock him. This section ends in the speaker's nadir of misery and self-pity, but out of it comes the realization, at the beginning of the third section, that the very strength of *their* attack is its vagueness: "Yea, they opened their mouth wide against me, and said Aha, aha, our eye hath seen it" (21). The "it," of course, the enemies will not or cannot define. The self-righteous, self-pitying enumeration of the crimes committed against the speaker has exposed the groundless basis of *their* charges, but as the speaker's thoughts return to God, his attitude toward himself changes, too. Since he has attacked only vague invective, only one conclusion is possible, given the premises advanced so far: "Judge me, O Lord my God" (24). This judgment will confound, shame, and dishonor *them* by the very person of the speaker. The speaker moves gradually into a state of responsibility, and this movement reflects the change in his attitude toward *them*: initially they are only opponents, but by the end of the psalm, they have become an attitude that he would abandon. The psalmist is not simply chronicling one of man's more dismal attitudes but is also probing the question of human responsibility and the manner in which spiritual strength can develop out of that dismal vision. The particular answer to his problem is of interest, too, for it would grant to the psalmist a distinctly personal revenge, instead of the satisfying but secondhand pleasure of seeing God attack his foes.

The psalms of more direct prayer and confession have the same end in view, although in them the speaker attempts, by experiential account rather than invective, to get control of his weaknesses and tasks. Here, too, the weakness the speaker seeks to lose may be the very attitude the psalm expresses so forcefully, the debilitating hostility toward oneself and others. The compensatory strength that one desires may be simply that of an open heart, exhausted of its rage. (An obvious parallel here is a poem such as Herbert's "The Collar," which I shall examine later.) There is a reverse side to all this, too, for the strength that one seeks to have his enemy lose—whether the enemy be physical, or a demoralizing attitude that one has oneself—may be purely temporal. In this case the surest way for the enemy to lose it may be for him to continue in it so long that he incurs God's wrath or correction.

By its very nature, the metamorphosis of weakness into strength is a process which confirms the essential unity of experience. One's growth, one's fullest spiritual enlargement, must rise out of the self of the present. (We are not likely to find David invoking a Last Judgment or a Resurrection.) The end and purpose of human strength must emerge from the present with all its limitations, not from some radical transformation of the soul. We must remind ourselves of the psalmist's lack of interest in fixed or finally static attitudes: if there are no psalms of total despair, neither are there any in which the speaker *becomes* God.[88]

The emphasis upon the weakness-strength pattern and the unity which it assumes may explain why the Genevan Calvinists could claim (as I shall show more fully under the next heading) that the psalter was a first aid manual for emergencies and Coverdale could call it a collection of work songs. More generally, this pattern may offer one reason why the Psalms adapted themselves so readily to interpretation as the prefiguring of Christian mysteries. It may also explain why it was so easy to make the Psalms coherent with Orphic religion. But speculation of this sort should not obscure the fact that the metrical psalms could present the pattern to the sixteenth- and seventeenth-century churchgoer in an unremitting and congenial form. To a poet like Herbert, whose main theme was the movement of his mind and spirit, as they grappled with the psychic problems implied in a fully trusting faith, this essential pattern of the Psalms was of central importance. To all metaphysical poets, in fact, the Psalms may have had something to say, and here it would be appropriate to return to the matter of the unity of experience. What Frank J. Warnke has said of metaphysical poetry in general may also be applied to the Psalms:

> Beneath the surprising, sometimes perverse surface of Metaphysical and Baroque poetry lie the related convictions that only the ultimate spiritual unity is real and that only the sensibility can be a source of knowledge . . . . The Renaissance poets . . . see experience on two levels, the finally real level of the spirit and the provisionally real level of the flesh . . . . Neither Metaphysical or High Baroque poets can rest content with the double vision of reality; they seek neither to reconcile the two worlds nor to resolve their conflict but to reduce them to a unity.[89]

Warnke's comments may suggest a reason why the Psalms were able to exert such a strong attraction for poets such as Herbert and Donne. The unitive impulse of both the Psalms and metaphysical poetry is

---

[88] On the general process of weakness becoming strength I have found especially stimulating Helmer Ringgren's *The Faith of the Psalmists*, trans. by the author (Philadelphia: Fortress Press, 1963), in particular chaps. 6 ("Lament and Confession") and 7 ("Thanksgiving and Praise"). Ringgren's comments are especially valuable on the psychological problems of praise and confession.

[89] Warnke, *European Metaphysical Poetry* (New Haven: Yale University Press, 1961), pp. 2, 23.

evident not only in their attitude toward psychological experience but also in the poetic concomitants of that attitude, which the Psalms and the metaphysical poems share: the dramatic positioning, the variation in form and structure from poem to poem, the employment of some-times violent contrasts in attitude, and the distinctive arrangement of whole collections of poems. I am inclined to think that the principle of arrangement in *The Temple* (and perhaps many other collections of sixteenth- and seventeenth-century lyrics) is the same as that of the Book of Psalms. By design or not, both collections have scattered groupings of poems within a larger apparently random order. The order is one which invites rearrangement, and the recombining and reintegration of a large number of variables, by the reader, is the same process that the poet performs within individual poems.[90] In both the Psalms and *The Temple*, as the poet faces the problem of his own unity of experience, he forces an analogous problem upon his reader.

Motives for Translation

Perhaps the crudest motive for psalm translation involves the amount of money to be made from having one's psalms and hymns authorized for exclusive church use. Here, at the low end of what educators would call the motivational scale, may be found George Wither, or at least part of him, living in poverty, grumbling at the way "we see the Flesh and the Devill, having for their service thou-sands of vaine songes, and prophane ballads, . . . and that many hundred pounds are yearely consumed upon them," and then asking himself, "what divine calling HOPKINS AND STERNHOLD had more then I have, that their metricall Psalmes may be allowed of rather then my Hymnes."[91] Like most writers. Wither cannot help dreaming of a best-seller; although in his dream-vision of success, the profits are mandatory and automatic, temporal as well as eternal. One does not encounter, in the early seventeenth century at least, devo-tional poets who write for money, nor can one imagine the circum-stances under which they would.

---

[90] Cf. R. P. Blackmur on the order of the Psalms: "the constant interflow of new relations, of new reticulations—as if the inner order were always on the move" ("A Poetics of Infatuation," in *The Riddle of Shakespeare's Sonnets* [New York: Basic Books, 1962], p. 131).

[91] Wither, *Schollers Purgatory*, p. 19.

The principal religious motive for psalm translation was, as we noted with Coverdale, a sincere desire to replace profane song and thereby spread the faith. As this view was given a Calvinistic extension it terminated in the view that the Psalms are the only proper hymns of adoration. It is a fundamental confusion of values that, as Wither says,

> hath made the common people leave the sacred *Hymns* of the *Holy Ghost*, for the imperfect inventions of Man . . . if they understood what puddle water they offer GOD, when they might present him with the living streams of his owne pure fountain, they would be ashamed of their choyce.[92]

More practically, as nearly every one of the translators pointed out, verse encouraged virtue by facilitating memory. This was especially desirable because the Psalms were held to be the best available handbook for resolving dilemmas of all sorts. One of the best examples of this is to be found in John Strype's account of the Genevan exiles presenting a copy of their psalter to Queen Elizabeth upon her accession to the throne. Strype quotes at length from the psalter's dedication, in which the Genevans assert that " 'they supposed in their judgments, that no part of the whole Scripture was more necessary for her Grace than that little Book of *Psalms*, if it were well weighed and practised.' " The dedication goes on to list the queenly problems that the Psalms might solve: for example, " 'If the outward Enemy threatned or invaded, she should remember also how God preserved his Servant *David*, and enlarged his Kingdom.' "[93]

But this sort of justification does not carry us far into knowing what psalm translation does for the individual psalmodist. If we go deeper we encounter Wyatt and Surrey, for instance, both of whom turned to psalm translation in times of personal danger. Without speculating on their personal motivations, we can observe that for them the Psalms seem to be functioning in one of their original capacities, that of exorcism. If it is correct to say that these two poets versified psalms as a means of removing a curse, then it may not be inaccurate to describe their practice as a spiritual analogue to the use of the Psalms as a moral guidebook. It is also perhaps the closest that the English ap-

[92] *Ibid.*, p. 40.
[93] John Strype, *Annals of the Reformation and Establishment of Religion*, 3d ed. (London: Edward Symon, 1735), 1: 111.

proached to the widespread European practice of meditating upon Psalms. The use of the Psalms in this manner was especially common in France, as we have noticed earlier; and although it may seem odd that the practice never took root in England, there is at least a parallel situation in the way that the Marot-Bèze psalter was generally ignored as well. (Or when referred to at all, it was scoffed at.) The absence of English meditations upon Psalms may be somewhat dubiously ascribed to a general anti-French, anti-Papist feeling, but whatever the cause, the fact that the Psalms could be adapted so thoroughly to the processes of formal meditation, even if not in England, might indicate the presence in the Psalms of an informing pattern, such as that described in the preceding section. (Pattern, rather than matter: a worshipper could after all meditate upon a bestiary, provided he had a model for an analysis and a rhetorical gift for colloquy.) Unless I am mistaken, what Wyatt and to a lesser extent Surrey have done in their psalms is work out inductively a form of translation which approaches the pattern of formal meditation. This may account for two distinguishing factors in their translations: an emphasis upon description and an exaggerated stress upon repentance, even given the Psalms before them. Their motivation and the subject matter of the Psalms may have committed them, however unconsciously, to some of the formal techniques that later poets found at hand in the manuals of meditation.

In discussing motives for psalm translation it is well to end on a note which stresses one of the strongest themes in the Psalms. We began by looking at translation for profit; it is appropriate to end with translation for pleasure alone. We know how the Psalms were playfully sung in the French court, and while the English did not unbend enough for that sort of frolicking, we do have the testimony of Giles Farnaby, who remarks in the dedication to his psalter (which like Matthew Parker's provides settings in four parts) that he has "a long time had a desire to present to the vew, Davids Psalmes into a more privatt exercise for Gentlemen."[94] One can imagine this attitude

---

[94] The MS exists in a unique copy at the University of Pennsylvania (Philadelphia); quoted by Morison Comegys Boyd, *Elizabethan Music and Music Criticism* (Philadelphia: University of Pennsylvania Press, 1940), p. 59. The entire dedication is reproduced in facsimile facing p. 60. There is general agreement that for difficulty in translation the Hebrew Psalms have rarely if ever been surpassed. In this respect it is pertinent that in the preparation of the New English Bible, the Psalms proved far the most difficult book to translate (*TLS*, December 4, 1969, p. 1382).

readily enough, and it hardly appears to have been unique to Farnaby. Translation has always been a socially acceptable outlet for the gentleman poet, who exercises himself today on Pablo Neruda or fifty years ago on Li Po or four hundred years ago on David.

But describing the social fun of metrical psalms is different from describing the poetry itself. I have suggested before that although the sense of worship as a joyful game is everywhere present in the Psalms themselves, it is a sense which one is unable to feel in many of the translations besides those of Sidney and his sister. Gratuitous exuberance is not a quality easily associated with Sternhold, or Hopkins, or even a bustling wit like Wither. A sense of play is not, on the other hand, simply a matter of verse technique. Questions of motivation and sincerity are hard to escape in criticism of poetry like this, and any reader familiar with I. A. Richard's discussion of these matters will be rightly warned of the dangers of judging a poem on the basis of its presumed sincerity.[95] At the least, though, it should be possible to isolate the sources of the sense of play in the Sidney psalter. First, there is the total absence of explicit monetary or missionary impulse; it is missing from even the marginal notes in the manuscripts. Further, remarks on the psalter by contemporaries of the Sidneys do not claim, after the fashion of most literate comments upon most psalters of the period, that it will deliver souls or spread the wings of healing. Second is the matter of tone. Divines like Joseph Hall, who made his translations of the Psalms expressly to replace the Old Version, are thoroughly sober in their poetic efforts, as Miss Campbell's lengthy quotations demonstrate.[96] Hall's psalms are no laughing matter, but David often laughs. So do Sidney and his sister. Finally, the Sidney psalter deliberately attempts to employ all the resources of poetry in the praise of God. Sidney and his sister are also not above calling attention to their ingenuity or smiling at it. As we shall see later, both poets allude to their technical virtuosity, which they regard not so much a product of pride as of magnanimity. Because God gave us everything, we should offer Him all we have. Clearly it helps if we have a lot to offer. But not all poet-translators admit, as do these two, that we never have enough.

[95] I refer of course to *Practical Criticism*, chap. 7.
[96] Campbell, *Divine Poetry and Drama*, pp. 34–54.

Translation and Impulse

In an age of belief, as we are persuaded the English Renaissance
was, the problem of translating Scripture is very different from that
of translating Petrarch or Sannazaro. For one thing, if the poet-
translator bungles a Petrarch sonnet he is not likely to have so much
as a legal suit filed against him, but if he bungles a Psalm he may be
summoned before God's aroused aesthetic sense. Or worse yet, he may
have been singing to the wrong God. The problem is epistemological,
for we all must translate whenever we speak to each other, and our
personal motives and abilities necessarily affect the quality of our
translation. A poet is in the same position as he writes. If he tries to
record or translate his own feelings for God, he may have to risk a
decision based on his faith which would make a bad poem, or a decision based on his poetics which would make for a bad faith. The
poet who sets out to translate another poet's feelings for God is,
therefore, in a doubly complicated position. While in the act of moving the original poet's words to a different culture, the translator has
to clarify his own motives, in one way or another, in order to prevent
coloring the translation. The devout translator may feel free to ignore
this last problem, although its existence may then be all the more
painfully evident to his readers. We can arrange the tasks in order of
their increasing difficulty: the poet has to move the literal poem from
one language to another; then register the state of the original poet's
mind upon that of his immediate audience, an act which will involve
the epistemological problems of translations on two levels; and beyond
this there is the final problem of how the translator is to treat the
original poet's problem of taking a spiritual experience and putting
it into words, the process that Herbert calls "discovery."[97] Perhaps
these dilemmas can be resolved by reference to the historical context
of psalm translation, for there is little chance that the translators
themselves were much concerned with these matters. If nothing else,
it might be possible to see how they avoided these questions, and how
their evasions proved of significance for devotional poetry.

Sixteenth-century proponents of the Old Version occasionally
pointed out, as something in its favor, that its text was faithful to that

---

[97] See Arnold Stein's comments on the two sonnets from Walton's *Lives*, in
George Herbert's Lyrics, pp. 2–6. This idea of translation has been treated suc-
cinctly by W. H. Auden in *Secondary Worlds* (New York: Random House, 1969).

of the original Psalms.[98] To some degree, this claim was only relative, for most of the Old Version psalms were faithful to the Hebrew only in the sense that they were not faithful to anything else. But when, after the turn of the century, poets such as George Wither started railing at the inaccuracies and improprieties of the Old Version, the reader may sense that these poets were facing any translator's unavoidable struggle to make an idiomatically current translation. For example, Wither's objections to the diction of the Old Version were only indicative of the expected changes in poetic diction from one generation to another.

However, it would be an oversimplification to say that the problem of idioms changing in translation can enclose all the spiritual problems of psalm translation in particular. Part of the tension between contemporary and anachronistic translation is associated with the problem of spiritual justification. If the poet's aim is to praise God in His inspired Word, then literary grace may not be far from immanent grace. For the writer who is lame and knows it, this would be discriminatory legislation even if it were of divine origin. There are two logical solutions to the problem, and both were used by poets and translators during the sixteenth and seventeenth centuries. If the poet has a historical consciousness, he can assume that God in His infinite wisdom has made allowances for changes in literary taste and convention. This assumption does not seem to have been popular although there is no doubt that Herbert was aware of it. The more common assumption among the psalmodists in particular was that literary grace may indeed be a relative of immanent grace but may still constitute a trap in itself, for extended concentration upon it may be a form of spiritual pride. As a result, most English psalm translators eschew grace in translation as worldly wisdom well avoided. The *locus classicus* would be Coverdale's doggerel protest to the effect that virtue is more important than verse, a justification which incidentally resembles that of another group of professionally outraged and virtuous poets, the Elizabethan satirists.

It is not surprising that in the face of this popular religious lyricism the devotional poets, all of whom write of the difficulties of faithfully translating their own impulses, should evolve what we think

---

[98] See Campbell, *Divine Poetry and Drama*, pp. 34–45. Needless to say, the poetic *form* of the versified translations was also a great argument for their fidelity to the originals.

of as uniquely personal styles. For these poets, the low popular style of most psalms is clearly unacceptable by the turn of the century, if not earlier; but by the 1630s the psalmodists' sturdy defense of the low style would seem to have made the unqualified use of the high style equally reproachable. Several solutions were possible, all of them present to a greater or lesser degree in Herbert:

1) Evolve a middle style in terms of Christian rhetoric, drawing on Scriptural and patristic thought and modifying it as necessary.

2) Use the low style and offer (often by means of the high style) a critique of its poetic and its defense of poetic crudity in the translation of spiritual impulse.

3) Use the high style and offer a direct critique of it by means of the low style.

The first of these possibilities has been explored by Stein; of necessity his approach must ignore the role of a popular low style. The second possibility is one I wish to associate with Herbert; it also may apply, though somewhat unevenly, to Henry Vaughan. Under this heading comes a particularly important development in devotional verse. The justification of crudity in psalm translation, on the basis of its fidelity to original inspiration and its virtue-inspiring qualities, quite often distinctly resembles the rationale behind Herbert's parodistic and often droll treatment of religious themes. The second heading describes what is in effect a pastoral mode working in terms of style alone, for which I can find no precedent in the writings of the Fathers of the Church. The third possibility is one which Herbert follows less frequently; I would associate it with the poetry of Richard Crashaw. Here we have a mode less amendable to ironic treatment if the poet has assumed the mask of a humble country parson (which Crashaw did not, either in his verse or evidently in his person).[99]

I have said that Herbert uses the apparent artlessness of the metrical psalms because of their presumed fidelity to inspiration. In this he is quite close to what A. O. Lovejoy described as the fifteenth sense of nature as an aesthetic norm: "self-expression without self-consciousness; freedom from premeditation or deliberate and reflective design, artlessness." Thus we may trace, in Herbert's verse, the "preponder-

[99] In 1668 David Lloyd described Crashaw's "thronged sermons," which "ravished more like Poems . . . scattering not so much Sentences as Extasies; his soul breathing in each word" (quoted by Austin Warren, in *Richard Crashaw* [Ann Arbor: University of Michigan Press, 1939], p. 41).

ance of feeling (as the spontaneous and therefore more 'natural' element in human nature) over intellection or deliberate aesthetic design."[100] Of course it is also true that in Herbert's design the apparently artless becomes the artful; what might at first be taken for violation of deliberateness in design may become, for the attentive reader, a highly deliberate stroke. Herbert considers this seeming contradiction in several poems, and resolves it by making God the source of all true art; He can modify the effect if the cause is valid. The merit of this aesthetic is that it works two ways, if the poem works or if it doesn't. Herbert never completely adopts this limited view; he is too aware of it as a trap or as an excuse for doing badly what he ought to do well. It is possible, then, to take Lovejoy's definition and turn it inside out: in Herbert's view, cultivated artlessness can become a trap as great as artfulness. It is here that the content of the Psalms—whatever the defects of their translations—can provide a stable center for the whole problem; this is vitally necessary, for as Lovejoy's listing shows, the concept of naturalness can be taken through so many convolutions that it is not hard to find one concept or definition rebutted by the very arguments that support it. (Thus, incidentally, the adoption, in eighteenth-century hymnody, of many of the homely touches the previous generation of decorous psalmodists had rejected.) Herbert's firm use of the Psalms behind the psalmody makes him end where he began.

The problem of exhibiting a revelation honestly, without the coloring of one's own desires, is common both to psalm translation and to *The Temple*, and in both cases the problem receives some similar solutions. However, most psalm translators rarely realize that in the poetry of worship, as in other poetry, one does not entirely escape literary convention. If the poet is alert, he can use it in full consciousness, rising through it to a poem that can describe a spiritual state and be understood by readers long after the death of the particular conventions within which it was written. Although this does not often happen in psalm translation, it does happen in *The Temple*, and the material for the description of the process was all present in the recurrent debate over psalm translation.

---

[100] Lovejoy, *Essays in the History of Ideas* (Baltimore: The Johns Hopkins Press, 1948), pp. 72, 74 (l). For specific illustrations of the matters discussed in this paragraph, see the comments in chap. 3 on "A true Hymne" and "Gratefulnesse."

Poetic and Spiritual Failure

Horace among others advised that the good metaphor will announce its presence in the poem by a break in the meter, and many of
the devotional and metaphysical poets took this advice to heart, either
consciously or unconsciously. The reasons why are not hard to see.
There are several connections between poetic and spiritual failure. If
for the devotional poet the supreme crisis is the failure to reach God,
then this failure will often manifest itself in the form of his poem.
There are Herbert's failure poems, for example, in which the rhymes are
dropped, or abruptly made, as a way of mirroring the speaker's shaky
spiritual state. Less obvious but equally valid examples may be found
in Donne and Vaughan, where contortions and clumsiness in syntax
or rhythm often indicate the presence or nature of a spiritual problem.
The most readily available examples for incompetence in lyric form
were the bathetic popular versions of the psalms, which present a
speaker in the same dramatic situations as the speakers in the devotional poems of spiritual crisis. There are complications of tone in
these poems, however, which make the metrical psalm quite useful
critically, for much of the mingled pathos and self-regard in the devotional poems may be the result of bathetic syntax and rhyming working their ways across elaborate stanzas or intricate logical structures.
This whole line of reasoning may be pushed to a perhaps speculative
conclusion: if the subject of baroque art is, as has been claimed, the
interplay of appearance and reality, and its characteristic mode of
treatment is the examination of mental process, or subject and object,
then it seems possible that in the English religious poetry of the late
sixteenth and early seventeenth centuries the metrical psalm played
a most important part. It did this by supplying, first, a flagrant crudity
of technique that could highlight extremely sophisticated statements.
More importantly, it permitted the speaker to comment upon the
manner in which he treated his subject, while in the very process of
treating it. As in Herbert's poems "Vanitie" (II), "Man's Medley," or his
translation of the "Twenty-third Psalme," the apparent technical incon-
gruities allow the speaker to comment on his own relations to God.

On the other hand, there is a narrow border between the poem that
attempts to describe spiritual failure and the poem that becomes a
legitimate failure in its own right. There are several strategies by
which a poet can balance on the border and not fall over. One

particularly ingenious solution may be found in Sidney's defense of the Psalms, cited earlier in this study. The fact that the Hebrew Psalms are poetry could be used to defend contemporary poetry, but since the metrical psalm also requires justification on its own terms as poetry, it is a weapon that has to be used with care. Just how much care may be seen as Sidney remarks dryly of David: "truely now having named him, I feare mee I seeme to prophane that holy name, applying it to Poetrie, which is among us throune downe to so ridiculous an estimation . . . ."[101] This double-edged attitude towards the Psalms—Sidney has managed to defend contemporary poetry with them while admitting his helplessness—resembles our modern thinking on thermo-nuclear weapons: as Herman Kahn says, the last thing these weapons are here for is to be used. Similarly, when most of the devotional poets come to justify their writing of poetry, they do it in the same backhand manner: the poem is justified in terms of its spiritual promise rather than in terms of its actual success as a poem. This disclaimer, it will be noted, is virtually the same that the apologists for the metrical psalm used when charged with poetic incompetence. Thus the spiritual defense of the devotional poets may be connected with their deliberate stumbles. These stumbles all share the same paradox: as one finds one's self by losing one's self, so the poem may complete itself by what may at first seem to be a loss of control.

[101] In Smith, *Elizabethan Critical Essays*, 1: 155.

TWO

Some Metrical Psalm Styles

I. SIR THOMAS WYATT

In chapter 2 of his essay on the Sublime, or the *Peri Hupsous*, Longinus used the term *bathos*, or "depth," to describe exaltation or elevation in writing. In his parody of Longinus, the *Peri Bathos*, Alexander Pope borrowed the term and inverted its usage, applying it to sublimely bad poetry that revealed "the *true Profound*; the Bottom, the End, the Central Point; *Vivacité de pesanteur*, or (as an *English* Author calls it) an 'Alacrity of sinking.'"[1] Pope was interested more in the narrative and logical qualities of "sinking" than in its stylistic qualities (in the sense of technical performance), but the two are related. We might see the connection by looking at some notorious lines from Wordsworth's "Vaudracour and Julia":

> To a lodge that stood
> Deep in a forest, with leave given, at the age
> Of four-and twenty summers he withdrew;
> And thither took with him his motherless Babe,
> And one domestic for their common needs,
> An aged woman. It consoled him here
> To attend upon the orphan, and perform
> Obsequious service to the precious child,

[1] Alexander Pope, *The Art of Sinking in Poetry*, ed. E. L. Steeves (New York: Kings Crown Press, 1952), pp. 6, 14, 15.

Which, after a short time, by some mistake
Or indiscretion of the Father, died.[2]

This is a masterly fusion of narrative and stylistic bathos. The last line is alarming for a number of reasons connected with its prose logic, such as the offhand dismissal of a character who had seemed important, and the vagueness as to the cause of death, compared with the precision of detail above ("with leave given," "four-and-twenty summers," and so forth). However, its stylistic features are equally responsible for this effect of bathos. If we can pass over the low burlesque of "some mistake or indiscretion," we might see that the final verb is surprising largely because of its distance from its grammatical subject. This long suspension is increased logically by the use of a less emphatic subordinate clause for the announcement of the death and rhythmically by the presence of the two parallel and dependent phrases between the pronoun and its verb. Without the numerous pauses within the lines, the verb would not have its impact. Finally, we should note the contrast between the polysyllabic abstractions dominating the second half of the passage and the monosyllabic final verb, which is not abstract and which has an emphasis of its own because of the repeated consonant. In all, the lines have a self-cancelling quality because of the contrast between the calm and serious tone Wordsworth desires and the disconcerting and pert tone he finally achieves.

In a poetry more strictly formal than this, poetry that is rhymed or stanzaic or both, the poet can create effects of bathos merely by abusing the form. The form itself, apart from the narrative line, can provide a structure for him to sink in. Sir Thomas Wyatt's psalms show him to be an artist with a taste for this sort of bathos, which is perhaps more fascinating intellectually than its counterpart of bathos in narration, because it is freed from the restraints of a coherent sequence of action. This bathos is first evident in Wyatt's rhyming. His *terza* and *ottava rima* stanzas, in a language not comparatively rich in rhymes, force him to adopt a number of desperate expedients, of which the most obvious is his closing a line with an exclamation or qualifier, usually one ending in a vowel and consonant for which rhymes are common. (The italics are mine.)

[2] William Wordsworth, *Poetical Works*, ed. E. de Selincourt (Oxford: Clarendon Press, 1949–63), 2: 66, ll. 271–80.

Thus drye I upp among my foes in woe,
That with my fall do rise and grow *with all*,
And me bysett evin now, I am *so*,
   With secrett trapps to troble my penaunce,
   Sum do present to my weping yes, *lo*,
The chere, the manere, bealte and countenaunce
Off her whose loke, alas, did mak my blynd.

(Ps. 6:79–86)

My hert, my mynd is wytherd up like haye,
   By cawse I have forgot to take my brede,
My brede off lyff, the word of trowth, *I saye* . . . .

(Ps. 102:13–15)

Let Israell trust unto the lord *alway*,
   For grace and favour arn his propertie;
Plenteous rannzome shall com with hym, *I say*. . . .[3]

(Ps. 130:28–30)

In each case, the bathetic effect is the same: the exclamations of emotional tension conflict with the manifestly practical function of the phrases. Thus the phrases have, on the stylistic level, a self-cancelling quality that is analagous to the narrative self-cancelling we noticed in the Wordsworth passage. Wyatt has two contradictory impulses, in trying to drum up emotions while killing time. Fortunately, Wyatt's amatory verse does not rely so heavily on the *lo*s and *I say*s; the size of the design, or incomplete revision, might be responsible for his carelessness in the psalms.

Wyatt as often twists a poem's logic in order to supply his needed rhyme words. Consider the start of Psalm 6:

   O Lord, sins in my mowght thy myghty name
   Sufferth it sellff my lord to name and call,
   Here hath my hert hope taken by the same;

---

[3] All references to Wyatt's psalms and lyrics are from *Collected Poems*, which is fully identified on p. 17, n. 42. Psalm and line numbers appear in the text. I was able to obtain the more recent *Collected Poems*, ed. Kenneth Muir and Patricia Thomson (Liverpool: Liverpool University Press, 1969), only after this book was in press. However, this newer edition makes virtually no significant changes in the passages I quote, although the psalms are now numbered consecutively. There is also a complete editorial apparatus which is quite helpful.

> That the repentance wych I have and shall
> May at thi hand seke marcy as the thing,
> Only confort of wrechid synners all;
> Wherby I dare with humble bymonyng
> By thy goodnes off the this thing require:
> Chastyse me not for my deserving,
> According to thy just conceyvid Ire.
>
> (1–10)

In order to find the rhymes he needs here, Wyatt creates a great tangle of language in which most of the important nouns and verbs have their own shadows, vague forms moving along with the real things. As nearly as I can puzzle out the first three lines, David says that his heart has taken hope because God's Name has allowed Itself to be uttered from his, David's, mouth. The first two lines are grammatically dependent upon the third, which makes a nice contrast between the true heart and the (formerly) false mouth. But when, at the end of the third line, the poet forgets he began with *sins* (since) and creates an anacoluthon by adding *by the same*, he seems less to be emphasizing the relation between the Name and his own mouth than he is making a convenient rhyme. This suspicion is confirmed by the fact that Wyatt usually employs conventional grammar. *Thing* brings the fifth line to a lame stop with a vague appositive that conveniently rhymes with *bymonyng*. One manuscript reads, "May at thi hand seke in the same thing," which makes the next line a more coherent direct object for *seke* but which still has a clumsy repetition in the phrase "in the same thing."[4] *Thing*, one of Wyatt's favorite fillers, returns in line eight to push *require* out to the end and seems to be unnecessary since *require*, in the obsolete sense of "ask or request one to do something," indicates that another statement, specifically a question, will follow. Finally, if chastisement is what David *deserves*, then clearly it is *just conceyvid*.

One could claim that Wyatt is only indicating in his syntax the agonized confusion of a sinner receiving his just deserts, but Wyatt's David talks this way even when he is hopeful or exultant. Ultimately

---

[4] *Collected Poems*, p. 276, n. 201. Wyatt's use of *thing* as a metrical filler is so consistent in his psalms that I would be reluctant to agree with Donald M. Friedman's view that the term denotes a specific state or attitude (see "The 'Thing' in Wyatt's Mind," *EIC*, 16 [1966], 375–81). In his psalms at least, Wyatt's *thing* seems to have about as much meaning as his *I say*, *lo*, or *eke*.

the padding seems to have no purpose beyond filling out the *terza rima*, and if one reads hurriedly or, like Wyatt's audience, with an eye turned to the moral sentence and subdued sensuality (neither of which is likely to invite the modern reader), most of the stuffing goes on quietly enough. Yet even an inattentive reader is awakened when Wyatt takes more desperate measures:

> He dare importune the lord on every syde;
>   (For he knowth well to mercy is ascrybid
> Respectles labour) Importune crye and call:
> And thus begynth his song therwithall.
>
> (Prol. 102:29–32)

As William Carlos Williams says in his poem "When Structure Fails Rhyme Attempts to Come to the Rescue,"

> > He
> does what he can, with
> unabated phlegm,
> ahem!

The abruptness and patent convenience of Wyatt's last modifier, and its virtual failure to add anything to the sense of the passage, would be more typical of the deliberate flounderings of Ogden Nash.

Two observations conclude these remarks on padding and rhyme in Wyatt's psalms. To position his rhymes, Wyatt is especially fond of padding with particles, conjunctive adverbs, and relatives in particular. In addition to these colorless terms, he uses in the middle of lines the same stock emotive phrases he uses at the ends, the *lo, alas, I say,* and so forth. Since examples of both of these may be seen readily in the quotations above and below, there is no need for fuller illustration here. These techniques of padding for the sake of rhyme may have recommended themselves to later psalmodists and poets—Sackville, for example—although there is no reason to suspect that as techniques they are so sophisticated that later poets could not have discovered them for themselves.[5]

---

[5] To Wyatt's credit, his psalms may be (as Kenneth Muir suggests, in *Life and Letters of Sir Thomas Wyatt* [Liverpool: Liverpool University Press, 1963], p. 257) only a first draft; but this fact (if it is) does not seem to have qualified their reception or imitation. Muir also prints (pp. 257–58, n. 9) some of Wyatt's revisions for

It would be an oversimplification to say that Wyatt's filler is present only to satisfy the rhymes of his *terza rima*, for it also helps satisfy a metrical pattern. I have chosen to focus on rhyme rather than meter as the chief benefit because of the difficulty of the rhyme scheme and the regularity of the meter. But one could make out a case for the filler as a purely metrical necessity, particularly when it is used in the middle of lines, where Wyatt is struggling to keep the accent. Perhaps because of this filler, Wyatt's management of the pentameter line is fumbling, and nowhere in his psalms do his rhythms have the control, clarity, and flexibility that they have in his satires.

With all their visible signs of hammering and patching necessary to stay close to the limits of five stresses and ten syllables, the Penitential Psalms should lend some strength to the idea that the erratic rhythms of Wyatt's lyrics are probably intentional.[6] As the psalms demonstrate, only a poet who had a fairly clear conception of iambic pentameter could perform such obvious tricks to get it. The result is a set of prologues and psalms almost entirely iambic, with the conventional substitution of trochees. Occasionally these will come two deep: "Whereby I dare with humble bymonyng/ By thy goodnes off the this thing require . . ." (Ps. 6:7–8). But the accentual rhythms of Wyatt's lyrics, the cadences that modern readers find so intriguing metrically—"Wherewithall, unto the hertes forrest he flieth"—give way in the psalms to rhythms that are based upon the syllable-stress meters that dominate the poetry of the coming generation. Although Wyatt's psalms are not usually brought into the definition of his role in the rise of English meter, they do suggest a crucial turning toward foot prosody, or to designate it more accurately, pedestrian meters. Recall-

---

Psalm 38, which show Wyatt casting for rhymes and inserting words to get metrically complete lines. In *Humanism and Poetry in the Early Tudor Period* (London: Routledge and Kegan Paul, 1959), H. A. Mason also discusses the possibility of revision in Wyatt's psalms; and makes in addition many valuable comments on the literary and spiritual background of the psalms. Mason finds much to praise, but points out that Wyatt's psalms are often incoherent, drastically limited, and technically clumsy.

6 For example, "To my mind it is impossible to believe that Wyatt could not quite easily have made his irregular lines regular had he wished."—D. W. Harding, "The Rhythmical Intention in Wyatt's Poetry," *Scrutiny*, 14 (December 1946): 93. Robert O. Evans, in "Some Aspects of Wyatt's Metrical Technique," *JEGP*, 53 (1954): 197–213, argues with some logic that through study of Wyatt's technique of elision we must conclude that Wyatt was working for regular iambic lines.

ing the popularity of Wyatt's psalms, we shall have to admit that they could have had a shaping force very nearly as great as his lyrics, even though these are admittedly more attractive to the modern historian of English prosody. In Wyatt's psalms the relation of prosodical regularity to meaning is especially evident in the lines which are logically redundant; here Wyatt rarely varies his iambic pattern. The rest of the time his variations are quite conventional. (Even if his psalms might have a metric full of sophisticated innovations that we simply are not hearing—an unlikely hypothesis, I think—the literary influence of those novelties would have been obliterated by the metrical primitivism of later psalters, the Old Version in particular.)[7]

Whatever his metrical practices, Wyatt is most closely related to later psalmodists in his use of rhyme and syntax. It is immediately apparent that the padding Wyatt adds for rhyme's sake has a shaping effect on his syntax. Several paragraphs above, I noted that Wyatt frequently stuffs a line with relative pronouns, relative clauses, and various redundant verb structures. By suspending the predication of his sentences, this padding creates many periodic rhythms, most of them handled with a heavy competence: "let by graunt apere/ That to my voyce thin eres do well entend" (Ps. 130:7–8).

Hardly Elizabethan grace; but the emphatic close on the verb does make the tone more serious. What the padding does more often, however, is create something like a periodic structure in reverse, in which the logical bulk of an idea, usually the predication, is given early in a group of lines, and its force then allowed to drain off in weak modifiers. This method can yield powerful effects in meditative passages, for it lends itself well to a slow and trailing motion of thought:

> Oh dyverse ar the chastysinges off syn!
> In mete, in drynk, in breth that man doth blow,
> In slepe, in wach, in fretying styll within,
> That never soffer rest unto the mynd;
> Filld with offence, that new and new begyn
> With thowsand feris the hert to strayne and bynd.
>
>   (Ps. 32:65–70)

----

[7] Of course, one could maintain that Wyatt's ineptitude was his sophistication, rough meters being a familiar item in the Renaissance poetic toolbox. Thus one would expect them in Wyatt's satires; but they are fairly smooth. Making a case for their sophisticated use in his psalms seems rather a modern line of reasoning, only possible through our historical hindsight.

A rambling motion is created by the prepositional modifiers that conclude the lines in the middle of this passage, and the lines show a happy fusion of poetic technique and slow reasoning. The method is less successful when Wyatt tries to become more intense. At the close of Psalm 102, when David comes to accept God's final power, there is a shift from lines of heavy strength into two final lines of turgid and sluggish movement:

> But thou thy sellff the sellf remaynist well
> That thou wast erst, and shalt thi yeres extend.
> Then sins to this there may nothing rebell,
> The greatest comfort that I can pretend
> Is that the childerne off thy servantes dere
> That in thy word ar gott shall withowt end
> Byfore thy face be stablisht all in fere.
>
> (85–91)

The syntax of the last three lines, each pieced out with the modifiers at the ends, establishes more limpness than submission. It is notable that although these modifiers may be placed as they are for their rhymes, the lines are run-on, and there are no necessary stops to emphasize the rhymes. Even without the effect of forced rhymes, the modifiers allow the lines to sink from within, as from a leak.

These qualities of bathos or sinking in Wyatt's poetic style correspond to a bathos in his picture of the relations between man and God. Piety for Wyatt most often takes the form of self-pity, and that is the quality of the Psalms that he has chosen to stress most heavily, just as Sternhold and Hopkins have chosen to stress violence. (Actually, the decision to emphasize self-pity was Aretino's rather than Wyatt's, but clearly Wyatt concurred in it.)

Wyatt's self-pity is complex, working on several levels. To illustrate this, we might explore his Psalm 6, as a coherent dramatic entity, and see how Wyatt relates David's self-pity to his sense of righteousness:

> I stopp myn eris with help of thy goodness;
> And for I fele it comith alone of the
> That to my hert these foes have non acces . . . .
>
> (94–96)

But this David is not entirely confident of his rectitude, for accompanying it is an equally strong sense of culpability:

> Chastyse me not for my deserving,
> Accordyng to thy just conceyvid Ire.
> O Lord, I dred; and that I did not dred
> I me repent and evermore desyre
> The, the to dred.
>
> (9–13)

At first it would seem that simultaneous convictions of one's righteousness and guilt do not go together, but Wyatt can reconcile them. David can ask God to make him stop his self-mortification:

> Reduce, revyve my sowle: be thow the Leche,
> And reconcyle the great hatred and stryfe
> That it hath tane agaynste the flesshe . . . .
>
> (46–48)

By doing this, God would conveniently affirm both David's guilt and righteousness. Wyatt also suggests that David's righteousness is a product of his guilt by having him say in effect to God, "Rather than chastise me for my crimes, you should pity me, because my repentance is so severe." (The argument is not unfamiliar to any teacher who has discovered a student cheating on an examination.) As Wyatt handles it, this plea often sounds like a threat: "But thow, O Lord, how longe after this sorte/ Fforbearest thou to see my myserye?" (40–41). It is not the self-consciousness of this statement that undermines the repentance and desire for reconciliation, but the fact that the speaker has made his suffering an end in itself. His suffering alone, or his awareness of it, presumably justifies God's mercy. The whole question has a lurking bathos in the direct object, *my myserye*.

If we step back from the immediate context of the Psalms, we can see that much of this pattern of rejection and self-pity also manifests itself in Wyatt's lyrics. As Wyatt frequently tells his mistress, "It is only my love for you that causes this pain":

> I love an othre, and thus I hate my self.
>
> ("I fynde no peace," l. 11)

> . . . with good will I lost my libretye
> To followe her wiche causith all my payne.
>
> ("My love toke scorne," ll. 3–4)

In Wyatt's psalms this sort of conflict can work on two levels. It applies to David the lover of Bathsheba: "My love for you has made me hate myself, insofar as I have abandoned my masculine integrity." And it applies as well to David the lover of God: "My love for You has made me hate myself, at least insofar as I have abandoned Your laws to satisfy my gross appetites." The bathos sets in as we move from these attitudes to the complaints that come out of them. The profane lover's complaint of his misery has a pleasing inconsequence, but in the sacred lover's mouth the same complaint—"I have forgotten part of my human nature!"—is only bathetic. The offenses and complaints are hardly similar.

To conclude these remarks on Wyatt's psalms, I would like to offer a proposal relating Wyatt's style and his self-pity. The difficulties that Wyatt faces in controlling the technical features of his verse are related to his chief theme, the outcast and imperfect soul seeking reconciliation, which is also one of Herbert's chief themes. Yet in his psalms Wyatt often forgets the *subject* of his address, that is, his God, and begins talking instead to himself, with all the hums and haws of most talkers-aloud. Similarly, he often forgets the *object* of his address and instead begins talking about himself or, rarely without ill effect, begins chewing on a metaphor for its own or the rhyme's sake, regardless of the dramatic context. Either way, he is liable to drop into the bathos we noted earlier. In short, it is Wyatt's dubious achievement to have devised a way by which his psalms could demonstrate, in their fumbling techniques, the enfeebled emotional state they describe.[8]

II. THE OLD VERSION

Although Sternhold and Hopkins (and the other contributors to the Anglo-Genevan psalter) may have won all the plumes for bathos in

---

[8] Wyatt's psalms were probably read by his contemporaries just for that self-pity. Surrey, for example, praised the way that Wyatt

> dothe paynte the lyvely faythe and pure,
> The stedfast hope, the swete returne to grace
> Of just Davyd by parfite penytence,
> Where Rewlers may se in a myrour clere
> The bitter frewte of false concupiscence.

("The great Macedon," ll. 7–11, in Surrey, *Poems.*)

lyric poetry, they still have their own strengths which are different from those of Wyatt's poetry or any other English poetry until Herbert's. Yet the weaknesses crowd them offstage; from the start the Sternhold-Hopkins psalter was a public joke as poetry. Forced rhyme and meter and wrenched syntax are not the least of the poets' offenses, and in these they show much greater ingenuity than Wyatt, who by comparison seems almost inhibited. One could exhume whole pages of examples like the following to show how bathos can be produced by careless technique:

> So I suppresse and wound my foes,
>   that they can rise no more:
> For at my feete they fall downe flat,
>   I strike them all so sore.[9]

> (Ps. 18:37–38)

Some of the flatness of this comes from narrative anticlimax and confusion of sequence, but the alliteration in the last two lines has a good deal of comic potential itself. Although the repetition between the second and third lines is perhaps occasioned by the mechanical necessity of the rhyme in line four, the alliteration is inspired beyond the call of necessity. The chief problem in discussing the Old Version may be to keep the psalter from seeming a comic anthology.

As for rhyming in general, the poets of the Old Version employ the same exclamations and qualifiers that Wyatt used, in perhaps greater profusion:

> The rich men of his goodly gifts,
>   shall feed and tast also:
> And in his presence worship him
>   and bow their knees full low.

> (Ps. 22:29)

The stock *also* in the second line and the weak adverb it rhymes with are typical of Wyatt's practice, although the rhyme scheme itself is not. Rhyming on fillers at least has expediency to recommend it, but the Old Version poets can even abandon the rhyme for the expedient:

---

[9] In citations from the Old Version, psalm and *verse* numbers (separated by a colon) appear in the text.

> And many dogs do compasse me,
> and wicked counsel eke:
> Conspire against me cursedly,
> they pierce my handes and feete.

(Ps. 22:16)

As Thomas Nashe says, "a leake of indesinence, as a leake in a shippe, must needly bee stopt with what matter soever."[10]

The above examples are taken from Sternhold, but as noted earlier, the level of poetic competence throughout the whole psalter is so remarkably even, in spite of the multiple authorship, that one could find examples of flagrantly forced rhyme by any of the contributors. Norton, for instance, begins Psalm 108:

> Oh God my heart prepared is,
> and eke my tongue is so:
> I will advance my voyce in song,
> and gevying prayse also.

(1)

Or as Kethe's God says:

> As for his enemies I will clothe,
> with shame for evermore:
> But I will cause his crowne to shine,
> more fresh then heretofore.

(Ps. 132:18)

Although the poets of the Old Version rhymed in the manner of many poets before them, including Wyatt, they also made some regressive stylistic contributions of their own. Most noticeable is their lack of awareness that the poetic line is a unit in itself. Individual lines often jump out of their stanzas because of the peculiar suggestions they make by themselves.

>   our God
> which is exalted hie:
> As with a buckler doth defend,
> The earth continually.

(Ps. 47:8)

---

[10] "Strange Newes, of the Intercepting Certaine Letters," in Nashe, *Works*, ed Ronald B. McKerrow (London: Sidgwick and Jackson, 1910), 1: 316.

> And as an Owle in desert is,
> loe I am such a one:
> I watch, and as a sparrow on
> the house top am alone.
>
> (Ps. 102:7)

In both cases the last lines form syntactic units that are very nearly viable on their own; they are the syntactic equivalent of dead metaphors suddenly brought to life by the context. Part of this carelessness with the lines themselves might be smoothed over by musical settings, but still we cannot disregard the lines as parts of *poems*. And there is ample evidence that contemporary criticism assumed that the Old Version psalms were, or should have been, poems in their own right.

Naturally it is easier to give a poetic line some unexpected syntactic life of its own if the line is not end-stopped. Thus, when the line that is not intended to stand alone syntactically suddenly does just that, the reader is left trying to balance the small phrase within the larger:

> And from the Lions mouth, that would
> me all in sunder shiver:
> And from the horns of Unicornes
> Lord safely me deliver.
>
> (Ps. 22:21)

It is the ballad stanza, as Sternhold and Hopkins handle it, that is responsible for their peculiar and bathetic lines. There is no question that the Old Version stanzas do resemble the Child ballad stanzas, at least in the number of lines, syllables, and stresses; but here the resemblance ends, for the two conceptions of the form are entirely different. The anonymous masters of the ballad stanza conceive of their form as four separate lines, each line with something of its own to do:

> Four and twenty ladies fair
> Were playing at the chess,
> And out then came the fair Janet,
> As green as onie glass.[11]

---

[11] "Tam Lin," stanza 9, in *The Ballad Book*, ed. MacEdward Leish (New York: Harper & Bros., 1955), p. 138.

The Old Version poets, on the other hand, persistently conceive of their form as a rearranged heptameter couplet. Here, too, each line has a function, each heptameter line, that is, and thus most of the quatrains logically split in two instead of in four. The syntactic consequences of this we have seen already, with the strange second and fourth lines left to hobble by themselves.

Difficulties for these poets enter when their lines are not end-stopped. This is most evident in Sternhold's stanzas, which have only one rhyme (*x a x a*) and are often not end-stopped, and less evident in Hopkins's stanzas, most of which employ end-stops and alternating rhymes. We would therefore expect Sternhold to generate the greater proportion of bathetic single lines, and this he does; but Hopkins, not to be outdone, achieves his own sort of bathos in the trimeter lines by repeating the idea of the tetrameter line above and adding a rhyme:

> By him I have succour at neede,
> against all payne and griefe:
> He is my God, with which all speede,
> will hast to send reliefe.
>
> (Ps. 42:5)

This stanza is somewhat atypical of Hopkins, who is more likely to come to a stop with his *a* rhyme, but it does show—I believe typically —how the habit of thinking in heptameter couplets could be retained in the ballad stanza, even with two rhymes in the middle. Although the rhymes give the stanza a greater unity than it might otherwise have, they cannot hide the fact that the trimeter lines involve duplication and often fail to advance the thought of the stanza.

The close relationship between Common Meter and the fourteener is indicated by the many versions of the Psalms (printed during and after the development of the Old Version) which were translated entirely in fourteeners;[12] and at least one version—Sir Edwin Sandys's —used both fourteeners and Common Meter. Another close relative to clumsily used Common Meter is Poulter's Measure. Like the fourteener, this stanza was greatly popular, and although it seems to have been used for relatively few psalms it may have had some influence upon the way the poets of the Old Version regarded stanza structure.

---

[12] Probably the best known was that by George Sandys.

Surrey's four translations are probably the best specimens, and his practice shows how the techniques of Poulter's Measure might have been adapted for use in Common Meter. When Surrey is not deliberately varying caesurae for emphasis, his Poulter's Measure resembles Common Meter manqué, or lacking one foot, as tinkering with his line divisions will quickly show. Here are rearrangements of the opening lines of the three psalms he completed:

> Thie name, O Lorde, howe greate
> is fownd before our sight!
> Yt fills the earthe and spreades the ayre,
> the greate workes of thie might.

> Thoughe, Lorde, to Israell
> thy graces plentuous be:
> I meane to such with pure intent
> as fixe their trust in the . . . .

> Oh Lorde, uppon whose will
> dependeth my welfare,
> To call uppon thy hollye name
> syns daye nor night I spare . . . .[13]

Many of Surrey's lines are more varied than these, but in the hands of poets less gifted, Poulter's Measure regularly falls into four short phrasal groups; and its light tail carrying the rhyme corresponds to the flimsy rhyming trimeter lines in, for example, the Common Meter stanzas of Hopkins. Both Poulter's Measure and Common Meter, for all their apparent brevity when printed in short ballad stanzas, are forms designed, as it were, for padding. They are to be distinguished from Wyatt's *terza rima*, which uses the padding only when necessary. Although Wyatt's plan commits him to extraordinary limitations in rhyming, it does not commit him to a stanza structure which openly invites ugly or incoherent lines.[14] As we shall see in a moment, how-

[13] As before, my text is Surrey, *Poems*.

[14] This use of syntactic movement across line-ends is not accounted for by most statistical studies of syntax in English poetry. Josephine Miles's *Eras and Modes in English Poetry* (Berkeley: University of California Press, 1957), for example, does not consider the line as a syntactic unit in relation to other syntactic units; nor for that matter do I see how the syntactic coherence of a line could be satisfactorily estimated for statistical purposes, much less the relation of a line's particular syntax to a larger syntactic pattern. There are, however, some helpful comments on this problem by William E. Baker in *Syntax in English Poetry* (Berkeley: University of California Press, 1967), especially chapters 3 and 4.

ever, there are several ways in which the rhythmic structure of the Common Meter differs from that of Poulter's Measure.

Consideration of stanza structure from the standpoint of syntax leads naturally to consideration of rhythmic structure within the stanza. For the ballad stanza of the Old Version, rhythmic analysis seems simple indeed, at least at first. If we read the Old Version as poetry, we find—not surprisingly—few if any variations from the prevailing iambic pattern. To stop the discussion here, however, would be premature, for the metric of the Old Version (unlike that of the psalms by Wyatt, for example, or the Sidneys) cannot be isolated satisfactorily from the context of congregational performance. The attempt to do so would, I think, be quite risky, for Englishmen of the sixteenth and seventeenth centuries would not have been likely (or easily able) to ignore the sort of metrical conditioning that any long-familiar tune can give to a poem.

The exact form which that conditioning might have taken is not beyond all conjecture. Although the metric of the Old Version psalms was in fact quite simple, it was not as a consequence so dull as modern readers at times imagine. Such evidence as exists shows that even though the psalms were, unlike contemporary art songs, unvaried in tempi, they were still sung quite rapidly, as fast as hornpipes, according to the Clown in *The Winter's Tale* (IV. iii). Further, it was customary to sing one psalm to the tune of another: since most of the psalms were in Common Meter, the switching posed no difficulties. It was an art form based, like the Model T, on interchangeable parts.

For these reasons, it is not difficult to describe a matrix for the metric rhythm of the Common Meter stanza:[15]

$$\cup \ \wedge \ \cup \ \diagup \ \| \ \cup \ \wedge \ \cup \ \diagup \ \|$$

$$\cup \ \wedge \ \cup \ \wedge \ \cup \ \diagup \ \#$$

$$\cup \ \wedge \ \cup \ \diagup \ \| \ \cup \ \wedge \ \cup \ \diagup \ \|$$

$$\cup \ \wedge \ \cup \ \wedge \ \cup \ \diagup \ \#$$

---

[15] Following the system initially set out by George L. Trager and Henry Lee Smith, Jr., in their *Outline of English Structure*, Studies in Linguistics Occasional Papers #3 (Norman, Okla., 1951; repr. Washington, D.C.: ACLS, 1956), I recognize four levels of stress and mark them as follows: primary ($\diagup$), secondary ($\wedge$), tertiary ($\diagdown$), and weak ($\cup$). Of course pitch and juncture (roughly, pause: long, #, and short, ‖) are also factors of meaning, but ordinarily it is difficult to find poems in which these factors are the sole determinants of meaning. As a general

The third and fourth lines are, of course, identical with the first and second, and although the pattern seems, in its bare bones, susceptible of an infinite monotony, we have to recall that variations in tune and the use of rapid tempi could keep the pattern from becoming offensively dull—at least to the true believer.

The paradigm can clarify several characteristics of Old Version poetic style. First, since the settings do not always place the notes of longer time value upon the syllables receiving the metrical stress, the nominally unstressed syllables (often articles, relatives, and the like) frequently bear a weight that works against the metrical paradigm and the literal sense of the lines. Second, the usual omission of caesurae in the six-syllable lines necessarily makes it difficult for these lines to establish contrasts, antitheses, or even distinctions within their bounds. (Even Dryden and Pope, in the second lines of their couplets, rarely manage to set up balancing or opposing ideas without the use of caesurae.) Without an enforced or demanded rhythmic pause within the lines to invite a break in the thought, it is inevitable that these lines should frequently be mere fillers, stretching out the matter of the preceding eight-syllable lines. Third, the eight-syllable lines, in which all the real work of the stanza gets done, usually consist of shorter phrasal units than do the six-syllable lines. This, like the previous two points, is an important reason why the Old Version's Common Meter, though derived from "fourteeners," still differs from them considerably. Even Poulter's Measure has more flexibility in its phrasal patterns. The Old Version's Common Meter is nearly always committed

---

guide I have found extremely helpful the monograph by Edmund L. Epstein and Terence Hawkes, *Linguistics and England Prosody*, Studies in Linguistics Occasional Papers #7 (Buffalo: University of Buffalo Department of Anthropology and Linguistics, 1959). Needless to say these writers are hardly responsible for my scansions. Often I shall juxtapose "linguistic" scansions with "traditional" scansions as a way of showing how poets can set up tensions within the called-for meter. Herbert himself recognized at least three components of verse rhythm in "measure, tune, and time" ("Grief," 1. 18).

The general distinction between meter and rhythm has received much attention; it is studied neatly and above all practically in Harvey Gross's *Sound and Form in Modern Poetry* (Ann Arbor: University of Michigan Press, 1964) and in the same author's collection of basic essays, *The Structure of Verse* (New York: Fawcett Books, 1966). Valuable linguistic studies in meter and style are too numerous to list here; but most of these, such as the various essays of Morris Halle, or most impressively, Roman Jakobson on Shakespeare, have seemed somewhat tangential to the historical task at hand.

to establishing contrasts or distinctions either within the long line or between the long line and the short line and almost never within the short line itself. Much of the monotony of the Old Version thus lies in the constant coincidence of metric, syntax, and meaning, just as much of it also lies in the unremitting repetition of the stanza pattern itself.

We cannot leave the Old Version without noting that its figurative language is one of its great strengths, although the terms *health* or *muscle* might better be used to imply the robust crudity of the psalter. This particular aspect of the Old Version is one that has been most consistently criticized from its own time; the reader is reminded of Wither's long reference to gross "improprieties" in many of its expressions. But even some of the most infamous of these often have a crude vigor. For example, Hopkins asks God

> Why doest thou draw thy hand abacke,
>   and hide it in thy lap?
> Oh plucke it out, and be not slacke,
>   to geve thy foes a rap.
>
> (Ps. 74:12)

Probably the modern reader would object first to the imperial tone of the passage, but sixteenth- and seventeenth-century hymnodists (and modern commentators on hymns as well) would probably object more to the breach of decorum in *rap*. There is a heroic disproportion here: a view of God through the wrong end of a telescope. The gesture seems more impatient than punitive. But if we have been reading the poetry of Herbert we may find in that rap a familiar note of whimsy; certainly Herbert describes exchanges no less startling or informal.

I am not arguing, however, for anything like direct correspondences in metaphor between Herbert and Sternhold and Hopkins, for the stanza immediately preceding the one above establishes a distinctly un-Herbertian context:

> When wilt thou, lord, once end this shame,
>   and cease thine enemies strong?
> Shall they always blaspheme thy name,
>   and raile on thee so long?
>
> (Ps. 74:11)

In this context, the rap that follows in the next stanza may be somewhat less than whimsical; it may in fact be only a handy rhyme for *lap*. The tone of the passage as a whole thus would seem to rule out any deliberate whimsy in the rap itself. The whimsy is apparent only out of context, as passionate demands for punishment of blasphemers are not likely to be satisfied (except in bad poetry) with a rap.

Perhaps the most absurd passages in the Old Version are those in which God speaks (here, through Hopkins):

> But to the wicked trayne,
>   which talke of God each day:
> And yet their workes are foule and vayne,
>   to them the Lord will say.
>
> With what a face darest thou,
>   my word once speake or name?
> Why doth thy talke my law allow,
>   thy deeds deny the same?
>
> Whereas for to amend,
>   thy selfe thou art so slacke:
> My word the which thou doest pretend,
>   is cast behind thy backe.
>
>   (Ps. 50:16–18)

With his vision of God as a Big Stick, Hopkins has a sort of insidious mastery of the genre:

> Leave off therfore (saythe he) and know,
>   I am a God most stout:
> Among the heathen hye and low,
>   and all the earth throughout.
>
>   (Ps. 46:10)

And critics complain about the way God speaks in *Paradise Lost*. Here the poetry rises to no occasion at all, with the result that the tone of the passages is surprisingly jaunty. Herbert's intimacy with the speech of God is always the result of skill and daring, as he realizes: Hopkins's is the result of incompetence and insensitivity, as he fails to realize. Yet in spite of these obvious dissimilarities, the "Old Version attitude" toward God has much in common with Herbert's, as we shall see later.

The unconscious whimsy in Sternhold and Hopkins' Godtalk is evident also in their use of imagery. Homely, abrupt, and intense, their metaphors seem to "happen" rather than grow naturally out of the logic or emotions. This perplexing spontaneity is emphasized by the violence of many of the comparisons:

> But flattring and deceitfull lips,
>   and tongues that be so stout:
> To speak proud words, & make great brags,
>   the Lord soone cut them out.
>
> (Ps. 12:3)

> And still like dust before the wind,
>   I drive them under feete:
> And sweepe them out like filthy clay
>   that stinketh in the streete.
>
> (Ps. 18:41)

> O God breake thou their teeth at once,
>   within their mouth throughout:
> The tusks that in their great chaw bones,
>   like Lions whelps hang out.
>
> (Ps. 58:6)

> a cup of mighty wine,
>   is in the hand of God:
> And all the mighty wine therein,
>   himselfe doth poure abroad.

> As for the lees and filthy dregs,
>   that do remain of it:
> The wicked of the earth shall drinke,
>   and sucke them every whit.
>
> (Ps. 75:7–8)

The relish with which this violence and vulgarity is brought in is not to be found in the Prayer Book psalter, and unlike the tone of Herbert's violent or homely images, it appears to be unqualified by any ironic or humorous qualities, at least none that are deliberate. Occasionally, the abruptness with which a metaphor is introduced will be intensified by the casual introduction of a second metaphor.

The following has a mixture of metaphors that is not to be found in any source or contemporary version: "Thy tongue untrue in forging lyes,/ is like a rasor sharp" (Ps. 52:2).

When the crudity and abruptness are properly tempered and directed toward the *persona* of the psalms, the result is an apparent self-mockery which, although it may be unintentional, is nonetheless effective:

> Unto thy house such zeale I beare,
>   that it doth pine me much:
> Their checks and taunts to thee to hear,
>   my very hart doth grutch.
>
> (Ps. 69:10)

There are some praiseworthy effects here; in this sober context the colloquial energy of *pine* and *checks* and *grutch* creates some human warmth, although the *much/grutch* rhyme looks suspiciously convenient. This sort of surprising energy is achieved the same way the sudden vapid line is achieved. When the rhetorical movement of a line or stanza prepares the reader for an important statement that never comes, the reader is almost as astonished as he would be by an image of violence:

> The seas that are so deepe and dead,
>   thy might did make them dry:
> And thou didst breake the serpents head,
>   that he therein did die.
>
> (Ps. 74:14)

> They shall heape sorowes on their heds,
>   which run as they were mad:
> To offer to the Idoll Gods,
>   alas it is to bad.
>
> (Ps. 16:3)

The airiest abstractions are reserved for the figure of God, and He often enters a poem in something like the emperor's new clothes:

> The voyce of God is of great force,
>   and wondrous excellent:
> It is most mighty in effect,
>   and much magnificent.
>
> (Ps. 29:4)

We should not leave the Old Version without remarking that although it was ridiculed for its inaccuracies of translation, it is more accurate than the poeticized paraphrases of Wyatt, Surrey, Hunnis, and others. Sternhold and Hopkins, for all their poetic shortcomings, do keep the psalms down near their original subjects and lengths, as Wyatt did not. But it is easier to compress a lyric than a romance; their design naturally demanded compression, just as Wyatt's demanded expansion.

It is difficult to make any short but accurate summary of the Old Version. As verse it is full of incompetence of every sort, on every level of poetic language, ranging from the abrupt *non sequiturs* of its violent imagery to the monotony of its forms. Nonetheless, the great popularity of the psalter decisively turned psalm paraphrase toward the grouping of independent lyrics; after the Old Version, attempts to integrate narrative groups of the psalms were neither numerous nor influential. (It is also likely that the Old Version was a major factor in the rise of the self-contained lyric as a genre, but there is hardly the space to show that here.) The Old Version also increased the number of tools available to psalmodists and, by extension, all poets. The commonplace imagery, the colloquial familiarity of diction, the emphasis on the handy ballad line, and indeed the very bathos of the psalter were all present in English poetry before, but by recombining these elements in a form for which there was an irresistible social demand, Sternhold and Hopkins made them a permanent part of English verse. As the most popular single work of poetry in sixteenth-century England, the psalter had an influence that would be hard to overestimate, even (or especially) for the poets who disliked it.

As we look back, Wyatt neatly balances the Old Version: the weight of each is best revealed by the other. Sternhold himself was almost exactly Wyatt's contemporary, and since the later contributors to the psalter worked in the poetic modes of Sternhold's generation, the whole production is in a sense contemporary with Wyatt. It is not surprising, then, that despite their working in different genres, Wyatt and the Old Version poets should employ similar poetic styles. Most of the differences between the two versions come down to the intentions of their authors, Wyatt having written his for reading and Sternhold having written his for singing. The secular concern of Wyatt's psalms, with their emphasis on the *parfite penytence* of the lover-worshipper, balances the churchly and congregational emphasis of the Old Version, just as Wyatt's narrative design is counterbalanced by the Old Version's commitment to the self-contained lyric. Some of these differences in turn come back to the differences in sources, Wyatt directly copying from European models and the Old Version using native English forms. In both Wyatt's psalms and the Old Version, though, there is a collocation of stylistic fumbling and emotional bathos that is not peculiarly "Drab" but is characteristic of the popular English psalm.

III. SIR PHILIP SIDNEY AND THE COUNTESS OF PEMBROKE

The Sidneyan psalms resemble Wyatt's in their use of Continental verse forms, but this is perhaps the only resemblance, for Sidney and Mary Herbert abandoned the whole modish idea of narrative structure in favor of self-contained lyrics. Their model, the Marot-Béze psalter, was like the Old Version a congregational manual. But this loose family relationship is all the Old Version and the Sidney psalter share. Once we begin looking for precise points of comparison between the two, the Sidney psalter seems the result of a conscious reaction to the technical practices and even the ideas of the Old Version, so far as the latter may be said to embody any. The distance between them is great. One version relies almost exclusively on one staple stanza; the other uses 148 different stanzas, the only similarly varied collection of English verse to this time being that in the *Arcadia*. One version often stretches a short psalm stanza with words alone, while the other moves toward condensation; one is violent and vulgar, while the other has the restrained singing strength of Dorus and Zelmane; and so on. But the Sidney psalter is not merely "original" in that it departs from the conventions of the Old Version. It has a freshness that remains startling not only because of the variety of forms but also because of the way these forms are suited to David's varied emotions.

Yet Sidney has always received little or poor notice for his translation of the Psalms. In 1619, only thirty-three years after Sidney's death, Ben Jonson had to assure Drummond of Hawthornden that "Sir P. Sidney had translated some of the Psalmes, which went abroad under the name of the Countess of Pembrock."[16] In modern times, ever since Grosart's edition of Sidney's poetry (1873), most critics have either rejected or ignored his psalms.[17] There may be some reasons for this; since the bulk of Sidney's poetry usually receives critical approval, the psalms may come in for keener "discrimination"; anyone who has heard of metrical psalms at all can safely follow Warton and condemn the whole lot as fanaticism. However, I propose to show that although Sidney's psalms are not a faultless collection, they do reveal a considerable skill in suiting form to meaning. In this, it seems to me, he far surpasses his sister. He also has a subtler musical sense; she is satisfied with coarser effects of rhythm and sound. Finally, there is an integration of rhythm, stanza, and idea which resembles that in the poetry of *The Temple*. Thus the psalms are important for the study of Sidney's poetry and Herbert's as well. Above all, they comprise a varied and brilliant collection in their own right, one of the best but most underrated achievements in the Renaissance lyric.

Yet if we could speak with some confidence of the uniform manner and quality of the Old Version, we cannot begin to do so with the Sidney psalter. In this case the collaborators have two different poetic styles, although the difference is not immediately apparent because of problems connected with the text. Sidney wrote only the first forty-three psalms, and none of his manuscripts have survived; for his texts

---

[16] *Ben Jonson's Conversations with Drummond of Hawthornden*, ed. R. F. Patterson (London: Blackie and Son, 1923), p. 19.

[17] Attitudes range from disgust—"There is no excuse for these absurdities" (Percy Addleshaw, *Sir Philip Sidney* [London: Methuen, 1909], p. 343)—to seeming evasiveness—"There is more poetry in any one complete passage of the Psalms in the inspired, unmetrical original [the critic apparently refers to an English edition, or does not remember that the originals were poems] than in all Sir Philip's ingenious versions" (C. Henry Warren, *Sir Philip Sidney* [London: Nelson and Sons, 1936], p. 161). More recently, Sidney's psalms have been ignored by David Kalstone, in *Sidney's Poetry* (Cambridge: Howard University Press, 1965), and Kenneth Muir, in *Sir Philip Sidney*, no. 120 in *Writers and Their Work* (London: The British Council, 1960). Robert L. Montgomery, Jr., in *Symmetry and Sense* (Austin: University of Texas Press, 1961), regards the psalms as a useful failure, "more primitive than the general run of poems in the *Arcadia*" (p. 23). Neil Rudenstine's recent *Sidney's Poetic Development* (Cambridge: Harvard University Press, 1967) comments only on the dating of the psalms, apparently to justify their exclusion from his critical study (see pp. 284–86). The most important appreciations are those by Theodore Spencer, "The Poetry of Sir Philip Sidney," *ELH*, 12 (1945): 251–78, and by William A. Ringler, Jr., who regards the psalms as an "exhibition of virtuosity" (Sidney, *Poems*, p. 501).

we have to rely on his sister, who had them copied into her own manuscript.[18] Unfortunately for students of Sidney, the Countess was, to use William A. Ringler's appropriately finical-sounding phrase, "an inveterate tinkerer," who repeatedly revised not only her own psalms but Sidney's as well, and thus Sidney's versions have to be obtained by working backward through her revisions. The process is not as tentative as it may sound, and Ringler's patient efforts have produced a text that would seem to be as near Sidney's as possible.

The Countess's psalms present almost the opposite problem, for they exist in a great scramble of fourteen manuscripts which provide innumerable variant readings. Clearly, the present time may not be ripe for a fully annotated edition—although if we are to have Walpole why not the Countess of Pembroke?—and in editing the only modern text of the psalter, J. C. A. Rathmell elected to follow what is apparently the final manuscript and not give variants. The edition is not definitive, but there is some consolation in the fact that the Countess herself seems to have been congenitally incapable of leaving a poem alone long enough to produce a definitive copy.

As we have noted before, several scholars have proposed that the Sidney psalter probably was the greatest single influence on George Herbert's poetic style. An obvious similarity lies in the immense range of stanza forms, but there are subtle differences in the ways that all three poets attempt to tailor a unique form to a unique experience. Yet the two Sidneys have their own characters. Sir Philip has a remarkable ear for song, which often leads him into brilliant interplay of rhythm and stanza but also occasionally into vapid lines; the dancing motion of a stanza sometimes seems of more interest than the idea. The Countess is careful of observed detail and rigorously logical, and as a result has a keen eye for metaphor; her figures are apt to seem more "metaphysical" than those of her brother. She has a cruder conception of form, notwithstanding the great variety in the number of lines in her stanzas and the number of feet in her lines. The press of her ideas occasionally leads her to mangle a form, and by coincidence, she often falls into the bathos of Sternhold and Hopkins.

[18] Ringler describes the manuscripts exhaustively in Sidney, *Poems*, pp. 501–5; there is a summary account by J. C. A. Rathmell in *The Psalms*, pp. xxvi–xxviii. The Countess completed the psalter before 1600; she died in 1621. It is a curious irony that she—with several other Countesses and Earls of Pembroke—is buried near the famous Lady Chapel in Salisbury Cathedral, where Herbert often went to play music with his friends. See Gleeson White, *The Cathedral Church of Salisbury* (London: Bell, 1908), p. 67.

They sink because they do not know any better, but she sinks because she has her eye on a metaphor. They are clumsy and lack ideas; she is clumsy almost because of them. All this is not to imply a qualitative distinction between her style and Sidney's; they are simply different, and Herbert, it seems, resembles both Sidney and the Countess. He has a lyric grace, much finer than Sidney's, and some of the muscular logic of the Countess at her best. Further, and it is on this level that I find the resemblances most interesting, Herbert can employ a simplicity, a near vapidity, like Sidney's, and a bathos like the Countess's.

Since it was Sidney who began the family psalm project, we might begin by looking at his contribution, first observing its relationship to previous English psalmody, the Old Version in particular. (Specific points of comparison with Herbert will be noted later; here our concern is more with the general characteristics of Sidney's style in itself.) We have already mentioned stanzaic variety. Stanza shape is not all there is to form, however, and we could narrow our focus even further, working down to the line and below. If we compare Sidney's psalms with contemporary lyrics and psalms, we soon notice that they avoid the monotony of the regular end-stopping which is characteristic of Tudor verse. Their enjambment has more than a negative virtue. Often two enjambed lines, with an advanced caesura in the second, can create a roll or flourish in emphatic statements:

> And so thereafter He, and all his Mates
> Do works which earth corrupt and Heaven hates,
>   Not One‖that good remaineth.
>
>> (Ps. 14:4–6)

> The Voice of that lord ruling us
> Is strong‖though he be gracious.
>
>> (Ps. 32:7–12)

> Thus I prest down with weight of pain,
> Whether I silent did remain,
> Or roar'd, my bones still wasted;
> For so both day and night did stand
> On wretched mee thy heavy hand,
> My life‖hott torments tasted.[19]
>
>> (Ps. 32:7–12)

[19] The text is that of Sidney, *Poems*; psalm and line numbers are given in the text after each quotation. I have silently supplied some end punctuation.

If we wish to overlook the apparently light logical pointing at the end of line eight in the last example, we have even another illustration. By running on only to pick up a few syllables before the pause, Sidney's lines have an elasticity that cannot be found in many lyrics of this kind, and certainly not in the Old Version. In either public or private song, in the early eighties, this practice is somewhat adventuresome, and Sidney can carry it still further. Often he will combine the long enjambed line with shorter phrases and more emphatic caesurae to set up an aggressive driving motion:

> Nay if I wrought not for his Freedome's sake
> Who causeless now, yeelds me a hatefull heart,
> Then let my Foe chase me, and chasing take:
> Then let his foot uppon my neck be set:
> Then in the Dust let him my honour rake.
>
> (Ps. 7:11–15)

The long phrase crossing over the line end (ll. 11–12) emphasizes the series of three verbs, turning around each other in their grammar, and the stanza closes with two direct shakes that contrast with the circular movement above. The lines animate the prose statement of the stanza, with respect to both the physical action it describes and the process of losing freedom.

This sort of line control is typical of the ingenuity and simplicity with which Sidney countered the practices of "Drab" verse and popular church song.[20] And *counter* must surely be the term, for Sidney writes as if he were searching for new and plain solutions to old problems: how to create an effect of expansion in a relatively short line; how to vary the tempo within a stanza, while still preserving the meter; or to state the whole lyric-psalm issue more broadly, how to achieve enough rhythmic variety to satisfy the mind, while writing lines that are uniform enough to be sung. Sidney's handling of the

[20] This at least was the way Donne regarded the Sidney psalms, which
> In formes of joy and art do re-reveale
> To us so sweetly and sincerely too,
> That I must not rejoyce as I would doe
> When I behold that these Psalmes are become
> So well attyr'd abroad, so ill at home,
> So well in Chambers, in thy Church so ill.

("Upon the translation of the Psalmes by Sir Philip Sidney, and the Countesse of Pembroke his Sister," ll. 34–39, in Donne, *Divine Poems*.)

run-on line is one simple and ingenious solution, and his use of feminine rhyme is another.

Sidney's critical attitude toward feminine rhyme is well known: one of the chief advantages of English, as a poetic medium, was that unlike the Romance languages it could place the rhyme on the last, next-to-last, or antepenultimate syllable.[21] Sidney himself never assigned any particular uses to the last two types of rhymes, but his contemporaries did, finding them too light, cloying, or trivial for serious poetry.[22] This may be why Sidney usually saves the feminine rhyme for emphasis among masculine rhymes. In this way the rhyme can be unobtrusive but emphatic in retarding the motion of an end-stopped iambic line, as here, for example, in suggesting the extent of God's dominion: "The earth is God's, and what the Globe of earth containeth,/ And all who in that Globe do dwell" (Ps. 24:1–2).

Somewhat more rarely, Sidney places the feminine rhyme at the end of an enjambed line, using it to drive the dead syllables before it and speed the reader along:

> Even multitudes be they
>   That to my soul do say,
>   No help for you remaineth
> In God on whom you build,
>   Yet lord thou art my shield,
>   In thee my glory raigneth.

(Ps. 3:7–12)

The slight speeding up between the third and fourth lines emphasizes the crowd's peremptory dismissal; the connection between form and meaning is typical of Sidney's attention to detail.

But as Sidney says in his own concluding remarks on feminine rhyme, "already the triflingnes of this discourse is too much enlarged,"[23] and we must shift to more complex studies of motion within groups of lines. One of Sidney's particularly important contributions to psalmody is his use of syntax and stanza form to control the more

[21] See the *Defence of Poetry*, in Smith, *Elizabethan Critical Essays*, 1: 205.

[22] See the comments by Sir John Harington and Samuel Daniel in Smith, *Elizabethan Critical Essays*, 2: 221, 383. See also Puttenham, *Arte of English Poesie*, p. 80.

[23] In Smith, *Elizabethan Critical Essays*, 1: 205.

militant and aggressive impulses in the Psalms themselves. Much of the violence and abruptness of the Sternhold-Hopkins Old Version is, as we have seen, a direct product of the style. The very construction of the stanzas and periods seems designed to emphasize the aggression of the statement. The method in Sidney's psalms is distinctly different, for here the syntax often places the violence of the subject matter at a distance. Periodic structures, for example, can retard the effect of the violence:

> No sooner said, but (lo) myne Enemyes sink
> Down in the pitt, which they themselves had wrought:
> And in that nett, which they well hidden think,
> Is their own foot, ledd by their own ill thought,
> Most surely caught.
>
> (Ps. 9:46–50)

Like a slow-motion film of a knockout punch, the leisurely predicate makes the action seem more like a gallant dance than a struggle. The motion of the syntax itself supplies an element of meaning, and this is the sort of integrity we do not often sense in the Old Version. And Sidney is not limited to the use of periodic syntax in order to soften the violence of his subject matter. Just as often he will employ simple grammatic dependency and parallel structures, although with these the motion seems rather more jerky:

> O madness of these folks, thus loosely led,
> These Canibals, who as if they were bread
> God's people do devower,
> Nor ever call on God, but they shall quake
> More then they now do bragg, when He shall take
> The just into his power.
>
> (Ps. 14:13–18)

Abruptness and confusion are evident not only in the action but also in the grammatic style itself, in the verbs that hustle over one another in the parallels and the comparative. "These folks" are "loosely led" in more ways than one.

Sidney's rhythms provide an equally important element of meaning. It should be noted first that his rhythms are not based on exactly the same principles as the common psalter. When Sternhold and Hopkins and their fellows produced their psalter, they proceeded under the Lutheran principle of one syllable, one note. Considering their congregations, this was only sensible, but it meant ironing the verse entirely flat; no substitutions could be tolerated, and there could be no experiments in timing, as with a shifted caesura. Sidney expects a greater sophistication than this, although he does not require as much as one might expect. The rhythms themselves are not daring metrically compared with those of the *Arcadia,* and although there are some simple metrical substitutions, no halfway cultivated voice would have trouble with a shifted accent now and then:

> He did himself to me ward bend,
> And hearkned how, and why that I did cry,
> And me from pitt bemyred,
> From dungeon he retired
> Where I in horrors lay,
> Setting my feet upon
> A steadfast rocky stone,
> And my weake steps did stay.
>
> (Ps. 40:3–10)

For vocal performance, Sidney rarely offers any greater difficulties than that in line eight above. The stanzaic variety of the psalter as a whole would have presented more of a problem to contemporary congregations, since there are more tunes to memorize, after thumping along so easily with Sternhold.

However, Sidney's songs are more than song in this simple sense. Verse, he reminds us in his *Defence of Poetry,* is "the onely fit speech for Musick."[24] Further, the Psalms are first of all in his view "a divine Poem"; the fact that they have been sung he only considers as part of his proof that they are preeminently poems offering an "unspeakable and everlasting beautie to be seene by the eyes of the minde."[25] The consequences of this distinction are extremely significant when applied to matters of rhythm. For if we failed to grasp the essentially literary nature of Sidney's psalms, if we took them on a simpler level, as tunes for congregational performance, we would miss the cross-rhythms and overtones that hold them together and distinguish them

[24] *Ibid.,* 1: 182.
[25] *Ibid.,* 1: 154–55.

from other metrical psalms. Sidney's psalms have rhythms too elaborate to be expressed completely in musical settings.[26] They carry their
own music with them, and it is not the subtlety of instrumental music
—even if it is more complex than the instrumental music of the Old
Version. A good illustration of this is Psalm 6:

> Lord, let not me a worme by thee be shent,
>   While Thou art in the heat of thy displeasure:
> Ne let thy rage, of my due punishment
>   Become the measure.

                                                    (1-4)

The verb phrase of the last line provides much of the logic or
rationale for the stanza. Further, as it is employed in subsequent
stanzas, it develops a gradual tension in the rhythms. That is, besides
the activity of the verb phrase there is also a source of strength in the
disposition of stresses. However, this would be difficult for us to note
by means of ordinary metrical notation, and thus I shall employ once
again a simplified Trager-Smith notation for four levels of stress. The
advantage of this system is that it allows us to see how in each stanza
Sidney gradually drops the secondary and tertiary stresses, giving the
stanza its sense of gathering motion for the final phrase:

> Lord, let not me a worme by thee be shent,
>
> While Thou are in the heat of thy displeasure:
>
> Ne let thy rage, of my due punishment
>
> Become the measure.

This tension in the meter does not violate the essentially iambic pattern; in fact it depends upon that pattern for its strength. All of the
stanzas follow this rhythmic pattern, except the third, in which the
speaker's direct appeal to God reaches a peak, and the last line of the
stanza is accordingly more strained:

---

26 On this general problem I have already mentioned V. C. Clinton-Baddeley's
excellent short study, *Words for Music* (Cambridge: Cambridge University Press,
1941); for comparison, see John Stevens, *Music and Poetry in the Early Tudor
Court* (London: Methuen, 1961), pp. 139 ff., and Wilfred Mellers, *Harmonious
Meeting* (London: Dennis Dobson, 1965), pp. 107-8.

Nay ev'n my soul fell troubles do appall;

Alas, how long, my God, wilt Thou delay me?

Turne Thee, sweet lord, and from this Ougly fall

My Deare God stay me.

(9–12)

It is pertinent here that the poem as a whole has only ten run-on lines, and eight of them introduce the short final lines at the ends of the quatrains. This accords with what we have observed earlier about Sidney's enjambment; here the speed of the movement across the line end, up to the caesura that is only two or three syllables into the last line, emphasizes the rapid meter and the spasm of anguish in the short final line.

Sidney's skill in relating syntax, stanza, and idea is evident even in more conventional forms. In some respects, Psalm 33 is similar to Psalm 6:

Rejoice in God, O ye
　That righteous be;
For that cherfull thankfulness,
It is a comely part
　In them whose heart
Doth cherish rightfulness.

O prayse with harp the lord,
　O now accord
Viols with singing Voice,
Let ten-stringed instrument
　O now be bent
To witness you rejoice.

A new, sing a new song
　To him most strong,
Sing Lowd and merrily,
Because that word of his
　Most righteous is
And his deeds faithfull bee.

> He righteousness approves
> And judgment loves,
> God's goodness fills all lands,
> His Word made heavnly Coast,
> And all that Host
> By breath of his mouth stands.
>
> (Ps. 33:1–24)

Partly by placing the verbs in the final lines of the stanzas, as in Psalm 6, and partly by repeating key ideas, Sidney has created an expanding motion at the end of each stanza. In every case, the second tercet provides a broad rationale for the first tercet: Rejoice, for it is comely; play instruments, because you rejoice; sing joyfully, because God is true; and God so loves righteousness on earth that he has made the universe righteous. The repeated shape of the ideas and the technical features of the last lines create much of the psalm's rhythm. This point is important, for in the remainder of the psalm—ten more stanzas—Sidney alters the pattern entirely, by separating the two tercets grammatically and making each a distinct and different thought. The fifth stanza clearly shows the break:

> The waters of the seas
> In heapes he layes,
> And depths in treasure his.
> Let all the earth feare God,
> And who abroad
> Of world a dweller is.
>
> (25–30)

The abrupt change in manner rather signals the end of the invocation to praise, and the beginning of a catalogue. The psalm shows conveniently the extent to which Sidney's stanza depends on relations between syntax and idea.

Somewhat more integrated in style is Psalm 16; but here, although the stanza is not particularly ingenious in form, it is still remarkably suited to the rhythms and the ideas. As a personal psalm that focuses on the relations of man to God, it necessarily involves some repetition of God's name and attributes. The stanza form is designed to emphasize this repetition by its arrangement of couplet and quatrain and its seven-syllable line:

> Save me lord, for why Thou art
>   All the hope of all my heart,
>   Witness Thou my soule with me
>   That to God my God I say
>   Thou my lord, Thou art my stay,
>   Though my Works reach not to Thee.
>
> (1–6)

The heavy repetition on Lord-God-Thou-Though-Thee becomes almost incantational. Almost; but Sidney is not a hypnotist, and the dominant drive of the poem seems rather more playful, the repetition of the Name Itself as a part of the description of God. It is the identity of God that is saving, and the repetition to this effect is used in other psalms of Sidney's, such as the Tenth, where the theme is even more explicit. Sidney is describing the pride of the wicked man:

> For he himself doth prayse,
>   When he his lust doth ease,
>   Extolling ravenous gain:
>   But doth God' self disdain.
> Nay so proud is his puffed thought
>   That after God he never sought,
>   But rather much he fancys this
>   That Name of God a fable is.
>
> (9–16)

As in Psalm 16, the repetition of the pronouns plays an important part in the speaker's persuasive argument, although the points of view are of course very different. Psalm 16 is less concerned with the Name, as a holy object, than with the name in the sense of "to whom do I appeal." The repetition is the speaker's way of focusing his attention, and it is important that among all the pronouns and names floating through that first stanza, only once does the first person pronoun take a conventional metrical stress:

> Witness Thou my soule with me.

The rhetoric of this is rather bold: Sidney is introducing the last tercet, affirming God's name, by asking God to witness the speaker's soul, to witness his witnessing. The syntax and the heavy stress on *me* ultimately turn the logic of the line back to God, as is clarified in the fourth line, "That to God my God I say," in which the *I say* is not merely a convenient rhyme, as it would be say, in Wyatt's psalms. The delicate overlapping of rhythm and meaning, and the wholly subordinate *me*, is typical of both Sidney's tact and craftsmanship. (The technical practice itself is rather like that of Herbert, although Herbert does not often indulge in wordplay as elaborate as this.) And if we have failed to notice the coincidence of rhythm and meaning, Sidney neatly informs us of it in stanza 2, with a sally that is as grim as it is witty:

> This all the best I prove,
>   Good and godly men I love
>   And forsee their wretched paine
>   Who to other Gods do run,
>   Their blood offrings I do shun,
>   Nay to name their names I disdain.
>
>   (7–12)

In a tactic as subtle as that of stanza 1, the stress finally comes down on *I* only to identify the speaker as one of the Lord's, and to introduce the wry last line rejecting other gods' names.

Many of Sidney's other psalms have similar rhyme schemes handled very differently. Psalm 38 has the same tercet foundation and odd-syllable-count meter, now with the so-called counterpointed rhyme:

> Lord while that thy rage doth bide,
>   Do not chide
>   Nor in anger chastise me;
>   For thy shafts have pierc't me sore,
>   And yet more,
>   Still Thy hands upon me be.
>
>   (1–6)

The value of this apparently arbitrary stanza becomes obvious when Sidney begins to employ a mixture of high- and low-key language, which is strangely emphasized by the enjambed stresses of his meter:

> My wounds putrify and stink,
>   In the sinck
>   Of my filthy folly lai'd;

Earthly I do bow and crooke,
        With a look
Still in mourning chear arayd.

(13–18)

The first tercet is at once like and unlike the overstated and violent
manner of Sternhold and Hopkins; the metrical effects are sophisticated, although the imagery seems rather coarse for Sidney. However,
the violence of the Psalms themselves seemed to remain attractive
long after Sternhold and Hopkins, and it is almost certain that Sidney
is restraining himself here. The violent manner survived well past
Sidney in fact, and even as late as 1636, when George Sandys published his psalter, the same passage is rendered with even more relish:

My Ulcers swell,
        Corrupt and smell;
Of Folly the sad end.[27]

Perhaps more passages of this sort should be resurrected to suggest
Sidney's control. The reader who can separate himself from Sandys's
subject matter will notice that Sidney's version turns the wounds into
metaphor by means of the copula in the third line, while Sandys is
content to let the ulcers remain real.

Sidney's tercets, on the other hand, are more subtle in their effects;
the tone is lower, and the syntax expresses many of the psalm's ironies.
There is a distinct drop from the "sinck" into the "filthy folly," because Sidney has used one phrase across two lines. Similarly, the
speaker's bent posture points him toward earth rather than heaven. In
the first two lines of the second tercet, the syntax and line ends suggest that the speaker is looking for knowledge in the earth he came
from; but by the last line, we see that he "looks" only in the sense
that he has an appearance. By these subtle means rather than a
frontal attack like Sandys's, Sidney has suggested the bathos in the
speaker's attitude.

The rest of the psalm continues this static enumeration of bathetic
ironies, all or most of them dependent upon the stanza with its short
centers, where Sidney usually makes an abrupt change or turn in

---

[27] *A paraphrase upon the psalms of David* (London: A. Hebb, 1636), p. 57.

thought. The speaker's perspective shifts from time to time, as the stanza shape isolates small currents within the larger flow of the syntax:

> In my reines hot torment raignes.
>   There remains
> Nothing in my body sound . . . .
>
> (19–21)

> My God Thou wilt heare my voice;
> For I sayd, heare, least they be
>   Glad on me . . . .
>
> (45–47)

> Sure I do but halting go,
>   And my woe
> Still my orethwart neighbor is.
>
> (49–51)

To shift briefly to considerations of meter, we can see that trochaic lines that are run-on in this way are not without some dangers of their own, particularly in their movement between a singsong and a heavy clumping at the start of the line. To capitalize on this tendency, Sidney occasionally attempts iambic substitutions in order to move closer to the speed of speech:

> But Í like a man become,
>   Deaf and dumb . . . .
>
> (37–38)

> For on Thee, lord, without end
>   I attend,
>
> My Gód Thou wilt heare my voice.
>
> (43–45)

One valuable resource here is the monosyllable, an important part of Sidney's program for other reasons, too, according to Ringler.[28] The ability of several monosyllables to take a greater range of stresses than

---

[28] Sidney, *Poems*, p. liii.

a polysyllabic word allows the poet more freedom to set up cross-rhythms. But as the above examples show, the rhythms still remain difficult to control; and several of the psalms (numbers 28, 42, and 43, for example) show a strain between the meter and the voice or dramatic situation.

After picking through this assortment of psalms, we might conclude with what is probably the most impressive in the group, the Thirteenth. The psalm's distinctive form is derived from the opening words of the Prayer Book version: "Howe long wylt thou forget me (O Lorde) for ever: howe long wylt thou hyde thy face from mee."

> How long, O Lord, shall I forgotten be?
> What? ever?
> How long wilt Thou Thy hidden face from me
> Dissever?
>
> (Ps. 13:1-4)

The few changes that Sidney makes create a work with its own character. Sidney is not just versifying or metaphrasing his source, and this is immediately evident in the form of the psalm. As the stanza shape displays the questions and answers, it imposes a new pattern on its original: in Sidney's version, the questions imply their answers in the rhymes. There is a rising and falling of hope which the original does not have, and this is depicted in the form itself. Successive stanzas repeat the mental and visual pattern:

> How long shall I consult with carefull sprite
> In anguish?
> How long shall I with foes' triumphant might
> Thus languish?
>
> Behold, lord, let to Thy hearing creep
> My crying:
> Nay, give me eyes, and light, least that I sleep
> In dying.
>
> Least my Foe bragg, that in my ruin hee
> Prevailed,
> And at my fall they joy that, troublous, me
> Assailed.

No, No I trust on thee, and joy in Thy
    Great Pity.
Still therfore of Thy Graces shall be my
    Song's Ditty.

                           (5–20)

There are some affinities here, in form and movement of idea, with Sidney's experiments in the "echo" form, as in the Second Eclogues of the *Arcadia*:

What do lovers seeke for, long seeking for to
    enjoy?   Joy.
What be the joyes for which to enjoy they went
    to the paines?   Paines.
Then to an earnest Love what doth best victorie
    lend?   Ende.
End? but I can never end, love will not give me
    the leave.   Leave.
How be the minds dispos'd that can not tast thy
    physick?   Sick.
                            ("Philsides, Echo," ll. 13–17)

This sort of harmless amusement rises to some dignity in Psalm 13, where the narrative pretext that requires the echo is abandoned, and the repetition is (with one exception) limited to the feminine rhyme. The design is thus more complex than that of the usual echo poem, and the intricacy is enhanced by Sidney's having the echo lines answer each other. The centered lines almost comprise the poem in themselves: God is ever dissevered; I languish in anguish; I cry as I die; my foes assail and prevail; and pity is my ditty. This loose pattern stands out because of the rhyme and because the "refrains" often take two unexpectedly strong stresses:

What? ever?

Dissever?

In Anguish

Thus languish

My crying

In dying

Prevailed

Assailed

Great Pity

Song's Ditty

Like the echo poems, the psalm registers the strain of the speaker's situation in the tentativeness of the rhyme. But unlike the echo poems, the psalm has a stanza shape that emphasizes the unsure and groping logic. The exposed skeleton of its central lines makes it easier to see that the psalm is an expanded conditional argument: if the first stanza is true, then the next three are true, and if they are true, then the last must be true. Thus stanza 5 is not a *deus ex machina* ending, although it may seem to be one at first. The speaker's joy in God's pity, even though he is in agony, is a result of the way that agony is imposed. To give in to the foes, as other psalms make clear, would be to acknowledge the strength of their gods, or worse yet, the strength of their false idols. These adversities are a test of faith, but as the speaker realizes, even in making his song of complaint he has acknowledged God and His power. The fitness of the last stanza in particular is evident in the half rhymes between the *a*'s and *b*'s and the meaningful relations they suggest. Thine is pity, which is mine; my ditty, of your pity, is thine. Over the course of the psalm, a trade has taken place, and it is related to the psalm's central purpose of shifting a burden.

I have mentioned that Sidney's sister went on to revise many of his psalms, and it is possible that he left them to her in an unfinished state, expecting her to revise them. During the initial stages of the work, the two poets were probably in touch with each other, for in her dedicatory poem to Sidney, Mary Herbert does refer to the psalter as "this coupled worke." But how far Sidney's inspiration or direct planning had extended we do not know. What is certain is that Mary Herbert continued to rely on the French psalter and maintained Sidney's principle of stanzaic variety.

Yet the differences between their poetic manners are great, although there have been only two main lines of approach to the question of what, in fact, the Countess achieved in her own psalms. The older approach, after Grosart, sidesteps the whole problem by saying, in effect, that whatever the Countess's psalms may be, they are better than her brother's.[29] But in the absence of any sustained analysis this claim is not convincing, and it has been only recently that a different approach has been made in an effort to secure the Countess as a poet worth study. Louis Martz proposed several years ago that the Countess's psalms are not far from metaphysical poetry, to which the Countess's modern editor, J. C. A. Rathmell, has added that although her psalms "are not, in any useful sense of the term, 'metaphysical,' " nonetheless "their strong, energetic rhythms, the expressive stanza forms, the insistent verbal play, and the preference for a packed, concise line immediately differentiate them from conventional Elizabethan psalmody."[30] Despite the differences in their aims, Martz and Rathmell both admire the same qualities in the Countess and wish to have her considered as a figure of importance and ability. About her importance there is agreement, quite properly, I think, but about her ability there should be more discussion. As helpful as Rathmell in particular has been, through his editorial work and criticism, he and the few others who have commented on the Countess's psalms have avoided some serious problems, for example, her struggle with metaphors, and in the process have missed some of the Countess's very real individuality and poetic achievements. We can approach these problems by discussing some of the ways in which the Countess is *not* a metaphysical poet and from there move on to a study of her technical skills and the role of technique as metaphor in the psalms. Although the Countess is not a particularly good poet, she is historically important; her poems are uneven, but rarely ragged, and in some measure they are important because of the way they fail to attain the level of the truly second- or third-rate poems written in the nineties.

Certainly many of the Countess's psalms resemble metaphysical lyrics,

---

[29] There is a good summary and analysis of older criticism in Rathmell, *The Psalms*, pp. xi–xxxii. I have used this text for all quotations from the Countess; psalm and line numbers appear after each quotation.

[30] *Ibid.*, p. xii. Cf. Louis Martz, *The Poetry of Meditation*, 2d ed. (New Haven: Yale University Press, 1962), pp. 273–79.

whether we define the metaphysical poem in terms of the meta-physical conceit:[31]

> How fisshes die, what should I stand to tell?
> Or how of noisome froggs the earth-bred race
>   Croake where their princes sleepe, not only dwell?
> How lice and vermyn heav'nly voice attending
> Doe swarming fall, what quarter not offending?
>
> (Ps. 105:60–64)

or the *discordia concors*:

>   his sonnes, whom fathers love enderes,
> Shall find like blisse for legacie bequeathed;
>   A steadfast throne, I say, till heav'nly Spheares
> Shall faint in course, where yet they never breathed.
>
> (Ps. 89:77–80)

or the dark wit of "strong lines":

> The vulgar grasse, whereof the beast is faine,
> The rarer hearb man for him self hath chose:
>   All things in breef, that life in life maintaine,
> From Earths old Bowells fresh and yongly grows.
>
> (Ps. 104:45–48)

Perhaps the strength of all these figures lies in one of the Countess's contributions to psalmody in general, that is, her emphasis on the literal level of meaning, her tendency to view requests to God in terms of specific tasks on a specific earth. And she has had to work for this, for often she has clarified or elaborated, by means of second-ary sources, what was only feebly imaged in the original. Rathmell has pointed out that in her Psalm 139, for example, the Countess has

---

[31] Here the definitions of metaphysical conceit, *discordia concors*, and "strong lines" are the familiar ones; see, respectively, James Smith, "Metaphysical Poetry," in *Determinations*, ed. F. R. Leavis (London: Chatto and Windus, 1934); Johnson's "Life of Cowley," in *Lives of the English Poets* (London: J. M. Dent, 1925); George Williamson, "Strong Lines" (1936), in *Seventeenth Century Contexts* (London: Faber and Faber, 1960), and Joseph Duncan, *The Revival of Metaphysical Poetry* (Minneapolis: University of Minnesota Press, 1959).

borrowed a metaphor from Calvin's commentary on the psalm, re-shaping and modeling it enough to fashion her own stanza.[32] Indeed, by working with Calvin, Bèze, and the Geneva and Bishops' Bibles, on one hand, and the Countess, on the other, we may verify Rathmell's suggestion that in psalm after psalm the Countess has borrowed a gloss from a commentary, or a phrase from a prose or verse transla-tion, and adapted it to her own purposes. She seems to have worked deliberately for clarity in prose meaning, even going so far as to unite the frequently mixed metaphors of the originals. In a sense, there-fore, the "metaphysical" lines quoted above are somewhat misleading, for generally the Countess's wit is bright rather than dark. *She* would not think that she belonged in Joseph Duncan's book, for her effort throughout is toward a prose clarity that can hold up her com-plex figures and intricate meters.

Yet even the most penetrating exegesis cannot of itself make a good poem, and in spite of the Countess's reliance on Calvin and the two Bibles, she still has lapses, and they are hardly infrequent. Source study in the Countess's psalms may reveal her admirable, even exhaus-tive work on single poems; but in spite of her diligence, her style is often dissipated in conveying prose meaning or sinks into Elizabethan clichés. This generalization may be tested by comparing some of her translations with the contemporary prose of the Prayer-Book version.

Psalm 90, for example, lays out the lines of a synesthetic metaphor, relating time and sound: "For when thou art angry all our days are gone: we bring our years to an end, as it were a tale that is told" (Ps. 90:9). From this the Countess extracts a metaphor that seems to sug-gest a smoking lamp making a noise which stops twice. It is very uncertain:

> Therefore in thy angry fuming,
> Our life of daies his measure spends:
> All our yeares in death consuming,
> Right like a sound that, sounded, ends.
>
> (Ps. 90:33–36)

This groping after metaphor also produces a strain that is more Cowleyan and ornamental, as in Psalm 104. First, the Prayer-Book version:

32 Rathmell, ed., *Psalms*, p. xx.

All beasts of the field drink thereof: and the wild asses quench their thirst.

Beside them shall the fowls of the air have their habitation: and sing among the branches.[33]

(Ps. 104:11–12)

Now the Countess's version:

Of these the beasts which on the planes doe feede
   All drinck their fill: with these their thirst allay
The Asses wild and all that wildly breede:
   By these in their self-chosen stations stay

The free-borne fowls, which through the empty way
Of yeelding aire wafted with winged speed,
   To art-like notes of nature-tuned lay
Make earelesse bushes give attentive heed.

(Ps. 104:33–40)

Here the elaboration of metaphors, apparently intended to gratify a taste for embellishment, and the desire to see one relationship within another, only succeed in creating a busy picture with many ambiguous gestures and static epithets. At times the Countess is like Aldous Huxley's Mr. Barbecue Smith, who is very adept at drawing out a metaphor but often unable to understand why he has done it.

These details of metaphor have larger implications for stanzas as wholes. As I have mentioned before, when the Countess becomes preoccupied with the details of a metaphor, her thought will wander much in the manner of Sternhold and Hopkins: she searches for additional relationships to draw out; Sternhold and Hopkins search for rhymes. As a result, their psalms are often surprisingly similar. The Countess's Psalm 59:

Now thus they fare: when sunn doth sett,
      Retorn'd againe,
As hounds that howle their food to gett,
      They runne amayne
The city through from street to street
With hungry mawes some prey to meet.

---

[33] My text is *The Parallel Psalter*, ed. R. S. Driver, 2d ed. (Oxford: Clarendon Press, 1904). Psalm and verse numbers appear after each quotation.

Abroad they range and hunt apace
Now that, now this,
As famine trailes a hungry trace;
And though they miss,
Yet will they not to kennell hye,
But all the night at bay do lye.

(Ps. 59:67–78)

The same psalm in the Old Version:

At evening they returne apace,
as dogs they grenne and cry:
Throughout the streets in every place,
they run about and spie.

They seeke about for meat, I say,
But let them not be fed:
Nor find an house wherin they may,
be bold to put their hed.

(Ps. 59:14–15)

Hopkins's Double Common Meter (the above passage is split between two stanzas) creates a rhythmic monotony which the Countess has partially avoided by using the dimeter lines. Yet her version is longer, to no great effect, and in this instance I believe the Old Version may be preferred to hers, for it creates a good deal more terror by having the "dogs" descend upon the houses. The Countess's search for metaphoric resemblances has led her to mix metaphors from the city and the field, with a resultant dilution of visual image. In neither case does the texture of the lines provide much interest in itself.

In short, the Countess's lines are extremely uneven, and she can shift abruptly from the weak to the strong: "God of his enimies the heads shall wound/ And those proud lookes that stiff in mischief go" (Ps. 68: 57–58). The syntactic awkwardness of the second line is a felt sign of the rigidity of pride (the Countess's addition—the Prayer-Book version reads simply "such as goeth on still in his wickedness"); it forms a curious contrast with the sluggish first line. Contrasts of this sort are by no means unusual with the Countess, and they seem to show a mind drawn on by metaphor itself. Unlike Wyatt at psalms, she is not a ruminant who will sustain a metaphor over a number of lines. Hers is an appetite that demands constant satisfaction, and in this she is more in the line of the later devotional poets. For the Countess, a psalm is very nearly an emblem, which can stimulate and control the imagination and sometimes constrict it.

Perhaps because of her concern for the broad development of metaphor, syntax is the chief sensuous element in the Countess's psalms. She does not incline to easy mellifluousness, unlike Sidney at his worst, or to deliberate strain, unlike Wyatt at his best. Unlike her brother she favors frequent repetition, using parallel structures, possessives, and adjectival modifiers. These can create the sense of a mind working by distinct stages—

> Mark what thou hear'st, and what thou mark'st obey
>
> (Ps. 45:38)

> Thie beautie shall both breed, and bredd, maintaine
>
> (Ps. 45:42)

> If I weep, and weeping fast—
>
> (Ps. 69:33)

but when used only for repetition itself, rather than for logical linking, they become confusing or trite:

> For I, alas, acknowledging doe know
>   My filthie fault, my faultie filthiness . . .
>
> (Ps. 51: 8–9)

> if they thinck on ought,
> Their thought they have, yea have beyond their thought.
>
> (Ps. 73: 20–21)

> How long, O God, how long
>   Wilt thou winck at the wrong
> Of thy reviling railing foe?
>   Shall he that hates thy name,
>   And hatred paintes with shame,
> So do, and do for ever soe?
>
> (Ps. 74:49–54)

> And so him self most terrible doth verify
> In terrifying kings, that earth do terrify.
>
> (Ps. 76:29–30)

> To thee my crying call,
> To thee my calling cry
> I did, O God, adresse . . .
>
> (Ps. 77:1–3)

> Yea, God to mind I cal'd,
> Yet calling God to mynde . . .
>
> (Ps. 77:10–12)

Some of this repetition is of course present for the rhyme, and some of it for the meter, as in the invocation to God in Psalm 65:

> The fertile yeare is with thy bounty crown'd:
> And where thou go'st, thy goings fatt the ground.
>
> (Ps. 65:41–42)

Perhaps if this God sounds rather like Falstaff, "larding the lean earth as he walks along," that is a tribute to Shakespeare, who has shown that the clumsiness of "go'st, goings" might have been avoided. The point is that because she has a taste for convoluted syntax to begin with, the Countess is readier to employ the most complex inversions for a rhyme or stanza form. Indeed at times it would be hard to say whether she or Thomas Sternhold was more capable of puzzling inversions:

> O sound her ruptures make,
> Her quaking bring to stay.
>
> (Ps. 60:7–8)

> How oft againe his gratious hand,
> To watry pooles doth desertes change!
> And on the fields that fruitless stand,
> Makes trickling springs unhoped range!
>
> (Ps. 107:93–96)

> I sometime straitned lay in thrall:
> So lying I on God did call,
> God answere gave me, when I called,
> And me unlarging, me unthralled.
>
> (Ps. 118:17–20)

Soe never slide
Shall I from what thy statutes do ordayne.

(Ps. 119R:17–18)

The purpose of some of the inversions in the Old Version is equally suspect:

They are so fed, that even for fat,
    their eyes oft times outstart:
And as for worldly goods they have,
    more then can wish their hart.

Their life is most licentious,
    boasting much of their wrong:
Which they have done to simple men,
    and ever pride among.

(Ps. 73:7–8)

Yet sometimes the Countess can use this inversion to create a spontaneous and gracious movement: "O how in her shall sprowt and spring/ The scepter Davids hand did beare!" (132:67–68). To repeat, the Countess is uneven; she is not incompetent but only indifferent. When she strikes on a natural phrasing in her psalms, it is as much by accident as by design.

Strangely enough, many of her smaller revisions in Sidney's psalms show her moving toward a more colloquial syntax;[34] for instance, in Psalm 32, she has changed "For so both day and night did stand/ On wretched mee thy heavy hand" to the more direct "On wretched me thy heauie hand/ Both day and night did sorely stand." However, the Countess seems to have admired both the energy of spoken language and the cunning of literary rhetoric. Thus her frequent interjections and exclamations. Rathmell points to an example in Psalm 58:

And call yee this to utter what is just,
    You that of justice hold the sov'raign throne?
And call yee this to yield, O sonnes of dust,
    To wronged brethren ev'ry man his own?
O no: it is your long malicious will . . . .

(1–5)

---

[34] My text is that of Sidney, *Poems.* In this edition, Ringler also offers what appear to be the Countess's revisions of Sidney's psalms, cited later in this chapter.

As Rathmell shows, contemporary prose versions begin the rebuttal
with a bland "Nay," but "the insertion of the exclamatory 'O' gives
a characteristically personal weight" to that mere connective.[35] But
many of her other additions are characteristically personal in that they
are only padding:

> Play, sing, and daunce. Then unto him, I say,
> Unto our God, nam'd of eternal essence,
> Present your selves with song, and daunce, and play.
>
> (Ps. 68:6–8)

> To endlesse whom be endlesse praise assign'd,
> Be this, againe I saie, be this effected.
>
> (Ps. 89:127–128)

> Which when I say, thus said I, loe,
> These men are madd,
> And too too bad . . . .
>
> (Ps. 95:33–35)

In these examples the Countess is filling out her meter or stanza by
using terms that attempt to be emotive. But the terms themselves, *I
say, lo,* and the equally common *alas* denote little. The context must
invest them with emotion, but in these cases, the contexts are empty
and the syntactic repetition does not supply an emotive statement.

Psalm 103 could be a model of all these techniques; the elements of
bathos combine almost symphonically as the structure of the stanza
slowly sinks:

> His way and trade
> He knowne to Moses made,
> His wonders to the sonnes of Israell
> The Lorde, I meane,
> Jehova; who doth leane
> With mildest will . . . .
>
> (Ps. 103:25–30)

The casual tone of "I meane" is at sorts with the wrenched syntax
of the second line, and the distinction itself seems pointless inasmuch

---

[35] Rathmell, *Psalms*, p. xxi.

as the psalm has been using the two names interchangeably prior to this; the interjection is probably present for its rhyme with *leane*, which here has an unintentionally humorous aptness. As before, many of the Countess's personal additions fit her contexts, but many more are merely facile fillers. Properly speaking, they are not personal but anonymous, for they blur her individual expression.

Our movement now from stanza structure to stanza form is a natural one, and here we shall find the Countess at home. The metrical variety of her forms has been greatly but not overly praised.[36] Her one hundred and seven psalms contain seventy-one different stanza forms. And I am reasonably positive that no one poem is virtually identical with another in both stanza *and* metric. When the Countess uses the same rhyme scheme in two or more poems, she invariably changes the meter or the stress on the rhyme, often producing as she does the so-called counterpointed rhyme.[37] This variety is no accident, and in places the psalms show signs of deliberate experimentation. Psalms 81 and 84, for example, have an *a b a b c c d d* rhyme scheme, but in 81 the *d* rhymes are feminine, and in 84 all the rhymes are feminine except the *d* rhymes. Occasionally the same stanza will appear in iambic pentameter, tetrameter, trimeter, and counterpointed forms (as in 80, 107, 60, and 64). More rarely, a consecutively numbered group may comprise something like a theme and variations. The Countess's three opening psalms have this quality: all have an *a b a b b c b c* rhyme scheme, although 44 is in trochaic tetrameter, 45 in iambic pentameter, and 46 in mixed iambic tetrameter and trimeter. There are also smaller signs of experimentation, as in 130 and 132, which use an *a b a b c c* rhyme scheme but have metrical schemes that nearly mirror each other, with 2 2 2 2 4 4 and 4 4 4 4 2 3 feet respectively. Or one could point to 119B and 119C, which use an *a b a c b c*

[36] See *ibid.* and Martz, *Poetry of Meditation, passim*; cf. Joseph Summers, *George Herbert* (Cambridge: Harvard University Press, 1954), p. 148 *et passim*; and Alicia Ostriker, "Song and Speech in the Metrics of George Herbert," *PMLA*, 80 (March 1965): 62–68.

[37] Miss Ostriker, in "Song and Speech," has pointed out (p. 64, n. 10) that six pairs of the Countess's psalms are identical except for the feminine rhymes; but these exceptions are important, for the Countess has gone to some effort to write poems that depend, for their contrasts, on these shifts of stress in rhyme.

The term *counterpoint* was first used by Albert McHarg Hayes, in "Counterpoint in Herbert," *SP*, 35 (1938): 43–60; the misleading aspects of the term are well noted by Summers, *George Herbert*, pp. 228–29, nn. 4–5.

rhyme scheme with two different counterpoint schemes of 3 5 4 3 5 4
and 2 3 4 2 3 4 feet.

But as these comments suggest, the Countess's experimentation is
chiefly in the direction of mathematical ingenuity and not in the
exercise of a good "ear." Her metrical substitutions are rarely more
inventive than a reversed initial foot, and in all her psalms there is
none of the colloquially stressed metric that we may find in *Astrophil
and Stella*, and in fact little of the whole pull and push between form
and meaning at which Sidney excels, even in his forty-three psalms.

There is an opportunity to verify these claims, for in the process of
revising her brother's psalms, the Countess impoverished Sidney's rich
metrical textures. Psalm 42, for example, is curiously revised, and the
revisions show a surprising lack of concern for Sidney's rhythms. Sidney's version had been syntactically awkward but rhythmically quite
emphatic:

> To him my thanks shall be said
> Who is still my present aid;
> And in fine my soul be raysed,
> God is my God, by me praysed.

> (53–56)

The first line of this disturbs the falling rhythms that have dominated
the psalm up to this point, and signals the start of the psalm's closing
movement. The next two lines return to the dominant rhythm, which
the last line accentuates by means of the caesura, setting up two large
blocks. To indicate the tensions in the meter by a four-stress scansion:

$$\text{G\'od \v{i}s m\'y G\^od, } \| \text{ b\^y m\'e pra\v{y}sed.}$$

For these four lines the Countess has attempted four revisions. She
may have been disturbed by that final passive verb; her revisions all
end with more emphatic verbs. More important, Sidney's rhythms
seem to have perplexed her, and each of her revisions systematically
simplifies the rhythms of the lines, by using only slightly varied
falling rhythms:

> Trust in him, on him relie
> Yeeld him praise contynuallie
> Who hath beene (thee failing never)
> Thy true God, & wilbe ever.

To him my thanckfull hart singe
Who is still my god and kinge
& with ayde me neare attendeth
When my foes my thrall entendeth.

Unto him a songe of praise
Still my thanckfull heart shall raise
He who helps my case distressed
Even my God for ever blessed.

He it is who hath and will
Beene my comfort reddy still
   He it is who faild me neuer
   God my blessed God for euer.

Each of these has grotesque touches of its own, as the Countess must have realized, for in what is evidently her final copy she restores Sidney's wording. We may infer from her revisions that she was more concerned with the sense of the original than with its rhythmic balance, and this generalization may apply to most of her other revisions. Her concern with form is somewhat mechanical. For example, Sidney ends six psalms with extra couplets or tercets, which in every case the Countess has removed. Some of the mutilation is serious, as in Psalm 16. This is the final stanza as Sidney wrote it:

Thou the path wilt make me tread
   Which to life true life doth lead:
   Where who may contemplate Thee
   Shall feel in Thy face's sight
   All the fulness of delight,
   And whose bodys placed be
      On thy blessed making hand
      Shall in endlesse pleasures stand!

(16:37–44)

The first two lines begin the stanza with a fairly even trochaic pattern; there is a slight metric disturbance in the third line, then still more in the fourth, as the poet thinks of sensing God's face directly. At this point one steady metric current takes over the stanza; the run-on lines, by abutting the stresses at the ends and starts of lines, keep up the pressure on the periodic syntax; and the stanza as a whole

seems designed to emphasize the exultation and plenitude of the true
life.

In the Countess's revision, this time preserved in her final copy, the
stanza loses this surging movement and doggedly grinds to a halt. The
lines are more weary and resigned than joyful:

> Thou lifes path wilt make me knowe,
> In whose view doth plenty growe
> All delights that soules can crave;
> And whose bodies placed stand
> On thy blessed-making hand,
> They all joies, like-endless, have.

(16:37–42)

The stanza now matches the others, at least in number of lines, but at
the expense of Sidney's interplay between meter and meaning.

The Countess's revisions of Sidney's psalms, along with the sheer
numerical variety of her own poetic forms, might seem to imply that
she is a gifted versifier but not necessarily a poet. This would be a
premature conclusion, however, for her gift for experiment seems
beyond that of the mere versifier who is adept at tinkering with pre-
existing forms. Her study and care in versification as a creative disci-
pline is nowhere more evident than in her Psalms 120 through 127.
This extraordinary sequence shows the Countess attempting asso-
nantal and consonantal rhyme, mixed feet, and intricate forms that
seem daring even when set beside her brother's experiments. These are
not especially attractive poems, but their technical care and thought
are remarkable for their time. I would like to look at two of these, 123
and 124, which show well the Countess's peculiar gifts.

Psalm 124, to begin with the simpler of the two, initially appears to
be written in conventional iambic pentameter and hexameter lines:

> Say Israel, doe not conceal a verity
> Had not the Lord assisted us,
> Had not the Lord assisted us what tyme arose
> Against us our fierce enimies . . . .

(Ps. 124:1–4)

To describe these lines as iambic, however, would be to ignore both
the problem of rhyme in the poem and the peculiar rising and falling

of the meter. As another possibility, it may be that the Countess was
listening for a paeonic meter, because this particular foot (the second
paeon, *x / x x*) places stresses on syllables that rhyme, at least better
than an iambic foot would do. This foot also accounts for the numerous unstressed syllables and accords with the poem's phrasal groupings. Any scansion would be risky, but I would offer one like this
(the rhyme notation will seem less mysterious in a moment):

```
     ×  ⁄ ××    ×  ⁄   ×   ×    ×  ⁄××
Say Israel, | doe not conceale | a verity                       a

      ×   ⁄   ×   ×   × ⁄  ×   ×
  Had not the Lord | assisted us,                               b

   ×   ⁄   ×   ×   × ⁄ × ×   ×   ⁄    × ×
Had not the Lord | assisted us | what tyme arose               a

     ×  ⁄   ×   ×    ×   ⁄ × ×
  Against us our | fierce enimies:                              b

 ×  ⁄  ×   ×     ×   ⁄   ×   ×    ×  ⁄   ×   ×
Us all at once | long since they had | devoured up,            a

     ×    ⁄   × ×     ×   ⁄ ××
  They were soe fell, | soe furious.                            a

 ×  ⁄  ×   ×  ×   ⁄     ×   ×       ×   ⁄ ××
If not, the an|gry gulphes, the streames | most horrible       a

      ×   ⁄   × ×   ×  ⁄   ×   ×
  Had drowned us: | soe drowned us,                             a

  ×  ⁄  ×   ×      ×  ⁄   × ×   ×   ⁄   ×   ×
That in the deepe | bene tombed, at | least on the deepe       a

     ×    ⁄   ×  ×     ×    ⁄ ××
  Had tumbled, our | dead Carcasses.                            a

  ×   ⁄    ×   ×  ×   ⁄  ×   ×  ×  ⁄   ×   ×
But Lord, what ho|nor shall thy peo|ple yeeld to thee,         b

      ×   ⁄   × ×    × ⁄ × ×
  From greedy teeth | delivered?                                b

 × ⁄ ×  ×    ×   ⁄   ×   ×   ⁄   ×   ×   ×
Escaped as | the fowle, that oft | breaking the ginn,          b

     ×  ⁄   ×   ×   ×  ⁄ × ×
  Beguiles the fow|lers wilynesse.                              b

 ×  ⁄   × ×   ×   ⁄   ×   ×    ×  ⁄ ×  ×
For sure this is | thy work, thy name | protecteth us,         b

      ×    ⁄   ×   ×    ×  ⁄  × ×
  Who heav'n, who earth | hast fashioned.                       b
```

Of course the meter may be heard as iambic rather than paeonic; two
is a multiple of four. In that case, though, the last foot would not

take the rhyme; with the paeonic scansion it does, and furthermore, puts it on the stressed syllable where it belongs. The rhyme scheme appears to consist of an alternately rhymed quatrain followed by three couplets each in the two rhymes; and the rhymes are generally back vowels, the *a*-rhyme (*air-ur-ore-are-ow*, and so forth), and front vowels, the *b*-rhyme (*eh-ee-ih-ay*, and so forth). It is not a flexible meter, and yet within its bounds the Countess does manage some expressive variation; in the thirteenth line, the substitution of a first paeon, for the usual second paeon, is quite appropriate. (A somewhat less expressive variation is the use of the dipthong *ai* ["eye"] in the third and fourteenth lines, in order to make the needed rhyme.) This sort of scansion is not likely to satisfy many readers, and yet I think it more satisfactory than one cobbled together by other means. Whatever the reader may make of this analysis, I trust that my main point is clear enough: the psalm is essentially a theoretical exercise, and it is easier to admire the Countess's ingenuity than her ability to suit form to meaning.

Psalm 123 shows a similar literary craft. On a first reading, the whole poem seems to be in a state of rhythmic and rhymic chaos. As in Coverdale's psalms, which usually relied on tunes for their "meter," the meters seem to be in a radical state of deterioration.

> Unto thee, oppressed, thou great commander of heaven
> Heav'nly good attending, lift I my earthy seeing
> Right as a waiters eye on a graceful master is holden;
> As the look of waitresse fix'd on a lady lieth:
> Soe with erected face, untill by thy mercy relieved,
> O Lord, expecting, begg we thy frendly favour.
> Scorn of proud scorners, reproach of mighty reprochers,
> Our sprights cleane ruined, fills with an inly dolor.
> Then frend us, favour us, Lord then with mercy relieve us,
> Whose scornfull miseries greatly thy mercy needeth.

The rhymes are clearer than those in Psalm 124, for they seem to fall into couplets, formed by rhymes in the penultimate syllables. Again there are puzzles, though, as in lines 5 and 6 (apparently a half-rhyme), and 3 and 4 (the "rhyme" here not even a legal fiction). The metric appears to consist of five hexameter lines followed by five pentameter lines, each line made up of trochees and amphibrachs:

```
 ⁄ ×   ⁄    ×    ⁄     ×     ⁄      ×    ⁄  ×   ×  ⁄ ×
Unto | thee, op|pressed, thou | greate com|mander | of heaven
 ⁄    ×    ⁄    ×    ⁄  ×    ⁄  ×    ×  ⁄   ×    ⁄ ×
Heav'nly | good at|tending, | lift I | my earthy | seeing
 ⁄    × ×  ⁄ ×    ⁄  ×   ⁄     ×    ⁄    ×   ×  ⁄ ×
Right as | a waiters | eye on | a graceful | master | is holden;
 ⁄   ×    ⁄   ×  ⁄    ×    ⁄   ×   × ⁄ ×   ⁄ ×
As the | look of | waitresse | fix'd on | a lady | lieth:
 ⁄   ×    × ⁄ ×   ⁄   ×  ⁄ ×    ×  ⁄   ×    × ⁄ ×
Soe with | erected | face, un|till by | thy mercy | relieved,
 × ⁄    ×   ⁄ ×   ⁄   ×   ⁄   ×    ⁄ ×
O Lord, | expecting, | begg we | thy frendly | favour.

 ⁄   ×    ×  ⁄  ×   ⁄   ×  ⁄  ×    ⁄ ×   × ⁄  ×
Scorn of | proud scorners, | reproach of | mighty | reprochers,
 ×   ⁄     ×   ⁄ ×   ⁄   ×   × ⁄ ×   ⁄ ×
Our sprights | cleane ruined, | fills with | an inly | dolor.
 ×   ⁄   ×    ⁄ ×    ×    ⁄   ×    ×    ⁄ ×   × ⁄    ×
Then frend us, | favour | us, Lord then | with mercy | relieve us,
 ×    ⁄  ×    ⁄ ×   ⁄  ×    ×   ⁄ ×   ⁄ ×
Whose scornfull | miseries | greatly | thy mercy | needeth.
```

In principle the meter resembles that of Sidney's "Asclepiadickes"
in the *Arcadia*, which use three different feet in a pentameter line; as
Theodore Spencer says of these, "the 'versifying' experiments reinforced one very important metrical lesson, namely that the same kind
of foot did not necessarily have to be repeated throughout the
line."[38] Yet like her rhymes, the Countess's meter smells of the lamp.
This may be the sort of "massy cadence" that Ruskin found in the
Countess's psalms,[39] but its pleasures are more theoretical than auditory.

If we return to stanza form, we may tie together these diverse comments on the Countess's style. It is obvious that the Countess, more
than Sidney, is responsible for the technical variety in the psalter as a
whole, and not merely because she translated the larger number of
psalms. Sidney used stanzas of four, five, six and sometimes eight lines,
and experimented by adjusting meter and line length.[40] The Countess

---

38 Spencer, "The Poetry of Sir Philip Sidney," p. 258.
39 Quoted by Rathmell, ed., *Psalms*, p. xxv.
40 Louis Martz is one of the few critics who have noticed Sidney's really narrow
limits in stanza length (*Poetry of Meditation*, pp. 273–74). My own tally of the
Countess's longer stanzas is as follows: eight lines, forty-four (including parts, G,
K, M, Q, and T of Psalm 119; nine lines, three; ten lines, three; and twelve lines,
two. There is also one sonnet (Psalm 100).

wrote in short stanzas as well as long stanzas of eight, nine, ten, and twelve lines. At times the Countess's stanza variations seem to have become ends in themselves, as in the examples above, where the form is more decorative than functional. Of course every psalm must be judged on its own merits; any generalization is dangerous when applied to one hundred and seven poems. But I believe that integrity of form in the individual poems was of less concern to the Countess than total variety. Reading her poetry, I cannot avoid feeling that the variety itself is a long pretence, that the forms may not be doing all the work they could in determining poetic meaning.

As I mentioned earlier though, technique for the Countess may function as metaphor. For her, formal variety signifies something more than the statistics, more even than the sum of relationships with literal meanings. Her psalmody is a devotional act: to her brother more than to God. As the opening lines of her dedicatory poem state emphatically,

> To thee pure sprite, to thee alone's address't
> 　this coupled worke, by double int'rest thine:
> 　First rais'de by thy blest hand, and what is mine
> inspird by thee . . . .[41]
>
> 　　　　　　　　　　　　　　　　　　　　(1–4)

This note is repeated several times throughout the ninety-one lines of the poem, and it is important to realize that it is not idolatrous. For the Countess, Sidney was literally an expression of the divine. He was dazzling enough to ordinary sensual man, say, Thomas Nashe, and infinitely more so to a younger sister. When in her "obsequies" (85) she speaks of his "Angell's soule with highest Angells plac't" (59), she implies that worshipping Sidney is not far from worshipping God. Donne describes their relationship rather more decorously, but they are still a heavenly pair:

> 　　as thy blessed Spirit fell upon
> These Psalmes first Author in a cloven tongue;
> (For 'twas a double power by which he sung
> The highest matter in the noblest forme;)

[41] These lines and the following come from Rathmell's text of the poem in *Psalms*, pp. xxxv–xxxviii.

So thou has cleft that spirit, to performe
That worke againe, and shed it, here, upon
Two, by their bloods, and by thy Spirit one;
A Brother and a Sister, made by thee
The Organ, where thou art the Harmony.[42]

As the Countess says, Sidney gave the Psalms lustrous garments ("superficiall tire/ by thee put on" [9–10]) and now her job is to finish his "half-maim'd peece" (18). Thus the formal variety with which Sidney inaugurated the psalter is, for the Countess, a real part of its consecrated purpose. That variety *is* an end in itself and a meaningful end. We should not overlook the psalter's devotional purpose; but we should remember that part of that purpose is to create, as the Countess calls it, a "world of words" (28). Thus the ingenuity, the analysis, the arrangement, in short, the *criticism* which underlies the psalter, finally merges with her own loving purpose. Indeed, the Countess misses the second or third rank of Elizabethan lyrists for this reason, because her failure in individual poems is almost the result of her critical and devotional success. Her preoccupation with sorting, testing, and renovating must have displaced or become a substitute for the writing of poems in which form and meaning are stated one in the other. In this respect her failures, such as they are, are quite unlike those of her contemporaries in the multitudinous miscellanies. Most of these poems, when they fail, accomplish nothing; the Countess's psalms, on the contrary, are like those works in every art that we value for all they accomplish in the process of missing a working or lasting unity.

In this sense it is helpful to say, as does Hallett Smith, that the Sidneyan psalms as a whole "might be regarded as a School of English Versification."[43] They do constitute a school in that the psalter is a self-contained body or system of models. But the term *school* may exaggerate the psalter's importance. Only a few poets attempted to take advantage of or even imitate the stanzaic and metrical variety of the psalter, and to credit the Sidneys (even by implication, by use of the term) with the founding of a school might be even more of a distortion than to refer to Donne's school. Yet as one attempt to

---

[42] "Upon the translation of the Psalmes . . . ," ll. 8–16, in Donne, *Divine Poems* (my italics).

[43] Smith, "English Metrical Psalms in the Sixteenth Century and Their Literary Significance," *HLQ*, 9 (1946): 269.

arrange and renovate, the psalter is extremely important. Theodore Spencer, speaking of Sidney's poetry as a whole, located some of the fundamental assumptions behind Sidney's art and, I would argue, the Countess's as well:

> If English poetry were ever to have any music in it, if the rhythm of the lines were rightly to echo the rhythm of the thought, if there were ever to be any of that essential *drama* in English verse technique, by which a resolved conflict occurs between the basic metrical pattern and the necessary rhythm of the meaning—if all this were to happen, the situation which existed before 1576 [that is, the start of the *Arcadia*] had drastically to be changed. The practice of verse technique needed a violent wrench to get it out of its dusty rut. And this wrench, this virtual dislocation, was largely accomplished by the experiments in classical meters. . . . [Sidney and his circle] tried to make people *think* about words; in order to "versify," words had to be broken up, each syllable had to be weighed and considered, and new rhythmical combinations had to be found which were as far as possible from the unthinking jog-trot of the prevalent iambic habit.[44]

And the changing stanza patterns are, as Spencer showed elsewhere in his valuable article, an integral part of this weighing and testing and checking. Even if Herbert never saw the psalter, these critical acts make it important because they indicate a particularly advanced poetic consciousness for the time. The psalter is more important as a critical work than as a poetic work. It selects and discriminates; it presents a theory. T. S. Eliot has remarked on this discriminating process in his "Apology for the Countess of Pembroke," and although his main concern is with poetics and drama, his remarks also apply to the Sidney psalter, which demonstrates "the intimacy of the creative and the critical mind."[45] To adapt Eliot's thesis, the psalter is one manifestation of "the Elizabethan critical mind expressing itself before the greater part of the great literature of the age had been written."[46] This surely is no small accomplishment; and that in the process Sidney and the Countess each wrote some dozen psalms of permanent value, in their own right, testifies to their capacity for this important critical office.

---

44 Spencer, "The Poetry of Sir Philip Sidney," pp. 257–58.

45 In *The Use of Poetry and the Use of Criticism* (London: Faber and Faber, 1933), p. 37.

46 *Ibid.*, p. 53.

IV. GEORGE WITHER

To shift from the Sidneys to Wither is inevitably disappointing. By the time his psalter appeared, approximately thirty-three years after Mary Herbert had finished the Sidneyan psalter, enough battles in poetic technique had been fought that, given Wither's talent (or lack of it, rather), his chances of surprising us are few. By this time the triumph of Sternhold and Hopkins was complete, as it was not in the eighties and nineties; in 1631 alone, the year before the publication of Wither's *Psalmes*, the Old Version had gone through eight different editions. When the Sidneys were writing, the supremacy of the Old Version was still open to challenge; but so far had it succeeded in Wither's time that he was practically forced to adopt its poetic forms if his own psalter were to be used widely, and apparently Wither did want this sort of success. His *Psalmes* thus have a compromise character; his aim is to remove the vulgarity and sheer bad writing of the Old Version, while still retaining its static structures. The literary dangers of Wither's task are obvious. There would be a tendency to "translate," that is, to clean up or revise the Old Version's errors, rather than work out from a fresh conception; and there would be a tendency to work toward mere inoffensiveness. Wither seems to have been aware of these dangers, for his two earlier books on the psalter are full of observations on the beauty of language and justness of sentiment in the originals.

It is hard to assess how far Wither's concern for these beauties and sentiments went before it shaded into his Protestant capitalism, but it did not result in especially attractive or edifying psalms. The decision to "fit," as he called it, every psalm to one already in the Old Version committed him to a rhythmic and stanzaic monotony. On the level of prose meaning, Wither's primary concern, as I noted in the Introduction, is with the figures of the psalter and the supposed breaches of decorum the Old Version had introduced. But as critics have always pointed out, many of the effects of bathos or sinking are also those of rising: the abrupt introduction of a metaphor, the unexpected shift in rhythm, and the more subtle effects of syntax moving across line ends and cross-rhythms rising and falling across the main current of the meter. By removing the potential for weakness, Wither also removed the potential for strength. Even the most dignified figures, clothed in a blanched and insipid rhythm, become only statues, or worse, ghosts.

Although Wither's language has much of the toughness and casual violence of Sternhold and Hopkins, the figures are introduced more carefully and the clashing metaphors are harmonized. The result is a great gain in immediate coherence:

> For, lo; with mischeeves being bigg,
>   They first conceive a sinn;
> Next, bring forth lies; then pit-falls digg,
>   Where, they themselves fal in.
> Thus, on their heads, their mischeeve all
>   Do justly tumble down;
> And wicked mens devises fall
>   On their devizors crowne.[47]

(Ps. 7, p. 11)

Sidney's version is much more energetic rhythmically, which is appropriate considering the subject matter, and his syntactic confusion is equally appropriate:

> A pitt was digg'd by this man, vainly strong;
>   But in the pitt he, ruin'd, first did fall,
>   Which fall he made, to doe his neighbour wrong.
>
> He against me doth throw, but down it shall
>   Upon his pate; his paine, emploied thus,
>   And his own ill, his own head shall appall.

(Ps. 7:40–45)

Sidney's syntax is mimetic, tripping over itself like the vain man, and this is usually the sort of effect that Wither avoids. He smooths over the roughest passages, in which one hopes for excitement:

> But, God shall cut their lipps that gloze,
>   And, pluck away the tongues of those
>   Who proudly make their vauntings, thus:
> Wee of our tongues will masters be;
>   Our lipps are ours, & who is he
>   That shall have Lord-ship over us?

(Ps. 12, p. 20)

[47] All references are to Wither, *Psalmes*. Psalm and page numbers are given in the text.

> From greefs like ours, they seemed free,
> Their pride & Cruelties,
> To them as clothes or bracelets be;
> And, fatt stuffs out their eyes.
>
> (Ps. 73, p. 133)

Clearly some substantial gains have been made. The metaphors have a sharper visual basis than they have had most of the time before, with most of the psalmodists; the logical contrasts are crisper; and there is some knowledge of the proud heart. The verse is very tidy but very dull, for the lines have a rhythmic banality that the figures do not conceal. Wither's psalms form an interesting contrast with Mary Herbert's, for while her rhythms are also rarely exciting, her figures often have a novel insight that at least secures our attention.

When Wither's figures are thin, or absent altogether, he, like his predecessors, resorts to wordy inversions and fillers to satisfy his forms. His steady iambic rhythms almost succeed in covering them up:

> Unheard of thee, I crye whole daies;
> Whole nights the same I doe;
> Yet, thou art Isr'els cheefest praise,
> And, thou art holy to.
>
> (Ps. 22, pp. 38–39)

> They seek not Peace, but Projects lay
> For them that peaceful be:
> With gaping mouthes, AH! HA, say they,
> Our wish, we now do see.
>
> (Ps. 35, p. 67)

> Who, resteth in the shade of God most high,
> Within his privy-Chambers is reposed:
> And, therfor, in my selfe, thus mused I;
> Thee, as a Fort, thy God hath round enclosed . . . .
>
> (Ps. 91, p. 172)

In many ways this is worse than the craftsmanship of Sternhold and Hopkins. Their work had some naive energy, inflicting itself on the medium in unexpected ways; but Wither's verse is just enough closer to an ideal of "correctness" that it has lost energy without finding sophistication. To that extent, even these examples, by stressing his flaws, may create a misleading picture of him as a refined Sternhold. Most of the time his art is competently dull. I would suggest as an analogy the architecture of the typical modern state college, always correct and well finished and often having surface interest, but static in its masses and imitative in conception. Even on an occasion that calls for life and energy, Wither maintains his dull movement. His Psalm 150, the *Laudate Dominum*, will quicken no pulse:

> Come praise the Lord, come praise him,
>   With in his holy-seat:
> In all his glories, praise him,
>   And his great Acts repeat.
> As he excelleth, praise him,
>   With Trumpet, and with Flute;
> With Harp and Psaltry, praise him,
>   With Viol, & with Lute.
> Upon the Timbrel praise him,
>   In Song, his praise advance:
> Upon the Organs praise him,
>   And, praise him in the Dance.
> On tingling Cimballs praise him,
>   On Cymballs loud that sound;
> And, let all creatures praise him,
>   In whom, life-breath is found.

(pp. 294–95)

Something has gone out of the verse since Sidney. The reader may recall Sidney's Psalm Thirty-three, a similar song of praise by music which has a corresponding music in its sounds and rhythms. These qualities are lacking in Wither's psalm; there is a gap between the ideas and the style. Much of the style seems to point ahead to some of the worst aspects of Restoration verse: the triteness of the rhythm (there is not even a tentative modulation); the heavy stamp of the rhymes; the stanza that is formal but not functional (note the redundancy in the first two lines of the last quatrain). It is true that the Countess of Pembroke is often capable of writing nonfunctional stanzas; but those forms themselves, in their great variety, still have intrinsic interest. In Wither, the last of our psalmodists, we have reached perhaps a low point in lyric form, for the verse is merely inoffensive and monotonous.

It is fitting that Wither should be the last psalmodist in this study, for his *Psalmes* are one of the last attempts in the century, by a literary figure of any consequence, to provide a public or singing psalter. The Old Version, maintaining its position and not to be replaced in the church service until 1696, actually may have encouraged the growth of a literary and private psalmody. Wither's conspicuous failure to dislodge Sternhold and Hopkins, even though he had the blessings of the King, may have provided a sufficient example of how *not* to use the psalms. Another factor in the general decline of psalmody is the rise of the hymn, and in this, ironically enough, Wither is a key figure. That subject is another essay; but it is likely that the very fixity of the Old Version promoted the devising of lyrics that would eventually replace the psalm in popular Protestant devotion. And finally, the complex of rising problems in church and state must have precluded the comparatively sweet freedom that encouraged psalmody in the eighties and nineties.

V. CONCLUSION

The history of the metrical psalm can be seen, without great oversimplification, as the course of tensions between a variety of elements: the tension between high and low church elements over the use and significance of the psalter, between the courtly expression of repentant passion and the vulgar expression of "enthusiasm," between elegance and variety and bathos and monotony, or between the narrative and the lyric. Of course these tensions were not unique to the metrical psalm but were felt in other genres as well. However, one effect of these conflicts within psalmody was the increasing stabilization of the iambic line. The Old Version in particular established this rhythmic norm as a part of the English consciousness; it presented a metric, indeed, an aesthetic, which a poet could accept, modify, or reject almost wholly. In fact, the Old Version's negative example may have been one of its best aspects, for it may have demonstrated to the Sidneys and to Herbert the difficulties of using one limited form to express a variety of emotions. We should not forget to add, too, that the Sidney psalter itself, though not the commercial success of the Old Version, provided the right people with a whole cluster of ideas that the theoreticians had not yet described.

In reading *The Temple*, we shall see how Herbert found something of value in the poetic forms of the metrical psalms; we shall see also how he found value in the content of these psalms, with their recurrent theme of weakness becoming strength. This study will involve looking at Herbert's personal resolution of those tensions which affected sixteenth- and early seventeenth-century poetry but were most boldly displayed in the metrical psalm. When Herbert says that "affliction shall advance the flight in me," he is referring to the physical and spiritual suffering by which he is strengthened, and a similar process of amalgamation takes place in his poetic form. In *The Temple*, the devices of the Old Version obtain new energy and provide a wing on which to fly; and the sheer, sometimes arbitrary variety of the Sidney psalter becomes functional. Courtly and common aspects of religious song meet in Herbert, and though he is usually considered only a minor psalmodist himself, he has a clearer idea than the major psalmodists of the interrelations and separate prerogatives of lyric poetry and music. Herbert is able to exploit the clumsy musical sense of his predecessors (excepting Sidney), sometimes in a satiric context by directing its bathos at himself, and sometimes in the highest and most serious contexts by diverting it into painful self-knowledge. The self-pity into which psalmody can sink so quickly—*vide* Wyatt—with its attendant stylistic messiness, gives way in Herbert to self-respect and a restrained yet vigorous style. In every case, Herbert gives dignity and value to what he borrows.

Has the metrical psalm had an active influence on us, outside the poetry of Herbert? The absorption of its poetic modes—particularly those of the Old Version—has been so complete that we are inclined to look rather at the poets who absorbed it than at its innovators. The rise of Protestant hymnody in the eighteenth and early nineteenth centuries consolidated the positive achievements of the versified psalms but had in turn its own problems. Isaac Watts, Charles Wesley, and William Cowper, to name only three of the best-known writers of hymns within this period, achieved their own styles and yet wrote verse which, though often pedestrian, at least made good prose sense, was not repetitious or padded, and demonstrated the poet's ability to think through metaphor. More dubious accomplishments in this period included Common Meter "translations" of Herbert's poems (many, alas, still to be found in hymnals) and the poetically incompetent hymns of the mob of Methodists who wrote with ease.

Significantly enough, many religious lyrics of the later nineteenth century seem to have been written in reaction to the progressively more sentimentalized Protestant hymns, just as many religious lyrics of the early seventeenth century had shown a reaction to the clumsy technique and naive faith of the metrical psalms. Browning, Tennyson, and especially Hardy were aware of the effects to be gained by countering the conditioned response to the themes and forms of religious song; Hardy possessed a gift for serious parody along these lines which would be hard to underrate. Yet there is no question that their own religious verse owes much to the vigor of the eighteenth-century hymn, just as the hymn in turn had gained much from the controversy over the "poetic" of the Old Version. Even modern religious verse has been the inheritor of that reassessment.

In our time the metrical psalm has been of interest chiefly to scholars, and there has been no rush on the part of modern poets to revive it for its salutary effect on our sensibilities. Among modern poets there has been only one, as far as I know, both voracious and perverse enough to have read and seriously used the metrical psalm. Writing of her early friendship with W. H. Auden, the novelist Naomi Mitchison has recalled that he was "fascinated by the metrical versions of the Psalms with their curious inversions. The poem that begins 'Not father, further do prolong' is directly influenced by the metrical psalms."[48] The poem itself, the last ode in *The Orators*, is an important illustration of an idea Herbert would have understood, criticism by original composition. Auden is also the only editor of a popular poetry anthology who has stressed the historical importance of the metrical psalms, and he has mentioned elsewhere that the earliest poems he recalls include *The English Hymnal*, the Psalms, and *Struwwelpeter*.[49] There is a curious fitness in all this, that the metrical psalms should have found a modern reader who, in spite of some evident dissimilarities to Herbert in other respects, possesses a keen musical sense and a faultless ear.

[48] "Young Auden," *Shenandoah*, 18 (Winter 1967): 13. Unfortunately it was not possible to reprint the poem here.

[49] *Elizabethan and Jacobean Poets*, ed. W. H. Auden and Norman Holmes Pearson, Viking Portable Poets, vol. 2 (New York: Viking Press, 1950), p. xv; *The Dyer's Hand* (New York: Random House, 1962), p. 34.

THREE

Orchestral Form

One perpetually attractive aspect of Herbert's art is his use of poetic form to expand or shape religious ideas. The term *orchestration* might best describe the way in which Herbert's metrical structures, stanza forms, and patterns of sound and syntax become integral parts of his poetic meaning. By means of these elements Herbert can shape, color, or define the literal meaning of a poem, creating a rich and careful harmony between the different parts of his design. There is an especially articulate orchestration in the way Herbert uses the themes and conventions of the metrical psalms; in this he has gathered from the air a live tradition. Yet he does not rely upon those themes and conventions as his only means of orchestration; he also develops and clarifies his thought by means of formal devices themselves, giving rhyme and meter almost symbolic properties. By looking first at some of these simpler means of orchestration, then going on to techniques from the psalms, we shall see that for Herbert the psalms were not an unavoidable body of conventions but part of his poetic and his whole spiritual being.

I. ANALOGOUS FORMS

The simplest instrument at Herbert's disposal for orchestration is onomatopoeia, and the simplest use of onomatopoeia is animation, "the sound seeming an echo to the sense." There is no substantial

study of onomatopoeia in *The Temple,* and to some extent, the concept works better in the study of a self-consciously sensuous poet such
as Dylan Thomas than it does for a poet determined to copy out and
save expense. Doubtless it would be a mistake to press onto Herbert a
complete poetic based on onomatopoeia; but it would be equally a
mistake to say, as does George Herbert Palmer, that there is "no
group of lines in Herbert of which we may say, as we can of passages
in Spenser or Tennyson, that its vowel effects are an important part
of the poetry."[1] Palmer's Romantic gold standard may have misled
him here, for when Herbert wants to, he can handle onomatopoeia
with a sensitive ear.

The problem is that Herbert's onomatopoetic passages cannot be
isolated easily. We might look at two brief examples. The second
stanza of "Decay" has music of a fine Tennysonian kind:

> One might have sought and found thee presently
> At some fair oak, or bush, or cave, or well:
> Is my God this way? No, they would reply:
> He is to Sinai gone, as we heard tell:
> List, ye may heare great Aarons bell.

> (6–10)

The last two lines of the stanza reproduce with considerable fidelity
the repetition of one bell stroke over another. When the high vowels
are written out phonetically the effect is more obvious: *eye-ee-ear-eh/
ee-ear-eh-eh.* The rhythm of the last two lines is also instrumental in
creating the bell effect:

> He is to Sinai gone, as we heard tell:
> List, ye may hear great Aarons bell.

The first line is predominantly falling, while the second is a series of
pulsations in answer to the first. Again, the onomatopoetic effects in
the lines are not easily isolated, and they do not mix any lucent syrups,
but they are nonetheless present and functional.

Austin Warren has already called attention to the general difficulty

---

[1] George Herbert, *Life and Works,* ed. George Herbert Palmer, 2d ed. (Boston:
Houghton Mifflin, 1915), 1: 128–29.

of isolating lines of Herbert, in his discussion of the peculiar strength
of the phrase in "Prayer" (I), "Church-bels beyond the starres heard."
Warren rightly observes that the line "cannot be detached; for it is by
virtue of its position in the whole poem and as pervaded by what has
gone before that it acquires its light and warmth."[2] Warren's chief
interest is the emotional coloring of the phrase, but his point applies
equally well to the sounds. (I will pass over the onomatopoeia and
assonance in the phrase as slight effects at best.) In order to locate the
sources of the musical effect in the phrase, we are forced to look at the
whole context, and similar sounds seem to ring in many of the other
phrases in the poem:

> Engine against th'Almightie, sinners towre . . .
> A kinde of tune, which all things heare and fear . . .
> Heaven in ordinarie, man well drest . . .
> Church-bels beyond the starres heard . . . .

It almost becomes a jingle, the full and half rhymes within the last
two or three syllables of each line, which are also set off as appositives
or final terms in a period. One thoughtful analysis of the poem suggests that "rhythmically the stress and intonation pattern and the
phrase lengths of the tercet reflect the mounting ecstacy of the speaker
as in contemplating prayer he comes to feel himself contemplating
heaven itself. This élan is particularly reflected in the increasing
length of the phrases."[3] But these patterns in sound and syntax are
still not firm enough in themselves to account for the sense of echoing
in the lines; and perhaps there are intellectual echoes which correspond to the echoing sounds. Christian tragedy permeates the lines,
and in each line there is a reference to the Christian opportunity well
missed: the prayer turned against the god; or turned back against
itself; or as man's proper garb—and as arrogance in the face of
heaven; or as the sound of heaven itself, audible but infinitely distant.
And perhaps tragedy itself is like an echo in the mind, in which the
sufferer hears the sound of some similar but dissimilar action he might
have chosen: maybe this is, as Lionel Trilling has said in some remarks
on the novel, "that strange and beautiful sound we seem to hear gen-

---

[2] *Rage for Order* (Chicago: University of Chicago Press, 1948), p. 33.

[3] E. B. Greenwood, "George Herbert's Sonnet 'Prayer': A Stylistic Study," *EIC*,
15 (January 1965): 34.

erated in the air by a tale of suffering, a sound which is not always music, which does not always have a 'meaning,' but which yet entrances us, like the random notes of an Aeolian harp, or merely the sound of the wind in the chimney."[4] It is perhaps a blending of these intellectual echoes with the verbal echoes that creates the final peculiar color of the church bells, and it is a subtle onomatopoetic music of this sort that fascinates Herbert more than the "purling streams" of verbal sounds strictly echoing sense.

Herbert is perhaps better known for a different sort of onomatopoeia, the use of visually recognizable shapes in the stanza form. This use of form is conspicuous in only two of Herbert's poems, and possibly a third ("The Church-floore" has stanzas in inverted triangles which suggest the checkered floor of a church). Although these pattern poems are generally inferior to the best poems in *The Temple*, they have received considerable popular and scholarly attention, as if they constituted the major part of Herbert's poetic achievement. It is common knowledge that the pattern poem is by no means original with Herbert; poems in the shape of altars and wings may be found in the Greek Anthology, and there were numerous continental and English pattern poems in the century prior to Herbert.[5] The genre received its first critical analysis in English in Puttenham's *Arte of English Poesie*, and critics have reminded us that Puttenham had advised the poet to observe "your ocular proportion," according to the shapes he laid out in fifteen drawings of dummy poems and eight examples, two of which resemble altars or "pillers."[6] Albert McHarg Hayes, for example, says that Herbert "follows Puttenham's advice to construct well-knit stanzas . . . . Further, Herbert's use of pictorial stanza patterns may be due to Puttenham who praises the practice."[7] But clearly Herbert did not need to read Puttenham to learn about shaping a poem like an altar or a pair of wings. And there is no

[4] Lionel Trilling, "The Morality of Inertia," in *Great Moral Dilemmas in Literature, Past and Present*, ed. R. M. MacIver, in Religion and Civilization Series (New York: Institute for Religious and Social Studies, 1956), p. 40. Cf. Arnold Stein's comment on the relation between the metaphors and phrasing in the poem: "Much of the difficulty of the poem lies in what is held back until the last words are in place" (*George Herbert's Lyrics* [Baltimore: Johns Hopkins Press, 1968], p. 184).

[5] See Margaret Church, "The Pattern Poem" (Ph.D. diss., Radcliffe College, 1944).

[6] Puttenham, *The Arte of English Poesie*, ed. Gladys Doidge Willcock and Alice Walker (Cambridge: Cambridge University Press, 1936), p. 97.

[7] "Counterpoint in Herbert," *SP*, 35 (1938): 48–49.

direct resemblance between Puttenham's examples and Herbert's practice.

By coincidence, however, the rhetoric of Puttenham's description of the pattern poem seems to link him with Herbert. This may be seen by looking first at "The Altar." Joseph Summers has shown how the altar—not a conventional Christian communion table—is a "type of the heart of man, hewn not by man's efforts but by God alone."[8] The poem's other levels of meaning all build upon the idea that the poem itself is a poetic altar. Praise is offered upon it; and it is also the first poem one encounters upon entering that section of *The Temple* entitled "The Church." Herbert's poetic offering is also placed in a very real sense *on* the altar; the first editions of *The Temple* had the word *SACRIFICE* deliberately centered over the word *ALTAR* in the last line.[9] And finally, the altar of fitted stone is, like a poem, an artisan's product. Rosemond Tuve described in detail the history of the "motifs" of the heart and altar of stone, concluding that "in iconography they are assumed as immediately understandable."[10]

This traditional metaphor and the meaning that Herbert has added are relevant to Puttenham's description of "ocular proportion," for Puttenham considers pattern poetry to be a literature of artifacts. That is, the poem is not simply an image of an object; it *is* an object. For Puttenham, the pattern poem is most properly "engraven in gold, silver or ivorie, and sometimes with letters of ametist, rubie, emeralde, or topas curiousely cemented and peeced together . . ."; to give some authority to this notion, Puttenham goes on to mention "a great Emperor in Tartary" and "a certaine great Sultan of Persia" who presented gifts of girdles and ornaments that were literally poems,[11] like Herbert's literal "Altar."

Puttenham's idea of the poem as artifact is hardly novel, but it may clarify the functions of the shape of Herbert's altar. To adopt Puttenham's typographic literalism, it would be as much to the point to note that the table atop the figure is formed by the poet's praise, the upright is formed by the description of his heart, and the base is

---

[8] Summers, *George Herbert*, p. 141.

[9] See Anthony James West, "George Herbert—a Study in Unity" (M.A. thesis, University of Washington, 1954), pp. 14 (n. 18), 29.

[10] Tuve, *A Reading of George Herbert*, p. 197; pp. 182–201 are also relevant.

[11] Puttenham, *Arte of English Poesie*, pp. 92, 94–95.

formed by the praise of God and His sacrifice. The reader of "The Altar" works down into broader categories and deeper relationships, because of the visual relationships created by the poem's shape. Because the poet seeks to have God's sacrifice identified with his own, the altar is a peculiarly appropriate shape for the poem in that it is symmetrical top and bottom. In this respect the visual shape of the poem may be said to be orchestral. Conventional stanza structures in themselves could not have indicated the above relationships, and of this sort of craft Puttenham seems to have had no idea.

All three of Herbert's pattern poems ("The Altar," "Easter-wings," and, as I have proposed, "The Church-floore") take the same fundamental shape in expanding, contracting, and reexpanding. My particular concern in "The Church-floore" is with the first section of the poem, in which the broad-to-narrow stanza form suggests the geometric contrast and angularity of a checkered floor:[12]

> Mark you the floore? that square & speckled stone,
>> Which looks so firm and strong,
>>> Is *Patience*:
>
> And th'other black and grave, wherewith each one
>> Is checker'd all along,
>>> *Humilitie* . . . .

(66–67, 1–6)

Beyond this level of "ocular proportion," however, the stanza shape determines the argument of the poem, just as in "The Altar." "The Church-floore" is about metaphor-making. Every stanza begins with pentameter and trimeter lines of closely observed detail, then ends with a dimeter line drawing an analogy—the speckled stone represents patience, and so forth. The checkered floor that provides the subject of the poem is a figure for metaphor-making, one stone neatly

---

[12] The design is simply that of a checkerboard turned forty-five degrees, with diagonals passing (horizontally) through each square. The pattern is a common one at this time; there is an illustration of it in Sir Banister Fletcher's standard *History of Architecture on the Comparative Method*, rev. by R. A. Cordingley, 17th ed. (London: Athlone Press, 1961), p. 400, pl. B. The floor is that of the choir vault in Oxford Cathedral (Christ Church), built ca. 1480–1500. The floor of Herbert's own church at Bemerton appears, in photographs at least, to be completely plain; but I have been unable to determine whether it was plain in Herbert's time.

corresponding to another, just as a metaphor establishes an identity between two different qualities or things. Consequently there is a three-way correspondence between the stanza shape, the literal meaning, and the metaphor itself. In this sense the stanza form has directed and completed the meaning of the poem.[13]

"Easter-wings" probably demonstrates the most impressive use of the expanding-contracting form. On the simplest level, the poem has, like "The Altar," a close fit between form and intention. It may be, as Summers suggests, that "the pattern is successful not merely because we 'see' the wings, but because we see how they are made: the process of impoverishment and enrichment, of 'thinning' and expansion which makes 'flight' possible." And, to take a step further back, "the poem and its pattern constantly insist that for man only through the fall is the flight possible."[14]

However, this reading depends on the poem's being presented in a certain way. And it was only after Herbert's death, when *The Temple* began to be printed, that the poem was composed vertically. Thus, in the 1633 edition, for example, the poem was printed sideways on two facing pages, so that it might more literally resemble "wings." I do not believe that it is being too finicky to say that it makes some difference how the poem is printed. Herbert has observed birds closely; as Joan Bennett noticed some time ago, "the diminuendo and crescendo in the poem's form are expressive both of the rise and fall of the lark's song and flight . . . ."[15] Early editors hoped, we may assume, to "draw" the flapping wings of a bird by printing the poem vertically, in this way "picturing" the birds. But given Herbert's preoccupation with aesthetic and religious unity, he would be most unlikely to write a poem that had to be "viewed" vertically and "read" horizontally, as if he were expecting the sort of visual adjustments and readjustments suitable for the "appreciation" of a portrait by Salvador Dali. The

[13] In a provocative discussion of Herbert's ability to think directly by means of image, Robert Ellrodt says of this poem, "L'idée ne précède plus l'image, car l'image est tirée du *réel*. La composition même des premières strophes, avec le brusque rejet du mot abstrait, suggère la naissance soudaine de l'idée, révélée à travers la matière . . . . La contemplation et la méditation procèdent de pair, l'épithète concrète annonçant chaque fois la verue abstrait" (*L'Inspiration Personnelle et l'Esprit du Temps chez les Poetes Metaphysiques Anglais* [Paris: Jose Corti, 1960], 1:350).

[14] Summers, *George Herbert*, p. 144.

[15] Bennett, *Four Metaphysical Poets*, 2d ed. (New York: Vintage Books, 1958), pp. 73–74.

vertical format is flatly impossible: the bird cannot be viewed from above, for no bird's wings flap forward and backward, unless, of course, they have come out of their sockets. Even though the poem shows how "affliction shall advance the flight," Herbert cannot reasonably be expected to have intended so grotesque a metaphor. Nor can the bird be viewed head-on: the lines do not form an arc. The printed lines of the poem can only *circumscribe* the arc of the wings as they flap up and down. The lark is flying toward the reader: he and his wings are not *in* the poem. Herbert may have observed birds closely, but he has not attempted to draw one. The poem is more concerned with certain qualities of bird flight than it is with the shape of wings, and it shows two ways of looking at a lark, not one way of drawing a lark. If we recall the tenor of the metaphor, we see why the "bird" is *not* there: it is the risen Spirit.

Both stanzas of "Easter-wings" are concerned with motion, but they differ in taking the general and the particular as their respective topics. Stanza 1 shows how man's foolishness culminated in the Fall, while stanza 2 narrows to show how the poet's own sin leads to his punishment. The difference in emphasis is striking; the first points out man's general impoverishment, the second a particular depravity. (The distinction between general and personal in the two stanzas is more evident if we compare the texts of the poem in its two manuscripts; in the last line of the first stanza in the earlier version, Herbert writes, "Then shall my fall further the flight in me"; "my fall" later becomes "the fall.") The first stanza is concerned with the fall of all men, the flight of the poet as representative of man in general. The second stanza is more personal. For example, in stanza 1 the ascension of the spirit is all-inclusive, a union of man and the created world: "O let me rise/ As larks, harmoniously," that is, as larks in general, or all birds; yet in stanza 2 the focus shifts to one bird, the Spirit, upon whom the poet would "imp his wing." These shifts in focus between the two stanzas are revealed in the line-by-line development of the poem. The two stanzas have interlocking rhymes (2 and 12, 4 and 14, 6 and 16, 8 and 18, 10 and 20), and six of the ten lines in each stanza are refrains. The changes in imagery take place in these double-rhymed refrain lines and are more emphatic for it.

The structure of the poem imposes some limits as well as a framework for the contrast between particular and general. For example, as Rosemond Tuve suggests, Herbert, in his capacity as preacher, may be referring to his role as a wing upon which the church may rise. Citing various scriptural commentaries, Tuve says that "the silver wings of the dove are the preachers who carry aloft the glory of the Church . . . the Church is borne up, as on wings, by the faithful."[16] But this interpretation of the metaphor seems unlikely, inasmuch as the fastidious Herbert states clearly that he cannot fly, and that if he does arise at all it will be as passenger rather than pilot. Furthermore, although both stanzas work the same way in the movement of idea, Herbert distinctly shifts his tone and logic at midpoint, and so prevents our equating the movements of the two stanzas. That shift is quite literally the poetic equivalent of the lark's flight. And the long intellectual pull, from the low point at which the second stanza starts, is more dramatic (and convincing) for singling out one body to fall and rise.

Rather than cite references to the "wings of the Church," it might be more helpful to look at an analogue for the intellectual aptness of Herbert's typography. Appended to many editions of the Old Version was "A Prayer against the Devill and his manifold temptations, made by S. Augustine." The prayer asks for deliverance from sin (sloth, carnal sin, and so forth) and culminates in a description of the saved soul. Augustine's final metaphor is that of bird flight; and printers set the type after a familiar manner which, in this context, distinctly resembles that of "Easter-wings":

> . . . He hath set snares
> for us in our wordes, and our workes, and in
> all our life. But though O Lord deliver us from
> the net of the Foulers & from hard wordes
> that we may geve prayse to thee saying: Bles-
> sed be the Lord who hath not geven us
> up to be a pray for their teeth, our
> soule is delivered as a sparrow out
> of the foulers net, the net
> is broken and we
> escaped.[17]

---

16 Tuve, *A Reading of George Herbert*, p. 157.
17 Old Version, sig. [T 7r].

The prayer ends, like Herbert's poem, with a personal recognition drawn out of a general experience; in both cases the recognition involves a desire to be liberated from "harde wordes"—specifically, in "Easter-wings," the words "poore" and "thinne."[18] And Herbert's poem is, of course, a prayer. One final note on the typography of Augustine's prayer may clarify an important intellectual movement in "Easter-wings." The typographical form of the prayer has an appositeness that is quite different from that of Herbert's poem. The prayer for deliverance narrows down to one word; by implication, the prayer seeks a literal escape from words altogether. In "Easter-wings," however, the lines become fuller; Herbert seeks liberation *into* words. Not to generalize unduly upon one example, but to look ahead, I would add that the process is entirely typical of Herbert.

Some of the problems in recognizing the purpose of visual form in Herbert's verse are problems we shall encounter later in recognizing the purpose of more conventional stanza forms. At fault are some inherited preconceptions of form, and we might illustrate this with reference to Joseph Addison's remarks on Herbert. Most modern critics, while sneering at Addison, still share his basic preconceptions when writing about Herbert's pattern poems and thus miss the formal relation of these poems to the rest of *The Temple*. When Herbert's pattern poems are regarded as freaks, it may be because of an implicit acceptance of Addison's remarks. Thus C. S. Lewis—following the lines of Addison-Warton in general—dismisses the pattern poem as the product of "a taste for something curious and clever," and likens it to "the court poetry of Lilliput in the age of Gulliver."[19] This is simply an urbane rendering of George Herbert Palmer's manly disgust: "Of course we all know that every species of elaborate artificiality was then in fashion. Embroidery pleased. Probably Herbert himself did on occasion enjoy a ruffled shirt. I will not attempt fully to defend him."[20] Some of this attitude can be traced back to Addison's distaste for "false wit," although his use of this term was based

[18] In comments upon Psalms 43 and 87, Augustine points out that prayer has two "wings," alms and fasting, which may correspond to Herbert's "poore" and "thinne." See *Expositions on the Book of Psalms*, ed. A Cleveland Coxe, Nicene and Post-Nicene Fathers of the Christian Church, vol. 8 (Grand Rapids, Mich.: Eerdmans, 1956), pp. 140*b*, 423.

[19] *English Literature in the Sixteenth Century* (Oxford: Clarendon Press, 1954), p. 432.

[20] Herbert, *Life and Works*, 1: 147.

on a conception of poetic form that few modern readers would accept, were it stated by itself. In the composition of the pattern poem, according to Addison, "the Poetry was to contract or dilate itself according to the Mould in which it was cast. In a Word, the Verses were to be cramped or extended to the Dimensions of the Frame that was prepared for them; and to undergo the Fate of those Persons whom the Tyrant *Procrustes* used to lodge in his Iron Bed . . . ."[21] But it is difficult to apply this sort of judgment to Herbert. Although Herbert was a master at deliberately letting his language be restrained by form—"Deniall" is the best example of this—he does not do so without an evident and self-conscious purpose. One logical end of restraint on language is restraint on language as a visual medium. A writer can work with and against form, and Herbert's practice shows how he extracted all the strength that the pattern poem could offer. The shape of "The Altar," for example, is not as it is merely to provide ocular pleasure. The form is functional, not decorative, and it would be pointless to speculate whether Herbert first conceived of the altar shape for a poem, or saw in a poem under composition the narrowing and expanding shape of an altar. What Addison failed to realize was that the pattern poem, as Herbert uses it, exists not so much to create an image in itself as to suggest, by physical correspondents, the shape of conceptions. In this respect it is really quite accurate to say with Northrop Frye that poems like "The Altar" and "Easter-wings" are "picture writing, of the kind most familiar to us in comic strips, captioned cartoons, posters, and other emblematic forms."[22] And if, as Frye suggests, the next stage in the development of this art is a sequence like Hogarth's *Rake's Progress,* we may be thankful that Herbert seems to have been growing out of the genre; "The Altar" and "Easter-wings" appear in the Williams manuscript of *The Temple,* and "The Church-floore" is the only pattern poem added to the later Bodleian manuscript. More important, "The Church-floore" moves away from the literalism of the earlier poems, into a greater concern for the uses of a shape that has, in itself, no intrinsic symbolism.

These comments extend the definition of onomatopoeia about as far as legitimately possible. Ordinarily a literary document plays only on the senses of sight and remembered sound, and we may shift our

---

[21] In Addison, *The Spectator* (7 May 1711), 1: 247.
[22] *Anatomy of Criticism* (Princeton: Princeton University Press, 1957), p. 274.

ground to the so-called conceptual onomatopoeia, in which the lines duplicate the movement of an idea. "The Church-floore" tends in this direction, and this use of form is more typically Herbertian than the strict "ocular proportion" poems. The movement of an idea may be caught in many ways, in sound patterns, rhythm, stanza form, and syntax. However, insofar as onomatopoeia is conceptual—that is, insofar as it loses its representational basis in sound, for example, as in bowwow theory—we should recognize that the term is somewhat misleading, even if it has been sanctioned by use. Hence the broader term *orchestration*. Although by using it we risk cluttering an already-cluttered critical vocabulary, at least we avoid having to draw an arbitrary line between matter and manner.

Stanza form itself is the most commonly discussed aspect of Herbert's craft, and the stock examples for this are "Home" and "Deniall." One is the reverse of the other. After using a regular rhyme scheme for twelve stanzas, "Home" finally shifts in the thirteenth to an unexpected rhyme:

> Come dearest Lord, passe not this holy season,
>   My flesh and bones and joynts do pray:
> And ev'n my verse, when by the ryme and reason
>   The word is, *Stay*, sayes ever, *Come.*
>
> (73–76)

"Deniall," on the other hand, uses incomplete rhyme schemes throughout the first five stanzas, and then completes the form in the sixth:

> O cheer and tune my heartlesse breast,
>   Deferre no time;
> That so thy favours granting my request,
>   They and my minde may chime,
>   And mend my ryme.
>
> (26–30)

In each poem, the form itself has a simple purpose of illustration: in "Home" the form is broken to show the speaker's "unreasonable" attachment to God, and in "Deniall" the form is completed to show the sort of unity the speaker wishes to achieve. (It is sometimes claimed that the rhyme shows he has achieved the unity, but this overlooks the fact that the speaker is still in the process of requesting.)

These pleasures are as much intellectual as auditory, and much of our own pleasure on reading the poems comes from seeing the formal pattern disturbed and rearranged. There is a sense of satisfaction in seeing the pattern fulfilled, and this we have desired and expected; but we have not desired or contemplated fully the possible course the fulfillment could take. There is no surprise but much suspense.

There are other examples of disturbed form in Herbert's poetry besides these, but they have been long overlooked, perhaps because they do not appear to be disturbed on the simple level of stanza form. Herbert is a meticulous craftsman, and it is important to realize that sometimes his craftsmanship requires disturbance rather than conformity. Thus in "A true Hymne," for example, Herbert says that

> if th'heart be moved,
> Although verse be somewhat scant
> God doth supplie the want.
>
> (16–18)

Canon Hutchinson may have made a mistake in his editing of this poem, for he emends the second line above (I have given the Bodleian manuscript and the *editio princeps* reading) by inserting *the* before *verse*. The line as written, he says, is "a slip, as the meter requires another syllable" (p. 168). Yet it seems much more likely that Herbert wants precisely that, a scant verse, and the missing article is not just a trick of demonstration. By leaving out *the*, Herbert makes clear that the "scantness" is purely technical; it is not a deficiency of spirit that God makes up—only a mere article is missing—but a deficiency of numbers. The skip in the meter determines the meaning of the line. As a deliberate violation of form, it is the metrical equivalent of the rhyme in "Home," and no editor has proposed emending the "defective" rhyme in that poem's last line. One recent commentator even points out that "A true Hyme" is "the overt statement of the poetics practiced so well in 'The Collar' and in 'Grief,' the irregularity of whose lines accords exactly with the state of the poet's soul," but fails to note the textual emendation in the line making the most overt statement.[23]

[23] Rosalie Colie, *Paradoxia Epidemica* (Princeton: Princeton University Press, 1966), p. 203. See also A. S. P. Woodhouse, *The Poet and His Faith* (Chicago: University of Chicago Press, 1965), pp. 8–9: "Nowhere is it perhaps more necessary

A similar meeting of form and idea through the agency of apparent error occurs in the sonnet "Josephs coat." The theme of the poem, stated simply, is that the many different pains in the poet's life save him from one great pain which would surely kill him. The poet concludes then that the joy which relieves those pains gives the pains some value, and he emphasizes this acceptance in the final couplet: "I live to shew his power, who once did bring/ My *joyes* to *weep*, and now my *griefs* to *sing*" (13–14). This radical mixture of pains and joys is symbolized by Joseph's coat of many colors, and it is also registered in the lively motion of the opening lines. Their tossing motion rolls over the second *a* rhyme:

> Wounded I sing, tormented I indite,
> Thrown down I fall into a bed, and rest:
> Sorrow hath chang'd its note: such is his will,
> Who changeth all things, as him pleaseth best.

> (1–4)

Palmer emended the third line, changing *will* to *right*, which brings the line into conformity with our natural expectations. But as the line is written, it conveys a very real sense of arbitrariness, not only in the connotations of *will* as opposed to *right*, but in the rhyme as well. In poetry as in life, God "changeth all things, as him pleaseth best." God's will, working itself out through human joy and grief, is often as contrary to human desires or expectations as the rhyme.

II. ORCHESTRAL FORM

This prelude to the study of Herbert's psalm material has shown, I hope, that Herbert expects much of his meaning to be understood on

---

than in dealing with religious poetry to distinguish between the attitude required in the poet and that in the reader. In the poet, the affirmation uttered (which includes, of course, whatever reservations he introduces), whether as an initial assumption or as a conclusion reached by virtue of (that is, by means of) the poem itself, must, at least at the moment of utterance, command his wholehearted belief and response; for this is the condition of that merging of religious and aesthetic experience which is the mark of religious poetry. George Herbert phrased it his own way: 'The fineness which a hymn or psalm affords/ Is when the soul unto the lines accords.' " The astuteness of Woodhouse's judgment is even more apparent when the poem is left unemended.

the level of poetic craft. In many ways, the psalm material is similar
to the material we have been discussing: it supplies a level of meaning
which is related to, but separate from, the typological or "meditative"
or even literal meanings. Because Herbert's style has this flexibility
and range, and can so completely approach the function of metaphor,
it probably would be best for us to begin with the poems closest to
popular psalms and then move to large structures and fusions of the
popular and elegant styles.

There is only one natural place to begin, that is, with Herbert's
version of the Twenty-third Psalm. This, Herbert's only psalm, is
entirely within the genre, and as Hutchinson has pointed out, it has
served as a congregational piece since 1645. Its family resemblances are
evident in the awkward syntax, unusual for Herbert, which opens the
psalm: "The God of Love my shepherd is." The queerness, even the
rusticity of this, is maintained throughout; Herbert has appropriated
all the clumsiness of the traditional psalm. Here are the abrupt con-
tradictions and the puzzlingly contracted parallelisms:

> Yea, in deaths shadie black abode
> Well may I walk, not fear:
> For thou art with me; and thy rod
> To guide, thy staffe to bear.
>
> (13–16)

Radical and abstract understatement, a common feature of the Old
Version, is employed with some dignity:

> He leads me to the tender grasse,
> Where I both feed and rest;
> Then to the streams that gently passe:
> In both I have the best.
>
> (5–8)

To say that "he has the best" is to imply an earthly standard of comparison, in a delicate and vague way, and the effect is dryly humorous.
Here as elsewhere in the poem, Herbert's own strengths are totally
bound up with these "weaknesses."

We can observe some of the formal resemblances quickly. Although
conceived in the heptameter-derived form of the Old Version, the
psalm makes every line do its own work, as does the true ballad. Yet

the psalm is still tuned to the longer duple movement of the Old Version, and every two successive lines consist of a statement and expansion or a developing antithesis:

> The God of love my shepherd is,
> And he that doth me feed:
> While he is mine, and I am his,
> What can I want or need?
>
> (1–4)

Within this long movement there is still the opportunity, as with Sternhold and Hopkins, to let some single lines stand alone. But these, unlike free-floating lines in the Old Version, have relevant possibilities of meaning:

> Or if I stray, he doth convert
> And bring my minde in frame.
>
> (9–10)

The first of these lines shows the tradition of the psalm alive and functional: the stanza is no longer a liability but an asset. The gentle shepherd can convert the speaker's mind, and will even come near to do it. The regular end-stopping of congregational singing would actually permit both meanings to be entertained at once. Herbert's lines have their strength because he is aware of this reality, as the Old Version poets were not. Similarly, the heavy sound patterns of the Old Version here form useful contrasts, as in the start of the third stanza: "Yea, in deaths shadie black abode/ Well may I walk, not fear" (13–14). The alliterative hardness in the first line meaningfully contrasts with the open sounds and voiced consonants in the second line. Here, too, it should be noted that the commonplace "Yea," like the "Nay" and "So" elsewhere in the poem, are far from being merely the convenient fillers they are in previous psalms, for here they reinforce valid distinctions.

Finally, the metric also shows some flexibility, while still remaining within psalm conventions. The rhythms have enough regularity for group performance but still retain some variety for the reader: "Surely thy sweet and wondrous love/ Shall measure all my dayes" (21–22). Dudley Fitts has called attention to the way Herbert has, in this psalm, "strangely touched" the Common Meter: "The vowel pattern

and disposition of pauses in the second stanza alone are an indication
of the care that has been taken with the composition."[24] The psalm
remains uniquely Herbert's, and even in its thought Herbert has
introduced his own unobtrusive signature. The third stanza closes by
stressing the speaker's humility; God's gifts are "not for my desert,/
But for his holy name" (11–12). This humility is not present in the
"original"; as the Book of Common Prayer and King James versions
have it:[25]

> He shall convert my soul: and bring me forth in the paths of
> righteousness, for his Name's sake.

> He leadeth me in the paths of righteousness for his name's sake.

The note of humility that Herbert has introduced in the third stanza
is answered at the close of the psalm, where he makes another addition that creates a symmetrical pattern of worship:

> Surely thy sweet and wondrous love
> Shall measure all my dayes;
> And as it never shall remove,
> So neither shall my praise.
>
> (21–24)

Again, neither the Book of Common Prayer nor the King James text
has this personal cast:

> But loving-kindness shall and mercy follow me all the days of my
> life: and I will dwell in the house of the Lord forever.

> Surely goodness and mercy shall follow me all the days of my life:
> and I will dwell in the house of the Lord for ever.

In his last line, Herbert has made the humility go out from the poet
and has given the psalm a personal weight while still remaining faithful to the sense of the text. Even though the Twenty-third Psalm is

24 *Herbert*, in the Laurel Poetry Series (New York: Dell, 1962), p. 15.

25 I would agree with Louis Martz in his emphasis upon the 1611 Authorized
Version as a useful tool in studying Herbert (see Martz, *Poetry of Meditation*,
p. 280); but there are also many specific parallels with the Book of Common
Prayer (on which see Herbert, *Life and Works*, p. 537). It is perhaps significant
that most of the scriptural quotations in Herbert's notes on Valdesso appear to
come from the Authorized Version.

not usually considered one of Herbert's great poems, it does show him in the process of assimilating and adopting the craft of the popular metrical psalm.

Herbert's extraordinary care with this craft may be seen by comparing his psalm with the seven psalms attributed to him in John Playford's *Psalms and Hymns in Solemn Musick* (1671). Playford himself was quite vague in suggesting Herbert's authorship, but before Hutchinson, modern editions usually included the psalms in the Herbert canon. After examining Playford's books and the psalms themselves, Hutchinson concludes that "the evidence for assigning them to [Herbert] is happily slender" (p. 555). Yet the evidence for rejecting them is equally slender, unless the reader can rely on their poetic style. As an editor Hutchinson is rightly reluctant to go so far, but I might rush in here, for by any stylistic test the seven psalms show a surrender to popular psalmody rather than an engagement with it. Indeed, it is unlikely that these are even early works, for they are unlike Herbert's early knotted Donnean poems that Walton records.

All of these psalms are written in Common Meter or Double Common Meter, or the "four-square" quatrain. The casual craftsmanship in the form is immediately evident in four of the psalms (2, 3, 4, and 7), which have unrhymed *a* lines after the manner of Sternhold, in contrast to the usual care of Herbert's rhyming. There is also a curious disregard for the line as an entity.

> Therefore shall not the wicked be
> able to stand the Judges doom.
>
> (Ps. 1, p. 215)

> Thou art my glory, Lord, and he
> that doth my head advance.
>
> (Ps. 3, p. 216)

> Yea, he my prayer from on high
> and humble supplication hears.
>
> (Ps. 6, p. 220)

Unlike Herbert's Twenty-third Psalm, these psalms have stanza forms that are superficial, as is evident in the strenuous rhyming:

> Rebuke me not in wrath, O Lord,
> nor in thine anger chasten me:

> O pity me! for I (O Lord)
> am nothing but Infirmitie.
>
> (Ps. 6, p. 219)
>
> Arise in wrath, O Lord, advance
> against my foes disdain:
> Wake and confirm that judgment now,
> which Thou did'st preordain.
>
> (Ps. 7, p. 221)

The relatively heavy use of auxiliaries and intensive verbs, which we have noted before in psalms from Wyatt to the Countess of Pembroke, here creates some unintentional levity:

> For wickedness their insides are,
> their mouths no truth retain.
> Their throats an open Sepulcher,
> their flattering tongues do fain.
> . . . .
> Yea, shout for joy for evermore,
> protected still by thee:
> Let them that do thy name adore
> in that still joyful bee.
>
> (Ps. 6, p. 219)

More fundamentally significant is the fact that the syntax and stanza form are handled in a way very unlike Herbert's. Two short examples must suffice:

> Salvation unto thee
> Belongs, O Lord, thy blessing shall
> upon thy people be.
>
> (Ps. 3, p. 217)
>
> Many there are that say, O who
> will shew us good? But, Lord,
> Thy countenances cheering light
> do thou to us afford.
>
> (Ps. 4, p. 217)

The inversion in the last line, for example, is a very different thing from that in the opening line of Herbert's Twenty-third Psalm: "The

God of love my shepherd is." The final verb in the doubtful passage seems patched on to match *Lord* in the second line, whereas Herbert's inversion is part of a pattern of inverted syntax which the whole stanza employs for a purpose. The rhyme that Herbert constructs for *is* is a firm one, "While he is mine, and I am his," whereas the second member of the rhyme in the doubtful passage is almost an afterthought. It seems that the author of these seven psalms, like the author of the Old Version, must build as he goes. Thus when a stanza does not come together he is forced to patch in conspicuous places. The method is to be distinguished from Herbert's, in which even the touches that would be most awkward in themselves are integrated into a total effect. The deliberate awkwardness that runs throughout the Twenty-third Psalm is partly designed, I suspect, to clarify the pattern of humility that Herbert has introduced into his materials. The logic of the psalm, as Herbert has paraphrased it, is to be found in the strained passages, and the seven doubtful psalms have no sign of this control.

To shift from the study of these psalms to small psalm effects at large in *The Temple*, we may observe that one of Herbert's most frequent appropriations from the popular metrical psalm is its facile and clumsy end rhyme. For Herbert this is a far more flexible device than it was for the psalmodists, and it rarely if ever turns back upon him. When he describes human frailties, for example, in "Mans medley," he uses the lame rhyme to suggest the flatness of man's "music":

> Heark, how the birds do sing,
> And woods do ring.
> All creatures have their joy: and man hath his.
> Yet if we rightly measure,
> Mans joy and pleasure
> Rather hereafter, then in present, is.
>
> (1–6)

The final bump is created not only by the speed with which the rhyme is introduced but also by its comparative verbal weakness; it is a static verb in what is usually one of the most heavily stressed positions in a stanza. Of course, Herbert is not limited to using verbs for this sort of lumpiness, and we might refer to another passage describing the roughness of the melody that is human life. "The Storm" employs the image of the "throbbing conscience spurred by remorse" (9), which

> stands knocking, to thy musicks wrong,
> And drowns the song.
> Glorie and honour are set by, till it
> An answer get.
>
> (13–16)

In this case, two monosyllables *get* and *it* are made to bear the rhyme, yet are as vague and lacking in color as the *is* in "Mans medley." This is part of their function of course, to create some sense of the neurotic and unlocated fear, to which their rhythmic uncertainty also contributes.

Fortunately Herbert does not always employ the Old Version's obtrusive rhyme with this same negative purpose; he spares the reader the pain of too many deliberately limping or vague rhymes. More typical and more significant is the example provided by the sonnet "Redemption." After thirteen lines in which the speaker searches for his "rich Lord," he finds him in the fourteenth:

> there I him espied,
> Who straight, *Your suit is granted*, said, & died.
>
> (14)

The abruptness of the rhyme owes something to the offhand closes in the Old Version:

> And for the nonce full craftily,
> he croucheth downe, I say:
> So are great heapes of poore men made,
> by his strong power his prey.
>
> (Ps. 10: 10–11)

In each case the lines run out to a syntactic brink, and the rhyme announces the accomplishment of the leap (almost unsuccessful in Sternhold's case). Herbert's abrupt turn on the rhyme is a device familiar from the lyric genre of the psalm, and it gains much of its surprise by appearing suddenly in a narrative context. Herbert was quite aware of its effect, and in "The Sacrifice" it appears twice, emphasizing rhythmically the abruptness and violence of Christ's death:

> Then they condemne me all with that same breath,
> Which I do give them daily, unto death.
>
> (69–70)
>
> Betwixt two theeves I spend my utmost breath,
> As he that for some robberie suffereth.
> Alas! what have I stollen from you? Death.
>
> (229–31)

As these examples should suggest, the pivotal *& died* in "Redemption" is not a shortcut but a phrase in the form of a shortcut, for the rhyme is largely responsible for connecting the death and the granting of the suit. The care with which Herbert has used the sudden rhyme may be seen by comparing it with similar turns in Wyatt's psalms. With Wyatt, the final additional phrases rarely change the direction of a passage; the thought stops rather than expands back into the poem. Herbert has utilized bad practices creatively, and the ending of "Redemption" is similar to that of "Home," in which the final rhyme "makes the plea itself bring back the subject of the poem: 'Come' rhymes with 'Home.'"[26] In "Redemption," the sudden appearance of *& died* not only brings us back to the title but also suggests (by the psalmist's rhyme) the abrupt violence of the act itself.

Apparently artless turns on stanza ends may be found in innumerable poems in *The Temple*. The first part of "Easter" shows a great variety of these deliberately lame effects put to good use, and the poem itself seems to allude to the process. Each stanza begins with a pair of counterpointed couplets that might be taken for a caricature of Common Meter, in view of the other devices present:

> Rise heart; thy Lord is risen. Sing his praise
> Without delayes,

[26] A. Alvarez, *The School of Donne* (London: Chatto and Windus, 1961), p. 62. This abrupt turn on the rhyme cannot resolve all the minutiae in the poem, nor does it seem intended to. An instructive example of taking the turn too strongly may be seen in Conrad Hilberry's "Two Cruxes in George Herbert's 'Redemption,' " *N & Q*, N.S. 3 (1956): 514. By ignoring the sequence of events in the sonnet, Hilberry has Herbert humbly taking orders, then returning to court to smile with the wise and feed with the rich. How the process of redemption applies to the speaker under these circumstances is not clear.

> Who takes thee by the hand, that thou likewise
> With him mayst rise . . . .

(1–4)

We need not delay over the half-rhyme between the two pairs of rhymes; the voiced *s*'s make it curiously harsh, probably because the poet's lute does not awake until the next stanza. The speaker's voice is having trouble finding itself, and the third line turns sluggishly around its rhyme. *Likewise,* the notorious lyric filler especially favored by psalmodists from Wyatt to the Countess of Pembroke, appears here for the only time in *The Temple,* and it has a deceptively off-hand air about it. However, it is not merely a filler, since it does express concisely the reciprocal nature of the heart's encounter with God. The relationship between God and the speaker is changed if the apparently superfluous rhyme is removed, even though the motion of the speaker's heart is the same.

Yet however concise *likewise* may be, I should not like to disregard a certain patchiness in its use, for this is part of the poem's larger meaning. As a psalm (in the literal sense) to the risen Lord, the poem's basic assertion is a recurrent one with Herbert: the quality of a hymn is of less importance than its intent. (The rest of "Easter" even insists on the difficulty of singing: the speaker has to "struggle" with his lute, and he is uncertain as to which key he should play in.) Once we see this element of meaning, we can observe that the first stanza concludes with another abrupt rhyme,[27] again not a mere short-cut but a functional part of the poem's thought: "That, as his death calcined thee to dust,/ His life may make thee gold, and much more, just" (5–6).

The second stanza begins as smartly as the first in managing the open clumsiness:

> Awake, my lute, and struggle for thy part
> With all thy art.
> The crosse taught all wood to resound his name,
> Who bore the same.

(7–10)

---

[27] Without explanation, Hutchinson has here adopted the punctuation of the Williams manuscript over that of the Bodleian manuscript and the 1633 edition, both of which delete the comma after *more.* As my subsequent remarks indicate, however, the abruptness of the rhyme is integrated with other qualities of the poem, including the moral distinction that the punctuation creates.

Since *crosse* may refer to the bridge of the poet's instrument or the Crucifixion, *same* has in one sense the straightforward redundancy of the psalmodist's *same:* the Cross (like the bridge of my instrument) taught all wood (including all the wood in my lute) to vibrate in sympathy with the Cross that Christ bore. However, Herbert is employing the couplet in a second way as well, and its pivot is that ambiguous *same.* The Cross taught all wood (including the cross in this lute) to vibrate in sympathy with the cross in Christ's instrument, that is, Himself. It is on this level that we find what Tuve referred to as "the basic metaphorical identification of *caritas* with music, or harmony."[28] Since the symbol of the Cross itself suggests this *caritas,* it seems likely that the first and apparently redundant reference of *same* gives the lines much of their depth. What is surprising—and characteristically Herbertian—in the lines is the way that the sophistication of the thought finds expression in the psalmodist's stock rhyme.

In the case of "Charms and Knots" we can see Herbert deliberately working to achieve a strained and "faulty" quality in rhyme. The poem is in nine tetrameter couplets, each a paradoxical proverb, most with designedly simple or even homely imagery. (In revising the poem, Herbert cut out two couplets on sophisticated topics: optics and courtiers.) The final couplet is the most emphatic, and in its original form in the Williams manuscript, the lines move with the energy and simplicity of some of Samuel Johnson's couplets: "In small draughts Heau'en does shine & dwell:/ Who dives on further may find Hell" (p. 97, n. 17).

But the final form of the couplet uses an inverted clause that is short and brutal: "In shallow waters heav'n doth show;/ But who drinks on, to hell may go" (17–18). The justification for this bathetic drop lies in the persona of the poem, the didactic preacher, who belongs in the family of moralists in rugged verse, such as the Donne of the satires. Of course that genre is very different from that of Herbert's lyrics, which is just the point, for the idea of roughness is relative, and in Herbert's case roughness usually consists of deviation from the lyric style, as in Donne's case (and in "Charms and Knots") it consists of the manhandled couplet. Herbert's cultivation of his order of lyric roughness is every bit as deliberate as Donne's, and may be demonstrated by three further examples of the same technique in the lyric genre.

[28] Tuve, *A Reading of George Herbert,* p. 145.

"The Pilgrimage" describes life as a journey through an allegorical landscape. Throughout the poem, Herbert takes great care with onomatopoetic effects of movement, and he pays particular attention to the short final line of each stanza. Most deliberately whimsical is the second stanza:

> And as I came to Fancies meadow strow'd
> > With many a flower;
> Fain would I here have made my abode,
> But I was quicken'd by my houre.
> So to Cares cops I came, and there got through
> > With much ado.
>
> > > > (7–12)

If the jesting of this is not immediately evident, we need only begin the next stanza, in which the context is even more definitely one of intellectual play, though not here involving the handy unhandy rhyme:

> That led me to the wilde of Passion, which
> > Some call the wold . . . .
>
> > > > (13–14)

This stanza clarifies, for our purposes, the humorous context of the *through/ado* rhyme; the idea of Passion as a wild wold is playful enough in itself to deflate some passions, but if as Hutchinson suggests "a pun may be intended on *would*" (p. 527), we are clearly in the realm of the comic.[29] Unrestrained passion may well be a wild wold of the would, like the Rabelaisian injunction to "Do as thou wilt," but it is also possible that the irrepressible rhyming itself partly triumphs over the excess of passion. It is parody in the vein of William Carlos Williams' *phlegm/ahem*, although the foul journey that "The Pilgrimage" describes is not entirely humorous.

In "The Jews" Herbert employs one of his few stock rhymes, the staple *alas* that carried many a psalmodist through a lean stanza, but Herbert's use of it is highly self-conscious. The first stanza is an ex-

---

[29] William Empson proposed this earlier, in *Seven Types of Ambiguity*, 2d ed. (New York: New Directions, 1947), p. 129; but he fails to consider the context of the punning. Thus he seems to me to mistake the tone of the passage when he refers to it as "prosaic, arid, without momentum"—a curious judgment from a critic whose own prose depends so much upon verbal play for its momentum.

tended apostrophe in regular and somber cadences, depicting the drying up of the Jews through the Christian scion, and it is answered by a stanza that is as serious as it is outrageous:

> Oh that my prayers! mine, alas!
> Oh that some Angel might a trumpet sound;
> At which the Church falling upon her face
> Should crie so loud, untill the trump were drown'd,
> And by that crie of her deare Lord obtain,
> That your sweet sap might come again!
>
> (7–12)

Instead of giving us the expected mass conversion at the sound of the "trump," Herbert has the Church accede to a great motion of pity; her tears flow from the second line through the fourth, and her falling on her face would verge on the bathetic if the seriousness of the first stanza had not prepared us for so absolute a reaction. But the key line in the stanza, perhaps in the whole poem, is the seventh, with its unusual stress pattern: "Oh that my prayers! mine, alas!" The point of view in the first stanza had been that of We, the Church, and this shift to the first person at the start of the second stanza is a grand thing. Were it not for the controlling signal of the subjunctive in *that*, we should have our speaker a redeemer himself. The function of the heavily stressed *alas* is to supply the speaker's balance, and in this respect the term is a functional rather than handy rhyme. And much of the force in the term is based on its inutility: the poet's own prayers are as lame as the poetical *alas*, so familiar are the connotations of the term.

Perhaps Herbert's most openly parodic use of clumsy rhythm and casual rhyme occurs in "Gratefulnesse." Each stanza has four lines, the last of which is always a doggedly abrupt monometer. The first stanza announces the technique and gives it a comic label:

> Thou that hast giv'n so much to me,
> Give one thing more, a gratefull heart.
> See how thy beggar works on thee
> By art.
>
> (1–4)

Each of the succeeding stanzas flaunts its final rhyme with a rhythmic sinking that far outdoes the drop at the end of the typical Old Version stanza. Many of the final lines, besides the first, allude to the homeliness of the rhyme:

> This notwithstanding, thou wentst on,
> And didst allow us all our noise:
> Nay, thou hast made a sigh and grone
>   Thy joyes.
>
> Not that thou hast not still above
> Much better tunes, then grones can make;
> But that these countrey-aires thy love
>   Did take.
>   (17–24)

"Countrey-aires," indeed: God's love for Man must be very great if it can work in spite of this sort of praise. The last two lines are another statement of the central paradox in Herbert's use of the technical crudity of the psalms: though rude and "countrified" as art, they still can win God's heart. Not a statement Donne would (or did) make, but a central conviction with Herbert, even though his own background is far more "aristocratic" than Donne's. Herbert is sophisticated enough to be aware of this double reaction and deliberately capitalizes on it. While we are told that the poem does have some effect upon the object of its address, we who are overhearing it are also allowed to react as another set of bystanders reacted to a similar set of rhymes so rudely forced:

> Come, tears, confound.
> Out, sword, and wound
> The pap of Pyramus.
> Aye, that left pap,
> Where heart doth hop.
>   (*Midsummer Night's Dream*, V. i. 300–304)

Herbert is directing this sort of technique upon the hymn form, and the final effect of "Gratefulnesse" thus "works on thee/ By art" posing as the very violation of art.

We have been working around to Herbert's use of flat rhythms, and

we may now approach it more directly. In *The Temple* spiritual defects and mendings generally manifest themselves in the movement of
the verse. Thus in "Easter" (I), the last line moves from heavy alternate stressing before the caesura to nearly uniform stressing in the last
three words: "And make up our defects with his sweet art." Herbert
typically conceives of resolution in auditory terms. Thus in "The
Call," the solid rhythms stress the finality of the mission:

> Come my Way, my Truth, my Life:
> Such a Way, as gives us breath:
> Such a Truth, as ends all strife:
> Such a Life, as killeth Death.

$$(1-4)$$

It is typical of Herbert that his statements of total dedication, such as
this, often move in the regressive and block-like rhythms of the chant,
while the delicate and musical variations that we prize so highly occur
most often in the poems of irresolution and torn sympathies.

This may be a good place to pause and consider Herbert's didacticism and its relation to his lyric style. If we accept Walton's account
of how Herbert gave Ferrar his "little book," we must assume that all
of Herbert's poetry is intentionally, if indirectly, didactic; and even if
we reject Walton's remarkable picture, there is plenty of testimony to
the same effect in the poems themselves. In *The Temple*, for example,
"The Church Porch" is clearly didactic but not on that account "anti-
lyrical," for the poem prepares us for the lyrical world we enter in
"The Church." The often homely tone, assumed as a mask; the themes
of prudential morality (here expounded, later examined); even the
techniques of low-to-middle style—all relate to the verse in "The
Church." More important than these, though, is the way that in both
sections the poet assumes a similar stance toward his reader. Joseph
Summers, in his introduction to a selection of Herbert's verse, has
developed a quite persuasive argument from the fact that the poem is
addressed to a young man who shares much of Herbert's own past
and is motivated by an enlightened self-interest.[30] When we read "The
Church" (as when we read the Book of Psalms), we are expected to

---

[30] *Selected Poetry of George Herbert* (New York: New American Library, 1967),
pp. xiii ff. The essay is reprinted, with some alterations, in *The Heirs of Donne
and Jonson* (New York: Oxford University Press, 1970).

begin with the assumption that people do—and should—place a value upon their good parts. To judge by "The Church Porch," then, much of the tone, style, and stance of the poem, although in themselves indicative of a "didactic impulse," are not opposed to a "lyrical impulse."

If we continue with the example of "The Church Porch," I think we may see the ways in which Herbert's lyricism pulls away from his didacticism *per se*. That is, there are many ways in which "The Church Porch" does not prepare us for the poems of "The Church": the subject of "The Church Porch," by being located in the world of social action, has deliberately few connections with the lyrics that follow; the poem has no lament, no thanksgiving for deliverance—of course this could scarely be expected, for the real terrors of the spirit have not yet struck nor have its even greater joys. Besides, how could one convince the worldly wise young man, before he has had the experience of the lyrics, that one cannot convert God and the world to his own image? Herbert instead holds out the opposite possibility, that God in man can be polished with only a little effort, a little self-interest:

> Stay at the third cup or forgo the place.
> Wine above all things doth Gods stamp deface.
>
> (47–48)

> Studie this art, make it thy great designe;
> And if Gods image move thee not, let thine.
>
> (101–2)

The possibility of giving and receiving love also seems deceptively simple. Here are none of the obstacles posed in the lyrics:

> Scorn no mans love, though of a mean degree;
> Love is a present for a mightie king.
>
> (349–50)

Direct love of God, with its trials and agonies, may be a matter too gauche to suggest to a young man of taste and breeding. Indeed these trials would seem almost incomprehensible in this context, just as the statements here on love would seem valid albeit oversimplified to the mind in "The Church." He has to have a "friend who whispers" to bring *him* back to the immediate issues of loving. There are great gaps between the experience of the person addressed in "The Church Porch" and that of the speaker in "The Church," though in each case experience is the focal point of the poetry. The person addressed in "The Church Porch" is at an early stage of moral development, and the speaker tailors his comments accordingly; the speaker of "The Church" has already taken a good deal of prudential advice and now has other problems, equally serious but by and large intellectual rather than social.

As a result, the rationale for the give and take of lyric form is not present in "The Church Porch." It is difficult to imagine, for example, the poem recast as a series of differentiated lyrics. One recent study has considered Herbert's lyrics as "re-invented" poems, which characteristically turn or reshape themselves under the poet's hand;[31] such "re-invention" never appears in "The Church Porch," or for that matter in "The Church Militant," which concludes *The Temple*. The design of these poems is to a very large degree predetermined, not so much in terms of prosodic or stanzaic form as in terms of organizational unity. Their centers of attention thus exclude dividedness of mind, or the crosscurrents of weakness and strength, and focus instead on comprehensiveness of pattern or the working out of all the implications of a set central paradox (as in "The Sacrifice"). It would be an error, though, to assume that Herbert's didactic poetry may be detected by particular stanzas, or tones, or ethical stands. While all his poems are didactic in one obvious sense, the term really applies best to those poems in which meaning and form exist in a congruent and fixed relationship.

It would be appropriate to return at this point to a lyric that has an immediately apparent didactic purpose, but lacks the didactic form I have just described. There are few examples of lyric form finer than that in "Employment" (I). Here the last line of each stanza openly invites a strain in rhythm, and in the technique appears much of the

---

[31] Helen Vendler, "The Re-invented Poem: George Herbert's Alternatives," in *Forms of Lyric: Selected Papers from the English Institute*, ed. Reuben A. Brower (New York: Columbia University Press, 1970), pp. 19–45. The practice may be observed in any number of lyric poets. Stanley Fish, in "Letting Go: The Reader in Herbert's Poetry," *ELH*, 37 (1970): 475–94, has also described this technique and related it to the self-diminishing of the speaker, reader, and author of a Herbert poem. However, I find that Fish himself often lets his reader go; his perceptive readings of the poems do not require, for their validity, our assent to his view of the reader and his mental adjustments.

poem's total statement on the speaker's lack of meaningful employment. Here, too, Herbert employs the last lines of the stanzas as his
fulcrum points; and in each case, although the line is strictly speaking
a dimeter, some pressure and concentration are required to hear the
pattern:

> If as a flowre doth spread and die,
> Thou wouldst extend to me some good,
> Before I were by frosts extremitie
> Nipt in the bud;
>
> The sweetnesse and the praise were thine;
> But the extension and the room,
> Which in thy garland I should fill, were mine
> At thy great doom.
>
> (1–8)

Here as in the three remaining stanzas, the final lines depart from the
even meters above and let the stresses fall seemingly at random. *Nipt
in the bud* might be an exception in that it employs a conventional
substitution, but *At thy great doom* calls for heavy stresses across the
last words. Generally, it seems safe to say that the final lines tend to
be prosaic rather than metric, by contrast with the lines above them,
and in each stanza the lines drop into unemployment, on the literal
and auditory levels. The last stanza, in which the speaker pleads for
a place in God's plan, shows how subtly Herbert can vary a pattern
to achieve resolution. The rhythm is approximately the same as that
in the stanzas quoted above, but its flatness is modulated:

> I am no link of thy great chain,
> But all my companie is a weed.
> Lord place me in thy consort; give one strain
> To my poore reed.
>
> (21–24)

By opening the vowels in the last line and avoiding stops between
them, Herbert is able to retain the same rhythm and still soften its
heavy drop. The effect is orchestral because it shows the shape of
unemployment, and the forced rhythms of the psalm provide Herbert's
metaphor of "give one strain."

Another important technique that Herbert's verse shares with the bathetic psalm is the use of the free-standing single line. It is not possible to generalize about its effects beyond noting that it allows Herbert to insert contrasts or additions to the tone and structure of the surrounding context. A clear example may be found in the last stanza of "Sepulchre":

> And as of old the Law by heav'nly art
> Was writ in stone; so thou, which also art
> The letter of the word, find'st no fit heart
> To hold thee.
> Yet do we still persist as we began,
> And so should perish, but that nothing can,
> Though it be cold, hard, foul, from loving man
> Withhold thee.
>
> (17–24)

Hutchinson clarifies the first four lines of this by quoting 2 Corinthians 3:3: "the Spirit of the living God is written not in tables of stone, but in fleshy tables of the heart." The second half of the stanza builds several ironies upon this: We, being flesh, might perish, were it not for Christ's love, which is now only flesh entombed in stone. However, not even the most obdurate stone can prevent that love. But this is not all the stanza can do, for as the syntax plays out across the end of the stanza, Herbert manages to suggest what is for him the central Christian paradox of men killing their Savior. The "loving man" has confined Christ in "cold, hard, foul" stone. This meditation before Easter (the event and the poem of the same name), is not merely a hymn to Christ's divinity but a statement as well of man's responsibilities. The violence implied in the syntax of the free-standing line is rather similar to that in the Old Version, as in Psalm 59: "Their wicked othes with lies and wrong,/ let all the world deride" (12). When the delayed predicate picks up the adverbial modifier in the line above, the result is more preposterous than grim. Like a chisel in the hand of an unsure carpenter, the tool cuts deeper than it ought to.

A similar depth of suggestion may be found in "Faith," the subject of which is man's ability to "bring by Faith all things to him" (4). After describing the power of the mind over the body (the mind is able to *imagine* the body out of hunger or illness or poverty), Herbert begins to treat the spiritual scale of the imagination:

> Faith makes me any thing, or all
> That I beleeve is in the sacred storie:
> And where sinne placeth me in Adams fall,
> Faith sets me higher in his glorie.
>
> (17–20)

The first line is free-standing because of its own syntactic integrity and because of the absence of a subjunctive verb in the second line. The context of the poem up to this stanza has been secular and physical, and the first line, in itself, is a witty way of affirming the role of the speaker's imagination in the "real" world. The second line, however, implies a complete opposition: the speaker's faith can make him anything he believes himself to be in the sacred storied world. Here again the line that unexpectedly takes on some coherence of its own turns out to have a relevant level of meaning.

We might be reluctant to go beyond this in describing syntactically independent run-on lines as having any relation to the bathetic metrical psalm. Unless the element of surprise carries with it an element of the grotesque or the humorous—the tonal effects most frequently created by the hobbling syntax of the Old Version—the basis of the identification is slim. For instance, the last stanza of "Mortification" involves a surprising and typical syntactic turn which derives its strength from grammatic independency. But the effect is unlike that of Sternhold and Hopkins, for the third line makes no suggestions beyond those it denotes, and the fourth line does not contradict it:

> Man, ere he is aware,
> Hath put together a solemnitie,
> And drest his herse, while he has breath
> As yet to spare.
>
> (31–34)

After observing these minor bathetic effects in *The Temple*, we might consider some poems that use elements from the metrical psalm in order to create unity in complete structures. Rhyme is again perhaps the easiest place to start. "The Starre" has many rhymes that have a deliberate clumsiness appropriate to the poem's tone and structure. In the opening stanzas praising God, these rhymes help create an effect of simple wonder:

Bright spark, shot from a brighter place,
   Where beams surround my Saviours face,
     Canst thou be any where
      So well as there?

Yet, if thou wilt from thence depart,
   Take a bad lodging in my heart;
     For thou canst make a debter,
      And make it better.

                        (1–8)

The speaker is mildly amazed, and his naive tone comes in part from the short trailing lines, the quiet addenda. Like the final short lines in the Old Version, these only qualify or extend the line above. In the middle stanzas, however, the apparently simple last lines become more intense. After describing his inadequacies in the opening stanzas, the speaker then requests a regeneration, the touch of God's "celestiall quickness" (14), and here the last line becomes more tightly integrated grammatically and logically:

Get me a standing there, and place
   Among the beams, which crown the face
     Of him, who dy'd to part
      Sinne and my heart.

                      (21–24)

In the four stanzas that now describe this wished-for union with God, the last lines are not stylistically parallel additions, as they were in earlier stanzas. The form shows one way, or the degree to which, the union can be achieved. When the poem closes with the speaker again realizing his present place, the stanza returns to its opening form, with the trailing parallel line:

Sure thou wilt joy, by gaining me
   To flie home like a laden bee
     Unto that hive of beams
      And garland-streams.

                      (29–32)

The poem has thus made a stanza-by-stanza transition out of, and back to, the rhythmic movement of the metrical psalm, and this makes the final affirmation seem both hard-won and graciously yielding. The casual last line, in its technical modesty, is almost the master's throw-away ending, like that at the end of the Beethoven Violin Concerto in D Major. In each case the artist is confident enough of his control of the material that he can afford the sudden turn that unites and closes the work in one stroke.

It might be helpful to pause here, after this initial example, to note some basic things about Herbert's quatrains and the Common Meter. We have seen that the Old Version poets tend to structure their stanzas so that the three-beat lines restate or parallel the four-beat lines. This is the easiest way to find the rhyme for the shorter line, but it is not the way that most "good" poetry operates, as we saw in the example of the true ballad. The law of the conservation of energy holds for good poems as for physical bodies: even in a lyric like *Paradise Lost* there are few if any wasted lines. In Herbert's case, repetition to fill out a stanza is rarely nonfunctional; it is used de-liberately to expose and perhaps cure a fatuous poetic attitude the poem itself is pointing to, and as often as not, when there appears to be no *conscious* exploration of this attitude, the style goes on to do its own work, setting up and resolving the conflict on its own terms. (Some poems of this type are treated in the next chapter.)

What we are concerned with then is a pattern that is rhythmic in the sense that it reflects a motion in the mind as much as or more than in the syllable-counting ear. A quatrain written in alternate pentameter and tetrameter lines may thus reveal some of the same motions as the alternating tetrameter and trimeter of the Common Meter; it is all a matter of scale, to which we shall find Herbert ex-tremely attentive. More irregular quatrains—with lines in 4-3-5-2 feet, for example—and some tercets and cinquains may be "derived" from the Common Meter in that they refer to it in their phrasal or syntactic patterns or generally bathetic manners. The compression of many of Herbert's tercets derives from their calling for a fourth line that is denied, just as many of the cinquains appear to close with the fourth line, then spring the fifth line as a surprise.

Arnold Stein has already demonstrated most thoroughly that Herbert is a poet who is fascinated, deliberately and perhaps instinc-tively, with pattern in itself. Although *The Temple* rarely descends to mere pattern, Herbert's great achievements in the lyric all derive much of their strength from the repetition and orderly arrangement of stresses, intonation, and other expressive elements of meaning. One pattern that Herbert was particularly fond of was the simple one of long-short-long-short, used to express his logic as well as his metrics and phrases: we could rewrite the pattern as complex-plain, or assertion-denial, or rejection-acceptance. Evidently the movement is ambiguous. In a description of this sort, however, it could hardly seem otherwise, since Herbert is not a poetaster who uses patterns that are separable from meaning. One generalization does seem possible (bearing in mind that a generalization exists for the sake of its exceptions): the pattern of diminutions in rhythm and thought is related to the repeated pattern in the Book of Psalms of strength coming out of weakness. Herbert's fondness for patterns that say more with less, that resolve a situation on minimal terms, in rhythm and in logical process, must inevitably lead us to believe that his stanzas related to the Common Meter have metaphoric significance. On the more practical level, the reader who seeks to relate a quatrain in an apparently arbitrary mixture of feet with the plodding Common Meter is taking some risks. Naturally the results of the relation are more important than the method, but any method is only as good as the reader's sense of tact.

In the same family as "The Starre" is "Frailtie," written in loose eight-line stanzas which may be regarded as a grotesque caricature of Double Common Meter; the lines have an alternating pattern of stresses (5-2-5-2—4-3-5-2) which group each stanza into a pair of quatrains (rhymed *a-b-a-b—c-c-d-d*). However, the technique of the poem is more suggestive of the metrical psalm than is the stanza form itself. The alternating short lines are handled clumsily and flatly:

> Lord, in my silence how do I despise
> What upon trust
> Is styled *honour, riches,* or *fair eyes;*
> But is *fair dust!*
> I surname them *guilded clay,*
> *Deare earth, fine grasse* or *hay;*
> In all, I think my foot doth ever tread
> Upon their head.

> (1–8)

There is an apparent slackness in lines 2, 4, 6, and 8; the implications of *upon trust* will not become apparent for several lines; the negligibility of earthly glory and pleasures is more restated in *fair dust* than it is informed; and the succeeding lines are more repetitive than additive. The thumping *Upon their head* would be typical of the Old Version tendency to close a flaccid stanza with a heavy hand were it not for the Hebertian *I think* in the lines above. Up to this point, the style of Herbert's genial expansiveness and bombast is very similar to that of the Old Version.

From this point, Herbert's treatment of the form becomes more intense. He is not often capable of the sustained heavy dogmatic faith of a Sternhold, no more than he is capable of the sustained heavy repeated stanza. The second stanza takes the repetitive form of the first and presses it even further into a series of parallels, as if to affirm the strength of worldly temptations:

> But when I view abroad both Regiments;
> The worlds, and thine:
> Thine clad with simplenesse, and sad events;
> The other fine,
> Full of glorie and gay weeds,
> Brave language, braver deeds:
> That which was dust before, doth quickly rise,
> And prick mine eyes.
>
> (9–16)

Again there falls the violent and rhythmically abrupt last line, but the mounting comparisons in the lines above give it a smartness and precision which contrasts with the thumping at the end of the first stanza. (In the Williams manuscript, the end of this stanza originally read "Troubling my eyes," a phrase which lacks the bright meter, sharp consonants, and vowel contrasts of the final version.)

The third and last stanza of the poem is a plea for stable values, and although it utilizes some of the phrases of the previous stanzas, its style has a smooth plainness which quiets the heavy concerns of the preceding stanzas:

> O brook not this, lest if what even now
> My foot did tread,
> Affront those joyes, wherewith thou didst endow
> And long since wed
> My poore soul, ev'n sick of love:

> It may a Babel prove
> Commodious to conquer heav'n and thee
> Planted in me.
>
> (17–24)

The absence of grammatic parallelism or even the appearance of repetition, and the long turns in syntax, attempt to lift the poem from the whole previous level of discourse, much as the poet requests that his worldly dust not "affront [that is, confront] those joyes" that draw him to God's service. The style of the poem itself tries to effect the sensual deliverance that the poet requests. As Herbert says in a marginal note on Valdesso's *Considerations*, "The natural concupiscence is not quite extinguished, but the heate of it asswaged" (p. 308, ll. 16–17), and this "asswaging" in the poem would not be possible without the rocking emphases derived from the conventions of psalmody.

Herbert's ability to control his rhythms—I am here using the term in the sense of metric and idea—is great enough that he can risk the most clumsy and indolent patterns, and unless we are willing to grant him this control we are likely to find many of his poems very puzzling. "Vanitie" (II) seems to me to be one such poem whose clunking rhythms out-Sternhold Sternhold and do so with announced intent. Both the peculiar structure of the poem and its consistently forced meter require quotation in full:

> Poore silly soul, whose hope and head lies low;
> Whose flat delights on earth do creep and grow;
> To whom the starres shine not so fair, as eyes;
> Nor solid work, as false embroyderies;
> Heark and beware, lest what you know do measure
> And write for sweet, prove a most sowre displeasure.
>
> O heare betimes, lest thy relenting
>   May come too late!
> To purchase heaven for repenting
>   Is no hard rate.
> If souls be made of earthly mold,
>   Let them love gold;
>   If born on high,
> Let them unto their kindred flie:

> For they can never be at rest,
> Till they regain their ancient nest.
> Then silly soul take heed: for earthly joy
> Is but a bubble, and makes thee a boy.

(111)

The apparent artlessness of this is deceptive. D. J. Enright, for example, takes the flatness of the final couplet simply at face value: "The couplet betrays, by its inept rhymes, the lack of personal feeling—a formula is being repeated." And more solemnly, "there is an unintelligent heaviness about such outbursts."[32] To some degree, Enright's charge about personal feeling, or the lack of it, is answered by the larger context of the poem; it is the first of a group of poems that are addressed to the idle or dry heart ("The Dawning," "Jesu," "Businesse," "Dialogue," and the best of the sequence, "Dulnesse"). But even within the poem's own context, the "inept" final rhyme is part of a pattern that conveys a considerable amount of emotion. The theme of the first movement is the low state of earthly pleasures, and the low words accordingly creep in not one but several dull lines, "Whose flat delights on earth do creep and grow."

For this part of the design the pentameter couplet is well suited; it would be more difficult to establish the level tone in a shorter lyric line. The tone itself is clearly not the result of any general inability with the couplet. ("The Church Militant" amply demonstrates Herbert's range in discourse with the couplet.) A more lyric or enthusiastic treatment of earthly delights would be a betrayal, considering the rest of the poem. The balance is delicate; Herbert must suggest the dullness of earthly pleasure and still write a poem that compels reading. Thus the metric shifts in the final couplet of the movement are designed only to reinforce the gravity of the situation:

> Heark and beware, lest what you now do measure
>
> And write for sweet, prove a most sowre displeasure.

The curious displacement on the sixth syllable is required by the

---

[32] "George Herbert and the Devotional Poets," in the *Pelican History of English Literature: Donne to Marvell*, ed. Boris Ford (London: Penguin Books, 1962), p. 146.

sense of the line; it is a fine adjustment of the thought rather than an emphatic turn.

Following this quiet set of couplets is an alternately rhyming quatrain and four couplets of mixed lengths, some counterpointed and some not. Although the tone of the lines above has been calm and insistent, Herbert now becomes more stubbornly emphatic. The rhythms are heavy and irregular, even crude, because of the frequent secondary and tertiary stresses:

> O heare betimes, lest thy relenting
>
> May come too late!
>
> To purchase heaven for repenting
>
> Is no hard rate.
>
> If souls be made of earthly mold,
>
> Let them love gold:
>
> If born on high,
>
> Let them unto their kindred flie:
>
> For they can never be at rest,
>
> Till they regain their ancient nest.

The obviousness and simplicity of the admonitions, their plain rigidity, coupled with the seeming clumsiness of meter and straining after rhyme, point the way to the final couplet, which again makes a metric shift late in the line:

> Then silly soul take heed; for earthly joy
>
> Is but a bubble, and makes thee a boy.

This does not seem to be so much ineptitude as deliberate experimentation. Herbert might just as easily have employed a participle in the last line, "Is but a bubble, making thee a boy," which would be rhythmically less offensive to the ear expecting a quiet and confident assertion. However, is it not possible that in the rugged meters we are being given one way of answering the great and often conflicting demands of art and faith, as posed, for example, in the "Jordan" poems? One way of rejecting earthly joys is to write an ugly poem, a poem in which the pleasures of graceful meter and rhyme are discarded in a convincing manner. Employing forced rhymes and wrenched meters is one way of rejecting the *false embroyderies* of artful verse. And in fact, we may regard the end of the poem's first movement as being a clue as to what is to follow and an allusion to its metrical roughness: "Heark and beware, lest what you now do measure/ And write for sweet, prove a most sowre displeasure."

Everything we know of *sweet*, as a term in literary aesthetics of the sixteenth and seventeenth centuries, suggests that nothing could be farther from the "sugred" style than Herbert's suggestion and parody of rough numbers and chaotic form. The labored second half of the poem is the "hearkening" that Herbert alludes to; it is the answer to the question of how to avoid sweetness in verse.[33] This is not a new question, but it is typical of Herbert that he should answer it by employing the "sowre" techniques of the mediocre psalm.

With all regard for the apparent intention of Enright's argument, it may seem that my approach to "Vanitie" (II) is one which ingeniously contrives to reduce the poem on several levels. If it were not possible to find Herbert commenting in other poems upon the uses of bathos, I should think that this interpretation does just that. But given these other signs of Herbert's interest in sinking, "Vanitie" (II) seems a quite self-conscious production. This may be its chief flaw, and it can hardly be called inconspicuous. At least the poem represents the sort of total experiment that Herbert did not repeat (or leave in manuscript).

Form this irregular is unusual with Herbert, and his more common method in making a negative statement is to incorporate the lame or bathetic features in a context which keeps them only at the level of suggestion. Placing them out in the open, as in "Vanitie" (II), is also a somewhat risky way of fulfilling his program that his *"Abilities in*

---

[33] Cf. Robert Ellrodt: "Le refus de la suavité, de la monotonie mélodieuse, est lié ici à l'acuité de la conscience critique. Si le contrepoint prosodique est un trait marquant de la poésie de Herbert, c'est que cette allure irrégulière épouse de plus près la démarche même de la pensée, rend plus fidèlement les surauts du coeur" (*L'Inspiration*, 1: 308–9).

Poetry, shall be all, and ever consecrated to God's glory." [34] The suggestion of bathetic elements can hold a larger structure together, and for an example we may look at "Repentance." Joseph Summers has pointed out the position of this poem in the sequence showing the speaker's triumph over affliction, [35] and we might qualify the idea of triumph by saying that with respect to technique the victory is a Fabian one. The speaker allows his imagination to carry him deeper and further into affliction until he has drawn it off. This description may sound more enigmatic than the poem is in fact. The poem uses a variety of clumsy rhythms to set up some of the poetic afflictions; and the stanza form shows a falling-away and a replenishment, as it narrows to a short couplet that usually repeats or clarifies, then widens out in one longer line. But the subject is not especially replenishing:

> Lord, I confesse my sinne is great;
> Great is my sinne. Oh! gently treat
> With thy quick flow'r, thy momentarie bloom;
> Whose life still pressing
> Is one undressing,
> A steady aiming at a tombe.
>
> (1–6)

The tomb naturally holds the possibility of life, at least if one has repented wisely, and after this first stanza the perception of life-through-death becomes the steady subject of the poem. After one stanza describing man's evanescence, we reach the height of the poem's conventional religious query:

> O let thy height of mercie then
> Compassionate short-breathed men.
> Cut me not off for my most foul transgression:
> I do confesse
> My foolishness;
> My God, accept of my confession.
>
> (13–18)

The casual, almost indolent dimeter couplet is "short-breathed" as a confession, and the final line is baldly prosaic as compared with the

---

[34] See the letter to his mother in Walton's *Lives,* reprinted in Herbert, *Works,* p. 363.

[35] Summers, *George Herbert,* p. 86.

somber line that ends the first stanza. The offhand tone can go further, however, and with some logic; for after confessing, one may as well wait out the steady passage of time with some detachment. Thus the poem begins to incorporate ignominious and faintly comic images and emphasize them by the verse technique:

> Sweeten at length this bitter bowl,
> Which thou hast pour'd into my soul;
> Thy wormwood turn to health, windes to fair weather:
> For if thou stay,
> I and this day,
> As we did rise, we die together.
>
> (19–24)

The stanza descends easily, through the couplet and into the last line, which turns the idea of creation on its head. Once the common perception is inverted in this way, Herbert can go on in the next stanza to show the dismemberment of man in all its variety:

> When thou for sinne rebukest man,
> Forthwith he waxeth wo and wan:
> Bitternesse fills our bowels; all our hearts
> Pine, and decay,
> And drop away,
> And carrie with them th'other parts.
>
> (25–30)

The pausing, offhand rhymes have something of a comically dread inevitability, and the step-by-step descent has man literally disintegrate before us, as he does, for example, in John Crowe Ransom's "Captain Carpenter." After our hearts have pined, decayed, and dropped away —and the singular in the first two lines suggests that Herbert means by *hearts*, "All of the hearts that each of us possesses"—the removal of "th'other parts" is not only irrelevant but absurdly anticlimactic. The stanza uses and controls the simultaneous vagueness and casual violence we have noted in the Old Version.[36]

---

[36] The Williams manuscript version of this stanza lacks the humor:

> Bitternesse fills our bowels; all our hearts
> Melt & consume
> To smoke & fume
> ffretting to death our other parts.

Smoke and fume, it should be noted, is written by a second hand cancelling *a salt rhume*, which is even sicker in both senses.

It is natural and inevitable that the final stanza of "Repentance" should reassemble man, and the understatement with which Herbert does this shows his "steadie aiming" at a looser style throughout the growth of the poem. The last stanza has a modesty and ease befitting the mind disburdened of guilt:

> But thou wilt sinne and grief destroy;
> That so the broken bones may joy,
> And tune together in a well-set song,
> Full of his praises,
> Who dead men raises.
> Fractures well cur'd make us more strong.
>
> (31–36)

The last line may seem a moralizing intrusion unless we see it as a part of the metaphor above and realize that Herbert has made an innovation in the dance of death. The doggerel rhyme, "Full of his praises,/ Who dead men raises," tells us nothing that the first three lines of the stanza have not. Its importance lies in its style: it is the *well-set song*—a jocular pun in itself—that the mended bones now sing upon resurrection. Because of the short end-stopped lines, the feminine rhyme here introduces a jigging motion appropriate to the dancing bones. In all, both the details and organization of "Repentance" show Herbert's great synthetic ability with the elements of popular religious song. The poem shows that sin is not so much destroyed as made a part of good, and the same process applies to the bathetic features in the poem's technique. On both levels, "Repentance" dramatizes the process of weaknesses becoming strengths.

Virtually the same theme is behind "Complaining," which pleads for either an end to the speaker's complaining or a speedy death and ascent to joys. The poem is formally composed of four stanzas, each consisting of two counterpointed couplets and a fifth line rhyming with the fifth line in the next stanza. Although the metrical and rhyme patterns are unique, the form is still a parallel one resembling Double Common Meter. The ideas are structured accordingly: the first pair of stanzas establishes God's power and the speaker's insignificance and misery; the second pair calls on God's other attributes and then names the speaker's desires. The pairing continues within the stanzas, each of which is built upon a pair of opposites. Partly because of this logical frame, and partly because of the syntax used within it, the poem emphasizes its rhymes and thus the differing lengths of the lines in which the rhymes appear. The poem begins with a somewhat jerky motion, the rhymes falling as if by accident or failed design:

> Do not beguile my heart,
> Because thou art
> My power and wisdome. Put me not to shame,
> Because I am
> Thy clay that weeps, thy dust that calls.
>
> (1–5)

Enjambing the short lines and making full stops within the following lines create some of this abruptness, which is linked to the developing theme of the speaker's lapsarian state. Herbert follows this pattern until finally he is able to clarify his dilemma:

> Am I all throat or eye,
> To weep or crie?
> Have I no parts but those of grief?
>
> (13–15)

Now understanding and confronting the question he has been circling, the speaker finally considers the two possible answers, and the style becomes as parallel and plain as that of Sternhold:

> Let not thy wrathfull power
> Afflict my houre,
> My inch of life: or let thy gracious power
> Contract my houre,
> That I may climbe and find relief.
>
> (16–20)

By end-stopping the dimeter lines and running on the longer lines, Herbert has brought the sluggish form into tune. In technique, the poem's resolution is effected not by a change of modes but by a strengthening of the original modes. At first the rhythms are clumsy, and they eventually become mechanical; this parallels the development of the poem's thought, in which the speaker's torments and weaknesses become a solution, a parallel set of options.

"Complaining" is a poem depicting an essentially dramatic situation, and much of the drama is created and resolved in the motion of the form about a bathetic norm. But this use of poetic form as a "narrative" device is not limited to poems of dramatic situations. Herbert may also employ such a form simply to chart the growth of an idea. "The Rose," for example, builds upon a stanza that is structurally very close to Common Meter, and the variations that Herbert makes upon this form imply one of the levels of meaning in the poem. As a quietly insistent affirmation of faith, the poem would be somewhat static were it not for the tensions in the form. The poem consists of eight alternately rhymed quatrains in uniform trochaic tetrameter. The resemblance to Common Meter is underscored by Herbert's again having structured each stanza about two main ideas. At least that is the organization of most of the stanzas, and the deviations from it are instructive. As frequently happens in those poems of Herbert's that build upon psalm techniques, there is at first a clear announcement of the aesthetic:

> Presse me not to take more pleasure
> In this world of sugred lies,
> And to use a larger measure
> Then my strict, yet welcome size.
>
> (1–4)

This is the "measure" of many hymns, and the two-part division of thought and form is that of the Common Meter; Herbert uses this convention for the next three stanzas. Stanza 2 states that the world has more woe than pleasure; stanza 3, that the world's deceits please others but are nothing to the speaker. Stanza 4 concludes the conventional homily by having the speaker offer his own "measure":

> But I will not much oppose
> Unto what you now advise:
> Onely take this gentle rose,
> And therein my answer lies.
>
> (13–16)

The implications of this symbolic answer are explained in stanza 5, at which point the poem shifts from the simple two-part structure of idea into more complex divisions that cut across the form:

What is fairier then a rose?
    What is sweeter? yet it purgeth.
Purgings enmitie disclose,
    Enmitie forbearance urgeth.

                                        (17–20)

As it is referred to in some of Herbert's other writings, the rose is
not only the conventional symbol of beauty but also a physic, a simple
folk medicine, distributed through God's art and providence.[37] The
stanza insists on the purgation that must accompany physical pleasures, and the complexity of the thought requires a somewhat denser
use of the form than the previous two-part structure would permit.
The thought requires condensation, and in the sixth stanza the pressure against the form becomes even greater:

    If then all that worldlings prize
    Be contracted to a rose;
    Sweetly there indeed it lies,
    But it biteth in the close.

                                        (21–24)

The complexity of the thought is mirrored in the tensions against the
trochaic meter, and in the condensed, line-by-line development. In-
corporating the thought of the previous stanza, and extending it as
well, stanza 6 suggests that if worldly joys may be symbolized by the
rose, then the close of earthly life will be as painfully deceptive, in its
own way, as the rose that looks sweet but conceals a thorn. Yet if,
as the previous stanza has emphasized, the rose also denotes a simple
laxative, *close* may involve a pun on "closestool" or "closet." Herbert
rarely discards the literal level of meaning, and here that level makes
good practical sense. In any case, the developing compression of
thought and form suggests the need of a physic for a mental condition,
and perhaps for a physical condition as well.[38] The nature of the

---

[37] See "Life," l. 15; and especially "Providence," p. 119, ll. 77–80.

[38] Arnold Stein's remarks on the logic of the poem describe the same pattern
from a different point of view: "an explanatory introduction, both general and
personal, is conducted with imaginative and witty leisureliness, in sharp contrast to
the concentration of the following stanzas" (*George Herbert's Lyrics*, p. 148). If
the reader finds implausible Herbert's use of anal humor, he might look at the
disposition of Sin (like the old stage Vice) in "L'Envoy" to "The Church Militant":

rose-as-physic is further stressed in the seventh stanza by the literal statement and by the shape of the thought. Here we return to the clear and purged two-part division of the opening stanzas:

> So this flower doth judge and sentence
> Worldly joyes to be a scourge:
> For they all produce repentance,
> And repentance is a purge.
>
> (25–28)

The humor of the whole poem is especially evident in the final stanza, in which the speaker employs the form with some relish, tipping up his heretofore regular syntax as he insists on his joke at his questioner's expense:

> But I health, not physick choose:
> Onely though I you oppose,
> Say that fairly I refuse,
> For my answer is a rose.
>
> (29–32)

It is the sort of humor that Herbert's parishioners might well have understood and appreciated: he offers an honest and conventionally pretty refusal, a rose; disclaiming all general interest in physic, he

---

> Choke him, let him say no more,
> But reserve his breath in store,
> Till thy conquests and his fall
> Make his sighs to use it all,
> And then bargaine with the winde
> To discharge what is behind.
>
> (11–16)

Something of my argument is suggested independently by Robert Ellrodt, who says that "d'ailleurs, il est chez Herbert un goût du grotesque dans les choses sacrées qui ne saurait être naïveté pure, comme il arrive souvent chez les auteurs du Moyen Age. Il y a une jovialité presque Rabelaisienne dans ses apostrophes à la conscience qu'il menace de l'Eucharistie comme d'une purge . . . . Il y a chez le pasteur de Bemerton une gaieté et même une irrévérence qui sont précisément l'apanage des saints" (*L'Inspiration*, 1: 299). The gallantly overstated but patriotic comparison notwithstanding, Ellrodt might almost be bouncing his reading off Don Cameron Allen's, which studies the poem as a renunciation of pagan meanings and an acceptance of the beautiful but ephemeral flesh of Christ; see *Image and Meaning* (Baltimore: The Johns Hopkins Press, 1960), pp. 67–79.

offers a common laxative. And this elaborate mock recoil is largely effective because of the deliberate variation from, and return to, the thinking methods of the psalm in Common Meter.

So far we have been concerned with the way in which orchestration has been achieved by use of the bathetic metrical psalm; I would like to turn now to Herbert's use of the more elegant psalm, as handled by Sidney and occasionally by the Countess. Observing the resemblance between *The Temple* and the Sidneyan psalter is a critical commonplace, as we have noted before. In the previous chapter, we also noted some general resemblances in the counterpointed lines, the long stanzas with interlocked rather than separable rhymes, and the musical phrasing, with its variety-within-regularity of meter, flexible enjambment, and movement of caesura. We have also seen resemblances between a few specific poems. There might be a temptation, at this point, to make a minute comparison of Sidney's psalms and *The Temple*. However, this could be somewhat repetitive after the remarks already made on Sidney, and it could be a mistake in proportion, for as I have proposed, it may be that the bathos, the peculiar mixture of pride and humility that is characteristic of Herbert, is given expression in Herbert's fusion of elegant and bathetic styles derived from the metrical psalms. We would do better, therefore, to look at the poems in which this fusion takes place and make a distinction between the two fundamental ways in which Herbert fuses these styles. The simpler sort of fusion is a clear and visible weld between the two styles: Herbert will write a stanza that consists of a conventional and heavy set of lines followed by a lyric response or addition, and somewhat more rarely, a whole poem that has another poem in a different style for an answer. The more complex sort of fusion involves the assembly of a stanza which establishes a phrase-by-phrase synthesis or opposition between the two styles. (As far as I can see, the distribution of poems of both styles, throughout *The Temple*, seems to reveal no general order or purpose.)

The two poems grouped under the single title "The H. Communion" form the single most conspicuous example of mixed styles. The second part originally appeared in the Williams manuscript, under the title "Prayer," and was later revised to incorporate Eucharistic imagery. The first part appears later in the Bodleian manuscript and in the 1633 edition. There is also in the Williams manuscript another poem entitled "The H. Communion," but this was not included in the later manuscript or in the *editio princeps*. This poem, and the possible reasons for its rejection, we shall consider in a moment. The complete "poem" in the Bodleian manuscript and the 1633 edition actually consists of two poems, the first with twenty-four lines arranged in counterpointed six-line stanzas; the second has sixteen lines in conventional Common Meter. It seems reasonably safe to assume that Herbert sees some sort of connection between the two parts, and I believe that a study of their relationship can tell us much about Herbert's use of psalm materials.

The most obvious difference between the two parts, aside from their visible dissimilarities in form, is that of tone. The first part, in the more complex stanza, is simple and direct, consistently devout and extremely sober. The second part, however, has a jesting and ironic whimsy that complicates the tone not only of this part but of the whole poem. The first part describes rather exactly the working of the bread and wine through the system,

> Making thy way my rest,
> And thy small quantities my length;
> Which spread their forces into every part,
> Meeting sinnes force and art.
>
> (9–12)

The sobriety of this is evident in its slow meters and slow action; the parallel phrasing and the closely developed correspondences between *thee* and *me* slow the pace and require some concentration from the reader. The second part is more dramatic, and opens with the intimate and hyperbolical manner of typically "metaphysical" first lines:

> Give me my captive soul, or take
> My bodie also thither.
> Another lift like this will make
> Them both to be together.
>
> (25–28)

As the poem develops it makes several abrupt turns of wit: "A fervent sight might well have blown/ Our innocent earth to heaven" (31–32), or even more casually,

> when Adam did not know
> To sinne, or sinne to smother;
> He might to heav'n from Paradise go,
> As from one room t'another.

(33–36)

And the second part ends at some remove from the first part with a final flippant touch:

> Thou has restor'd us to this ease
> By this thy heav'nly bloud;
> Which I can go to, when I please,
> And leave th'earth to their food.

(37–40)

Thus on the level of tone, "The H. Communion" contains one obvious contrast, the complex form containing a relatively simple and public emotion, and the simple form, traditionally employed for public praise, containing a subtle and personal emotion.

But the rhythmic structures of the two poems prevent our assuming that this simple inversion is all that Herbert has to say about the two styles, for each poem demonstrates a rhythmic skill of an entirely different order. In this respect, the second of the two parts, for all its complexity of tone, is the simpler of the two; its rhythms are regular and almost entirely falling. The purpose of this regularity seems to be to prepare us for the one metrical surprise in the poem, the sudden and clumsy drop in the last line: "Which I can go to, when I please,/ And leave th'earth to their food."

That the flatness of the ending is deliberate may be shown by comparison with the final stanza of the poem as it appears in the Williams manuscript. The thought is neat and the rhythms are tidy:

> But wee are strangers grown, o Lord,
> Lett Prayer help our losses,
> Since thou has taught vs by thy word,
> That wee may gaine by crosses.

(53)

The imagery of the revision is sharper than this, and considerably more relevant; in all, the clumsiness of the later passage is more metrical than mental. Certainly the revision has helped to move the poem closer to a "personal" utterance. And although it has been pointed out, in connection with this poem, that the Holy Communion is one of "the three Services in the Book of Common Prayer with which a Cathedral Choir is concerned,"[39] it is difficult to see how the poem, particularly the last stanza, could be sung, let alone make a valid choral statement. As personal as is its approach to God—in the whimsy of its tone and sudden irregularity of meter—the poem is at once "closed" and "open." This is a perplexing mixture; and Helen White saw the problem when she implied that the first two lines of the second part refer to a state of "ecstacy" but concluded that "the verse never quite takes off into the free air of ecstacy. It remains cramped, and Herbert's verse is not usually cramped."[40] Part of the difficulty, I suspect, lies in the tone, and part of it lies in the contrast between the two parts of the poem.

Returning to the first part, we find the rhythms complex and subtly varied, dense, quite unlike the predominating thinness of the Common Meter in the second part. The lines are full of stresses and move slowly:

> But by the way of nourishment and strength
> Thou creep'st into my breast;
> Making thy way my rest,
> And thy small quantities my length;
> Which spread their forces into every part,
> Meeting sinnes force and art.
>
> (7–12)

The last line of this stanza—and the second line as well, for that matter—is an excellent example of a line drawn long by a careful choice of consonants and long vowels. The slow care in rhythm and the clogged sound patterns suggest that the first part of the poem could have been performed or set only with difficulty; the heavy use of intricate junctures and stops certainly would preclude group singing. Rhythmically, the first part is much less accessible than the second part; yet the thought, as we have noted, is public, formal, and detached, as distinguished from that of the second part. We may draw

[39] Summers, *George Herbert*, p. 157.
[40] *The Metaphysical Poets* (New York: Macmillan, 1936), p. 177.

the obvious conclusion that as Herbert's art matured, between the Williams and Bodleian manuscripts, his tone deepened and his verse technique became more intricate; but this is hardly the way to read the two poems. We still have to face the question of why Herbert revised one poem, making it technically cruder, then changed its title, and finally appended it to a later and very different poem.

The answer may involve Herbert's connection with the metrical psalm on the very deepest level. Herbert wrote a second part that brings out the poetic virtues of the first part; and perhaps more obviously, the rhythmic control in the second part is highlighted by the different sort of control in the first. It is as if Herbert were implying that the second part involves a skill as substantial as that of the first part; as the second of the two poems, it naturally receives this emphasis. And the sense of technical equivalence is mirrored somewhat in the thought of the two parts. The theme of the first part is the intricate, "privie," and "subtle" way in which Christ's sacrifice works into man's system, and the verse form is accordingly devious. The theme of the second part is the easy availability of Christ's sacrifice, which allows us to enter Paradise as easily as we might walk about a house, and the verse form is accordingly accessible and easy. The thought of the total poem should make clear what the technique implies: Communion (or Redemption) works experientially two ways at once, by closeness and openness. It is like the two halves of sacred poetry, fine and private, coarse and public. Both experiences make up the rite of Communion, as both forms make up the poet's praise.

This conjunction of meaning is confirmed by the "H. Communion" poem that Herbert abandoned. On the level of metaphor, the earlier poem is a highly conceited attempt to describe *both* the depth and the breadth of Communion. Herbert plays off the two stages of the Presence in the sacrament, as they are related to the speaker-worshipper:

> O Gratious Lord, how shall I know
> Whether in these gifts thou be so
>   As thou art every-where;
> Or rather so, as thou alone
> Tak'st all the Lodging, leaving none
>   ffor thy poore creature there?

(1–6)

The whole poem is on this order, a highly theoretical discussion of the same ideas presented by the two separate poems later given the single title of "The H. Communion." The inevitable density of thought in the earlier poem is apparent in the stanza quoted above, and when Herbert then becomes sportive and turns communion bread to metaphor, the result is rather ponderous:

> Then of this also I am sure
> That thou didst all those pains endure
>   To'abolish Sinn, not Wheat.
> Creatures are good, & have their place;
> Sinn onely, which did all deface,
>   Thou drivest from his seat.
>
> I could beleeue an Impanation
> At the rate of an Incarnation,
>   If thou hadst dyde for Bread.
> But that which made my soule to dye,
> My flesh, & fleshly villany,
>   That allso made thee dead.
>
> (19–30)

The whole poem is reminiscent of Herbert's brother Edward at his most jocular. As the lines fill up with wordy connectives, the dramatic situation becomes progressively more remote and the occasional "hard line" only serves to confuse the speaking voice. It should not be surprising that Herbert discarded the poem as he assembled his "little book," for it is very unlike the later poems; but the two poems that replace it present the two halves of the same contrast that was in the earlier poem. Rather than make his point by theological wit-writing, the later Herbert employs a contrast that is essentially dramatic, creating two speakers or two moods. The fate of the early poem demonstrates the truth of Eliot's remark that Herbert's work must be read as an *oeuvre*, for Herbert's thought on this aspect of Communion seemed to require the pair of poems rather than the single dense one. The revision also emphasizes what Eliot has called Herbert's "dominance of sensibility over intellect."[41] Instead of arguing out the ideas

---

[41] T. S. Eliot, *George Herbert*, Writers and Their Work, no. 152 (London: Longmans Green, 1962), pp. 15, 17.

in the manner of Donne, as in the earlier poem, Herbert chooses to present them as they are reflected in the mind receiving Communion. At this point we may pull closer to Herbert's use of psalm form. Herbert had, I suspect, by the time the poems in the Bodleian manuscript were composed, a conception of psalm material as being essentially dramatic. And to generalize further upon "The H. Communion," it would seem that Herbert conceives of psalm materials as an orchestral voice to be employed for contrast and emphasis. That in "The H. Communion" the conception was deliberate I take to be indicated decisively by the revisions in form and meaning.

The two parts of "The H. Communion" show a contrast between a flat psalmodist's style and a literary craftiness, but for a fusion that is more decidedly Sidneyan we may turn to other poems. The first poem titled "Praise" shows a delicate balance between bathetic and elegant styles. Structurally the poem is almost a parody of Common Meter. Each of the alternating short lines contains a quiet understatement, and to emphasize the turn of it, Herbert has used an asymmetrical tercet, followed by a *b* rhyme connecting every two stanzas:

> To write a verse or two is all the praise,
>   That I can raise:
> Mend my estate in any wayes,
>   Thou shalt have more.
>
> I go to Church; help me to wings, and I
>   Will thither flie;
> Or, if I mount unto the skie,
>   I will do more.
>
>   (1–8)

The peculiar flavor of this comes from the mixture of faltering understatement and lyric assurance. On the one side there is the confidence of the bargaining table (and this comes straight out of the Psalms), what C. S. Lewis has called "the suggestion of the very silliest Pagan bargaining, that of the savage who makes offerings to his idol when the fishing is good and beats it when he has caught nothing. More than once the Psalmists seemed to be saying, 'You like praise. Do this for me, and you shall have some.'"[42] This confident sort of Old Testament trading (which, incidentally, seems to be the basis of most of

42 *Reflections on the Psalms* (New York: Harcourt Brace, 1958), p. 91.

Herbert's "business" metaphors)[43] is at odds with much of the rest of the poem. The requests for succor and divine uplift are strangely followed by the vague promise to "do more." The promise is rather like that of the half-witted horse in *Animal Farm*, whose answer to every adversity is always "I will work harder." What more could or need be *done* after one's mortal estate is mended, or after one has mounted unto the sky?

However, the placid fatuousness of the requests is not the sole element in determining the tone, for the verse technique has a poise of its own. After the plodding and end-stopping of the first stanza, the enjambment that opens the second is typically Sidneyan, especially in its relation with the preceding caesura. The first line has two pauses, the first by far more important to the thought: "I go to church; help me to wings, and I/ Will thither flie . . . ." The hopeful leap in logic after "I go to Church" carries the thought straight down to *flie*, with only small flutters at *wings* and *thither*. In the speaker's desire to ascend to heaven he overshoots an important qualifying detail, the great *if* behind *help me to wings*. The result is very similar to the sort of dash in thought and rhythm we have found in Sidney: "to God my God I say/ Thou my Lord, Thou art my stay" (Ps. 16: 4–5).

The next stanza employs the same jumps and sweeps in rhythm and ideas as it elaborates on man's great potential in spite of his insignificance:

> Man is all weaknesse; there is no such thing
> As Prince or King:
> His arm is short; yet with a sling
> He may do more.
>
> (17–20)

In the case of "Praise" (I), the movement of the verse is integral with the logic; the lines have "the sound of sense," to use Robert Frost's phrase,[44] and they achieve it through the working methods of the bathetic and elegant psalms. The opposite case is illustrated by

[43] See Bernard Knieger, "The Purchase-Sale: Patterns of Business Imagery in the Poetry of George Herbert," *SEL*, 6 (1966): 111–24. Many of Knieger's examples of commercial metaphors are related to ritualized propitiation.

[44] See *Selected Letters of Robert Frost,* ed. Lawrance Thompson (New York: Holt, Rinehart and Winston, 1964), no. 53, pp. 79–81. Frost is referring not to "common sense" but to the inflectional patterns required by the context.

"Praise" (II), which we shall discuss later in the chapter on tentative form; there, the technique and meaning are working against each other, and comparison of the two poems will serve to define the value of each.

Although "Submission" is written in a standard Common meter stanza, a variety of effects both clumsy and lyrical give it more flexibility than the conventional poem in this form. In the opening stanzas, Herbert alternates short and long statements in end-stopped and run-on lines to create the mask of the querulous and unsubmissive supplicant:

> But that thou art my wisdome, Lord,
>   And both my eyes are thine,
> My mind would be extreamly stirr'd
>   For missing my designe.
>
> Were it not better to bestow
>   Some place and power on me?
> Then should thy praises with me grow,
>   And share in my degree.
>
> (1–8)

The monotony is both mental and poetical. The quietly parenthetical *Lord* in the first line gains some humor as the rhyme of *stirr'd* in line 3 reflects back on it; this I think is another instance of Herbert's using a padded rhyme first in a pair, rather than second, and the slight mismating of sounds calls attention to the surprising conjunction of ideas: "Make me powerful and rich and You too will look good." As we reach the end of the third line, I suspect that we begin to be aware of a distance between the title of the poem and the tone, as it has been developed so far.

During the rest of the poem, the speaker gradually bumbles his way into a state of submission. The process is not an easy one, and the speaker's puzzlement is conveyed in the fumbling and amateurish management of syntax:

> How know I, if thou shouldst me raise,
>   That I should then raise thee?
> Perhaps great places and thy praise
>   Do not so well agree.
>
> (13–16)

The difficulty of the word order and meter in the first line of this—as inside-out as a line of Sternhold—reveals the speaker's well-founded suspicions about the chances of his being raised, and the smoothness and clarity of the next line explains why he has *not* been raised. The ironic understatement of *perhaps* and *so well* in the next lines reveals the last stage in the speaker's movement to self-awareness: "The joke is on me, I mean, my life."

The fitting modesty of the next and last stanza is secured partially by Herbert's full employment of the stanza form:

> Wherefore unto my gift I stand;
>   I will no more advise:
> Onely do thou lend me a hand,
>   Since thou hast both mine eyes.
>
> (17–20)

The simplest way of revealing submission, for a poet of Herbert's temperament, is to submit to poetic form, even clumsy form. In this respect "Submission" is almost (but not entirely!) the poetic equivalent of *credo quia absurdum est.* There is an intentional homeliness in the first two lines, and the movement of verse and idea is almost exactly that of many psalms: "Therefore my soul as at pits brinke,/ most heavy is and sad" (Old Version, Ps. 42:4).[45] The third line of Herbert's stanza falters over the intensive and begins to close the movement of the stumbling pilgrim. As the poem shows, the only way for a poet to lose his eyes is to lose his ears. Again we see the ease with which Herbert can put even slight details from popular bathetic psalmody to surprising and constructive uses.

As we have observed before, Herbert does not necessarily employ a strict psalm form in those poems in which he uses psalm techniques. However, some of the poems do make obvious references to psalms, just as some bear obvious technical resemblances to psalms. We might now consider two poems from this group and see to what extent Herbert was able to regard his themes objectively. "Church-musick" and "An Offering" are both patterned on, and play off against, the

---

[45] This citation presents the textual problem mentioned earlier (p. 12, n. 31). The particular 1582 edition of the Old Version which I have cited throughout reads "Therefore my heart as at pits brinke/ is most heavy and sad." All other editions I have consulted read as above and keep the meter.

themes and conventions of popular congregational song. "Church-musick" has a prominent place in Herbert's Temple; the reader hears it soon after entering *The Temple*, immediately after seeing the church monuments and before looking at the floor, the windows, and the other details of the physical church and the services held within it. The position of the poem in the geography of Herbert's metaphorical Temple has been noted before, but if we redirect our attention to the poem itself, we shall find in it a penetrating study of worship and music. Yet at first the poem's figurative language seems weirdly mixed, its metaphors fundamentally discontinuous:

> Sweetest of sweets, I thank you: when displeasure
>   Did through my bodie wound my minde,
> You took me thence, and in your house of pleasure
>   A daintie lodging me assign'd.
>
> Now I in you without a bodie move,
>   Rising and falling with your wings:
> We both together sweetly live and love,
>   Yet say sometimes, *God help poore Kings.*
>
> Comfort, I'le die; for if you poste from me,
>   Sure I shall do so, and much more:
> But if I travell in your companie,
>   You know the way to heavens doore.
>
> (65–66)

In stanza 1 the music is a sweet conductress, an inn-keeper; in stanza 2 it becomes an angel; and in stanza 3 it is a traveler who appears to be riding a horse. This seeming confusion may be resolved by asking what kind of music Herbert is thinking of. The form of the poem itself is suggestive: it is a common hymn stanza, and its use here is reinforced by that literal reference in stanza 3 to the music's posting or galloping, which the poet has trouble keeping up with. (The two *if*-clauses in the last stanza would not make much sense if he were simply observing his reactions to something like a choral anthem—not that that would be likely in Bemerton anyway.) Herbert is describing what seems to be congregational song, although clearly his attitudes toward it are mixed.

Let us return to the house of church music itself. Herbert says two things about this lodging: first, it is imaginary, a refuge from the storms and pains of the body; and second, it is outmoded and maybe even a little amusing. "House of pleasure" recalls such lyric monuments as *A Petite Pallace of Pettie his Pleasure* (1576), at least when the phrase travels in the company of "daintie," a term of high praise from the poetics of two generations before. It is hard to see Herbert implying with a straight face that this church music was any kind of *Paradise of Dainty Devices* (by coincidence also from 1576). Yet the psalter out of which he and his congregation are singing comes from that time, and has some of the affectations of that style. Looking at the rather dated extravagance of the first stanza, someone unfamiliar with Herbert's temperament might think him ironic or even sarcastic, in his description of church music; Donne found it easy to be so in his comments on that conventional song. But Herbert emphatically rejects such a stance.

For in the next stanza the music carries him into a state of ecstasy. The poet flies on the wings of the music, transcending his body and its wounds; and more than merely an escape, this flight is creative, for in it he lives and loves. He and the music can transcend even the maker of the church song, as they do when they look down from their altitude and say, *God help poore Kings*—the burden of innumerable Psalms: "Help me, O Lord my God: O save me according to thy mercy" (King James version, Ps. 109:26). Even the "real" David can be left below as the music of the song carries them up. In a religious context and in its own quiet tone, the process resembles that described in the grander rhetoric of Wallace Stevens:

> And when she sang, the sea,
> Whatever self it had, became the self
> That was her song, for she was the maker. Then we,
> As we beheld her striding there alone,
> Knew that there never was a world for her
> Except the one she sang and, singing, made.
>
> ("The Idea of Order at Key West")

The comparison with Herbert should not seem striking if we recall that the problem itself is one of the great recurrent ones in Western art and might be as fascinating to a Christian as to a self-proclaimed pagan.

Out of his apparently ethereal moment the poet is jarred by the last stanza. The music has started to post. It is not surprising that this should conclude the poem; one does not need much experience with church music to notice the gallop at which a congregation will attack the final stanza of a hymn. Herbert's conclusion is natural, persuasive, and utterly consistent: if he can keep up with the music it will lead to *heavens doore.* There is no flinching before the public side of the music, however outmoded in form or awkward in performance; although the ecstasy may give a pleasurably vertiginous experience, the public moment *knows the way* and gives direction. The double awareness of the music's strength and surface clumsiness resembles that which we saw in "A true Hymne." For Herbert, private meanings and public forms finally and always come together.

I have remarked several times that Herbert seems to be alluding to his use of diverse materials in poetic devotion; and he does this in the second poem I wish to consider under this discussion of churchly mixtures. "An Offering" is in two parts: a snappish parson rebukes a dull worshipper, and then makes a hymn for him to sing. The first part has a Donne-like abruptness and simultaneously treats the real and the ideal:

> Come, bring thy gift. If blessings were as slow
> As mens returns, what would become of fools?
> What hast thou there? a heart? but is it pure?
> Search well and see; for hearts have many holes.
> Yet one pure heart is nothing to bestow;
> In Christ two natures met to be thy cure.
>
> (1–6)

The subject of the sermon that follows is the divided heart, which an All-heal, "a balsome, or indeed a bloud,/ Dropping from heav'n" (19) will cure. With the healed breast as an offering, the speaker says, the listener should come before God and sing his "hymne."

The hymn itself is spare in form and subject. There is only one image, the heart, and it is used only once and somewhat abstractly. While the first half develops an argument and establishes a *persona,* the second part works on the level of style and tone alone. Like other hymns, it begins with a long syntactic lurch:

> Since my sadnesse
> Into gladnesse
> Lord thou dost convert,
> O accept
> What thou has kept,
> As thy due desert.
>
> (25–30)

The singer's arguments are, given Herbert's usual conciseness, strangely redundant; if God has kept his heart, presumably He has accepted it, and any *desert* cannot avoid being *due*. Of course rhymes for *-ert* and *-ept* are rare in English, which may be the cause of the padding, but Herbert knew how to avoid this sort of workmanship if he wanted to. In this poem I cannot see that he wanted to, since the second stanza has many of the same problems. The repetition now verges on silliness, and the pointless elaboration is more typical of the Countess of Pembroke:

> Had I many,
> Had I any,
> (For this heart is none)
> All were thine
> And none of mine:
> Surely thine alone.
>
> (31–36)

Apparently the *All-heal*, which the speaker has recommended in the first part of the poem, has not wrought so complete a transformation that the speaker may write lines as concise and suggestive as those of George Herbert. Surely something is wrong somewhere; the lyric is not bearing out the promises made in the first stanza, or elsewhere in Herbert's verse, where proper devotion leads to clarity and the eye on the object.

Recalling the dramatic circumstances of the song, we see that this is the hymn recommended by the speaker of the first part, and we should be careful not to construe his haste, rudeness, and sententiousness as qualities Herbert might have approved of. There is no question of the dramatic effectiveness of the portrait; it definitely has some Donnean qualities, although the speaker is more surly than Donne, whom we might expect to explode but not grumble and fuss in this

manner. But the country parson whom Herbert describes, in order
that he might "have a Mark to aim at" (p. 224), speaks "seasonably
and discreetly" to all (p. 226); "his voyce is humble, his words treat-
able, and slow; yet not so slow neither, as to let the fervency of the
supplicant hang and dy between speaking, but with a grave livelinesse,
between fear and zeal, pausing yet pressing, he performes his duty"
(p. 231). We may make a mistake in assuming—as Joseph Summers
does—that the speaker's conduct is right or even acceptable in
Herbert's terms, for the listener whom the speaker has been address-
ing has committed no wrong save being slow or hesitant.

   We may rejoin the hymn now and see that its flaccid writing is
probably the result of the "sermon":

> Yet thy favour
> May give savour
> To this poore oblation;
> And it raise
> To be thy praise,
> And be my salvation.
>
>   (37–42)

The falling rhythms become even more obtrusive, as there are now
two feminine rhymes; a contemporary critic would have noticed the
lightness of rhythm in relation to the idea. And the idea is rather thin,
for again, the heart that has been treated by the *All-heal* recommended in the first part, "the balm of Gilead, the medicine of the
Great Physician whose own blood is his balsam,"[46] is a heart that has
been saved. This balm, which is identified with the "true bread from
heaven" described in John 4, is itself the gift of everlasting life, and
thus as the hymn becomes more and more circular, the authority of
the speaker's attitude becomes less and less certain. Yet if the first part
of the poem is unpleasant and overbearing, it is natural that the
second part should seem, as if in response, uncertain and repetitive.
The poem actually may have great integrity, insofar as it describes the
dynamic of one kind of catechism. Might not the whole poem be a
piece of extended self-satire? Lord Herbert said that his brother
George was not exempt from the choler that was typical of their

---

46 Noted by Summers, *George Herbert*, p. 236, n. 18.

family,[47] and the first part of "An Offering" may be a dramatic mono-
logue through this choleric mask, through someone more like the
speaker of "The Collar," in a direct (not self-descriptive) form. As a
lyric appendage to the poem proper, the song is dramatically fitting as
a response to the manner of the first speaker. Structurally the poem
may be contrasted with "The H. Communion," where the two parts
form two halves in idea and form. Here the two parts are two aspects
of the same meaning, a limited and impatiently expressed idea calling
forth a limited and uncertain song. Whether Herbert intended it to or
not, the whole poem shows how an overbearing and heavy inquisition
does little for the act of composing devotional poetry, for it can lead
one to overlook the premises of the poetry and concentrate instead on
the outward forms. Apart from a few phrases, the poem does not
particularly demonstrate the influence of the metrical psalms; I refer
to it chiefly for its subject and structure, and incidentally because it
shows a part of Herbert's poetic character. The point of the shift in
structure I hope will be apparent in a moment.

In a few intricate lyrics, Herbert adopts this same larger structure
for individual stanzas, that is, he makes a lyric shift at the end of a
stanza and by doing so indicates a shift in the poem's thought. To
conclude these remarks on mixed lyricism and bathos for orchestral
effect, we may look at "Giddinesse" and "Dulnesse." Although its form
is the simpler of the two, "Giddinesse" is a virtuoso display of lyric
style within the confines of a narrow form. On the page the poem
resembles Common Meter, but the lines have five, three, five, and two
feet, and are rhymed *a b b a*. The shape of the form is close enough
to Common Meter to provide some of the same technical challenges
and still allow the elasticity suggested by the title. "Giddinesse" is the
method as well as the title, and the frenzy is best displayed working,
as here, against a conventional form.

The first stanza states the theme in the familiar two-part form, breaking the two ideas about the middle of the poem. But the repetition
at the end of the stanza and the rush of time, logical and metrical,
immediately establish the whirling atmosphere:

> Oh, what a thing is man! how farre from power,
> From setled peace and rest!

[47] *Autobiography of Lord Herbert of Cherbury*, ed. Sidney Lee (New York, n.d.),
p. 11.

> He is some twentie sev'rall men at least
> Each sev'rall houre.
>
>   (1–4)

There is a certain looseness of form in this; the values of the slightly eccentric stanza are not yet apparent, and Herbert might easily have written

> O what is man! how farre from power,
>   From setled peace and rest!
> He is, in every sev'rall houre,
>   Some hundred men at least.

Although the words are roughly the same as those in Herbert's stanza, they do not say the same thing, for as rewritten, the interruption of that cascade of adverbs across the third and fourth lines gives the stanza a stability it says men do not have.

From this point on the two-part division begins to disintegrate. In a sporadic and jumbled movement, man

> counts of heav'n as of his treasure:
>   But then a thought creeps in,
> And calls him coward, who for fear of sinne
>   Will lose a pleasure.
>
>   (5–8)

For contrast the third stanza returns to a norm, but so abruptly as to seem artificial or stilted, which indeed the action is. Even the caesurae in the long lines are reversed symmetrically:

> Now he will fight it out, and to the warres;
>   Now eat his bread in peace,
> And snudge in quiet: now he scorns increase;
>   Now all day spares.
>
>   (9–12)

The poem now gathers for a rush to the end, placing together two dissimilar metaphors and letting the lines run out, jumbling the neat order set up at the start, then returning to it:

He builds a house, which quickly down must go,
    As if a whirlwinde blew
And crusht the building: and it's partly true,
    His minde is so.

O what a sight were Man, if his attires
    Did alter with his minde;
And like a Dolphins skinne, his clothes combin'd
    With his desires!

                                   (13–20)

We must remind ourselves that this picture of man, particularly the one in the second of these stanzas, is only partly true; there is an alternative method for the mind, but the speaker does not want to consider it. His chief concern is with the imaginative recreation of the giddiness, and our suspension in it is to be even greater in the next stanza:

Surely if each one saw anothers heart,
    There would be no commerce,
No sale or bargain passe: all would disperse,
    And live apart.

                                   (21–24)

The complete negation in this statement undercuts the entire subject, and the negation is total because of the emphatic repetition: the passing of sales and bargains is nothing but commerce; and living apart geographically is only an objectification of the conditions in each other's hearts. The lines overlap in meaning and affirm a unity in negation, our separate hearts driving us all apart. When, therefore, the last stanza proceeds to the mending of our hearts, it must of necessity assert that the mending is universal. Mending one heart requires mending all, but mending one heart requires mending it continually, because man's giddy nature has both extension and intension:

Lord, mend or rather make us: one creation
    Will not suffice our turn:
Except thou make us dayly, we shall spurn
    Our own salvation.

                                   (25–28)

It may be helpful to regard the poem as a dramatic embodiment of
what James Smith has referred to as the central concern of the metaphysical poem, a leading metaphor that is reducible to the philosophi-
cal argument of the Many and the One:

> That verse properly called metaphysical is that to which the im-
> pulse is given by an overwhelming concern with metaphysical
> problems; with problems either deriving from, or closely resem-
> bling in the nature of their difficulty, the problem of the Many
> and the One . . . . It is conceivable that there should be a few
> who, aware of the difficulty of metaphysical problems, see them
> lurking behind any action, however trivial, they propose. Such
> people will be in a state of great disturbance or at least excite-
> ment. Such excitement may well be an impulse to poetry, and the
> poetry it generates be metaphysical.[48]

The excitement of Herbert's poem comes about through the speaker's inability or reluctance to face his problem, and thus it is appropriate that Herbert directly present man's multiplicity, as opposed to
God's unity, through a series of rapid, stop-motion pictures. But here
I must diverge from Smith and the idea of a reasoned metaphysical
conceit, for Herbert has perhaps less concern for developing the argument logically than for presenting it sensuously. The verse technique
carries substantial weight, for the argument of the poem is elaborated
as much on the formal as on the verbal level. The One in the poem
is both the desired state of man and the orderly form of poetic expression, and the poem not only describes the frustrated desire for
unity but manifests it by control of form. The stanza structure proceeds from a clear two-part separation of ideas to a spreading and
rambling lack of form.

The penultimate stanza is the turning point; the eventual separation of all men is the extreme of giddiness, and the prayer in the last
stanza asks for a resolution of the giddiness on its own terms: *make
us dayly*. The stanza form obeys this principle of the extreme supplying
its own resolution. As we have already noted, the penultimate stanza
is repetitive, but beneath the metaphors, each two-line unit presents
the same two ideas: separate identities lead to no interchange; no
interchange leads to separate identities. In the most extreme statement
of the poem's thought, there is an underlying symmetry of expression.

---

[48] "On Metaphysical Poetry," in *Determinations*, ed. F. R. Leavis (London: Chatto
and Windus, 1934), pp. 24–25.

The final stanza, the plea for re-creation, implies an even neater and more circular order in spite of its irregular rhythms. As the speaker phrases it: Lord mend or create us, and do it constantly; and creating us constantly, You shall mend us or save us. The integrity with which Herbert pursues the form is no less than that with which he develops the prose meaning. We might, for example, note that the formal development of the poem parallels another tendency in the poem's imagery: the making of the Many, the different selves, takes place on the level of the body; and the making of the One, the single self, takes place on the level of mind. In almost every respect, the style of the poem moves out from order to disorder, and upon that disorder erects a new order. The lyric excursions in the middle of the poem eventually provide the material for the turning unity of the final stanza.

"Dulnesse" is one of Herbert's most successful fusions of lyric and bathetic styles, and it is a deepening, in every sense, of the themes and techniques of "Giddinesse." The poems have identical forms and there are numerous thematic connections as well: both begin with man's soul in a body of uncoordinated senses; and giddiness is the result of sensual action, as dulness is the result of sensual repose. Man attempts to define himself through violent physical action, and fails; or looks for definition through physical inaction, the "sugred lyes" of the inert body, and fails again. Both states are fully realized, but "Dulnesse" is perhaps the better poem because Herbert makes its form do more work, and eventually draws his answer out of it. But before this can be shown, there are some immediate problems to be solved, or at any rate approached. As the poem is not long I will quote it in full:

> Why do I languish thus, drooping and dull,
>   As if I were all earth?
> O give me quicknesse, that I may with mirth
>   Praise thee brim-full!
>
> The wanton lover in a curious strain
>   Can praise his fairest fair;
> And with quaint metaphors her curled hair
>   Curl o're again.
>
> Thou art my lovelinesse, my life, my light,
>   Beautie alone to me:
> Thy bloudy death and undeserv'd, makes thee
>   Pure red and white.

When all perfections as but one appeare,
          That those thy form doth show,
The very dust, where thou dost tread and go,
          Makes beauties here.

Where are my lines then? my approaches? views?
          Where are my window-songs?
Lovers are still pretending, & ev'n wrongs
          Sharpen their Muse:

But I am lost in flesh, whose sugred lyes
          Still mock me, and grow bold:
Sure thou didst put a minde there, if I could
          Finde where it lies.

Lord, cleare thy gift, that with a constant wit
          I may but look towards thee:
Look onely; for to *love* thee, who can be,
          What angel fit?

One puzzle in the poem is the ending. After exploring his own attitude toward religious praise as it relates to secular praise, Herbert appears to reject secular poetry and to ask for a clearing of his mind in order to see God. Yet the question in the final stanza may not be simply rhetorical. Is the poem an expression of a limited sort of feeling, in which an answer would be out of place? Or is the final question one which the preceding parts of the poem have in fact answered? And why does the question concern man in general rather than just the *I* of the poem?

The other puzzle concerns what might be called a doctrinal point. In stanza 6 the speaker laments that he is *lost in flesh*, and as the previous stanzas show, he does not mean by this merely carnal lust or its poetry; evidently his lament is more existential, a lament for his fleshly state. But as Christian orthodoxy emphasizes, Christ also was made flesh. Is it possible that in the speaker's rejection of the fleshly state and the poetry of the flesh, he has failed to see the fleshly existence of Christ and accordingly finds himself languishing and dull? Has he an implicit desire to avoid the imitation of Christ? Ultimately both of these questions come down to the problem of tone and attitude: Is "Dulnesse" intended to be a dramatic statement of a limited attitude, or is it intended to show the mind's movement up and out of a limited attitude? Or should it be viewed simply as an examination of an attitude, without any scoring and grading of answers?

The poem can give specific answers to these questions, answers which are clarified by the verse technique. Moving through the poem more or less methodically, we may see the speaker testing and discarding alternatives that are as much stylistic as theological. As is characteristic of Herbert, these two levels of meaning are thoroughly integrated. This is immediately apparent in stanza one:

> Why do I languish thus, drooping and dull,
> As if I were all earth?
> O give me quicknesse, that I may with mirth
> Praise thee brim-full!

As Arnold Stein has shown, the paradox of the matter is that for all the speaker's announced heaviness, this is one of the lightest and most carefully balanced stanzas in *The Temple*.[49] Indeed, when the speaker takes a look at what the secular lover is doing next door, *his* verse is flat by comparison and flatter still in the imitation that the speaker offers:

> The wanton lover in a curious strain
> Can praise his fairest fair;
> And with quaint metaphors her curled hair
> Curl o're again.

> Thou art my lovelinesse, my life, my light,
> Beautie alone to me:
> Thy bloudy death and undeserv'd, makes thee
> Pure red and white.

The pun on *strain* is a preparation for the third stanza, and links it with the first; the speaker is, as we are told in the first stanza, *all earth, drooping and dull,* and some of the compensatory, overstated

---

[49] Stein, *George Herbert's Lyrics,* pp. 46–50; and see in relation to these comments pp. 97–101, which discuss the role of lament and praise in the speaker's reconciliation to his humanity. Although the emphasis I would place upon the poem is very different from Stein's, the two readings are not mutually exclusive. The problem of sensation and perception, which Stein sees as central to the poem, is implicit in the passages from Augustine which I quote later; my own effort goes into relating that theme to the lyric style of the poem.

assurance of technique in the third stanza is thus the result of the
curious strain imposed upon the dull body. The psychological fidelity
of the picture is readily apparent. The usual reaction to the third
stanza (and its relation to the two preceding) was perhaps best stated
by J. B. Leishman:

> There is that same blend of wit and tenderness which is charac-
> teristic of some of the best love-poetry of his age—even that con-
> ceit about red and white, which many would find offensive, seems
> to me, I must admit, entirely in keeping with the whole tone of
> the poem, and not at all extravagant.[50]

Rosemond Tuve pointed out, in response to Leishman's remarks, that
Herbert's use of the red and white symbolism to connect sacred and
profane love is "witty, radical, and apt—and thoroughly conventional." Tuve went on to show that authority for the red and white
conceit, as applied to Christ, can be traced as far back as Augustine
and that "the connection doubtless sprang from the words applied to
Christ as the soul's lover, 'My beloved is white and ruddy' . . .; no one
was unaware of the secular uses of the phrase."[51] But here Tuve's
habit of reading Herbert's poems only in terms of their sources led her
away from the explicit statement of Leishman's paragraph. In fact he
claims no uniqueness for the subject matter of Herbert's conceit, and
is doubtless aware of its history, but is more concerned with the tone
of Herbert's stanza, "the blend of wit and tenderness" which is expressive of a particular person rather than a cultural tradition. "The tone
of the whole poem" is Leishman's proper concern, because once we
have understood the traditional nature of Herbert's conceit, we still
must decide what he, George Herbert, does with it. I believe that what
he does is reject the symbol and the whole machinery of praise of
which it is a part.

The *red and white* stanza is simultaneously sweet and horrifying,
for under its conventional passion is a rather eerie detachment. The
first two lines are pretty in an ordinary way, and could have been
lifted from any of several dozen lyrics and sonnets from the generation
preceding Herbert. The cliché quality of Herbert's lines is evident in
their vagueness and lack of imagery and in the overstated meters and
sound effects. The first two lines are conventionally tripping:

50 *The Metaphysical Poets* (Oxford: Oxford University Press, 1934), p. 137.
51 Tuve, *A Reading of George Herbert*, pp. 149, 151.

> Thou art my *love*linesse, my *l*ife, my *l*ight,
> Beautie a*l*one to me.

And the next two lines surprise in every expected way: imagery suddenly appears, the meter treads more heavily, and the sounds shift dramatically to hard *d*'s: "Thy blou*d*y *d*eath an*d* un*d*eserv'*d*." The tongue stops where it had made the *l*'s; the place of death is the place of love, in more than one sense. No one was unaware of the secular uses of the image.

Yet the stanza is considerably more than an extended exercise in parody, as these remarks might seem to suggest. In spite of its heavy-handed sound effects and familiar, even trite imagery, the stanza has some serious thought in it. The logic is dense, cutting across the two-part division we have just noted. And at every point, the logic is bounded by the clichés in sound and image. *Undeserv'd*, for example, is deferred to the center of the line for very good reasons, apart from its position in the sound pattern and its delayed Petrarchan sob for the unfortunate lover. Its isolation emphasizes the contrast between the active death of Christ and the inertia of the speaker, and it also tells us something about the speaker's point of view. His superimposing the theme of the unfortunate undeserved death rather ignores the usual value of the Redemption, which holds that Christ's sacrifice was meaningful precisely because it was not deserved but voluntary. The emphasis that *undeserv'd* receives in its position in the middle of the line—and we should observe that Herbert might just as easily have written, in the same meter, "Thy undeserv'd and bloudy death" —heavily qualifies the thought of the rest of the stanza. *Pure red and white*, for example, is a red and white as pure as an over-simplifying secular lover can see it. And although this speaker may writhe over the cruelly undeserved death of Christ, the Herbert of "The Sacrifice" sees the sustained paradox in Christ's deliberate submission. The speaker of the third stanza does not rise to this view and perhaps cannot, for although the verse technique in the stanza may be heavy or trite, the thought is elaborated in so intricate a manner, cutting across the two-part division of the stanza, that it gives the appearance of being as profound an utterance as the speaker is capable of making.

But if we step back from the stanza and look around at its context, we may see that the speaker in it does not seem to be the same as that in most of the other stanzas. His sort of praise seems more a mask tried on for effect and discarded. The failure of the speaker's experiment in adapting secular verse is immediately asserted in stanza 4, as he draws a comparison between himself and his loved Christ, using more clichés from the earthly lover's repertoire:

> When all perfections as but one appeare,
> That those thy form doth show,
> The very dust, where thou doth tread and go,
> Makes beauties there.

Augustine's comment on Psalm 116 may be relevant here: "I was aroused by those beautiful feet, that I might call upon the Lord's Name."[52] But exit the Christ (*tread and go*), in beautiful dust, while our speaker is still without a song, as he will explain in the next stanza. But even in this stanza his invention has begun to flag, and the *curious strain* of clichés has begun to be more obvious. Half of the second line, for example, consists of relatives and connectives to support his flimsy lover's Platonism, and the third and fourth lines are similarly (but not so flagrantly) stretched to complete the rhymes. Bad secular verse and bad religious song have come together for a moment; the subject is one that has been worn down for a generation, and the verse technique is neither graceful nor meaningfully crude, except insofar as it shows the speaker's emotional bankruptcy. There is the same sense of killing time for the sake of form alone that is common in the bathetic style.

> It is to manifest alas,
> That first I was conceived in sinne:
> Yea of mother so borne was,
> And yet vile wretch remayne therein.
> (Old Version, Ps. 51:5)

Our consciousness of this strain in style keeps us from saying that Herbert actually wants to be a combined secular-religious lover. Rosemary Freeman has said that this fourth stanza is "an immediate statement of the degree of perfection represented in his subject," which is apparently designed to contrast with the third stanza. "The sharp-

---

[52] *Expositions on the Book of Psalms*, ed. Coxe, p. 555a. It may be pertinent that Athanasius recommends this psalm "for his dominion and presence in the flesh"— the central problem in "Dulnesse." (See Old Version, sig. [B 4ᵛ].)

ness of the context for 'pure red and white,'" Freeman says, "places that well-known phrase in a way that condemns the whole standard assumed by secular poets." About the condemnation in stanza 3 I would agree, but the context of stanza 4 seems quite as "sharp," and both the images and style in it are as much clichés as those in the stanza preceding. Thus it seems erroneous to say that "the achievements of amatory verse are imitated yet made merely contributory,"[53] when the rest of the poem seems an outright rejection of that amatory imitation.

What is left to the speaker after his four stanzas? After those Petrarchan indulgences, the speaker's first step is to return to a colloquial movement within a straight two-part form and to use this for some sarcastic comments on the sort of praise he has been attempting:

> Where are my lines then? my approaches? views?
> Where are my window-songs?
> Lovers are still pretending, & ev'n wrongs
> Sharpen their Muse

The lovers' wrongs only heighten their invention, while the great Christian wrong, at least when viewed through a lover's eyes, does nothing for Herbert's invention, and he now repudiates the lover's mode:

> But I am lost in flesh, whose sugred lyes
> Still mock me, and grow bold:
> Sure thou didst put a minde there, if I could
> Finde where it lies.

These are both crucial stanzas, the second especially so. The chief obstacle to achieved repose is the flesh; and unfortunately the trials of the flesh alter the mind. Psalm 116 says (I quote here from the Old Version), "I sayed in my distresse and feare,/ that all men lyers be" (p. 286). Herbert's own context is narrower but nonetheless emphatic: "Lovers are still pretending, & even wrongs/ Sharpen their Muse." Even his own heart lies, mocking and bold; but this vision or hallucination of universal lying can lead to revelation, for it is hard not to

---

[53] Freeman, "Parody as a Literary Form," *EIC*, 13 (October 1963): 314–15.

see a parallel between the "sharpened" muse of secular verse and the
aggressive lies of the flesh. *Sugred lyes* is itself a cliché (as the repeti-
tition of the rhyme in line 4 emphasizes), and the only answer to it is
the dogged stumbling of the third line, where there is a fleeting suggestion of "You got me into this." (Maybe there is still in him a trace
of the lover after all.) The pun in the last line qualifies the stanza,
and it is a turn in the thought that leads into, or more exactly, *allows*
the last stanza; the mind perceives the lies of the body. But the last
two lines also emphasize that the mind itself can lie: it can lie in a
stupor, and it can also indulge in the mental equivalents of the *sugred
lyes*, that is, the *approaches, views,* and *window-songs.* We should also
observe that for all this punning, we continue to move away from the
densely locked lover's stanza, into a plain two-part structure that is
now becoming clearly antithetical. The eccentric form has now begun
to fumble its way back to orderliness. I would like to quote a stanza
from the Old Version to show just the quality I am describing:

> Thou madest a spring with streams to rise,
>   from rocke, both hard and hie:
> And eke thy hand hath made likewise,
>   deepe rivers to be drie.
>
>   (Ps. 74:16)

In spite of all the differences between this and the Herbert stanza
under discussion, both have the same fundamental arrangement of
thought, a statement and counterstatement turning about the center
of the stanza. As we have observed in the previous pages, Herbert is
fond of moving to this pattern of thought as his submission increases;
and here the shifting word order is accompanied by an increasing
closeness to a regular meter. He is approaching a moment of clarity
and recognition, and it is therefore appropriate that, after he has
diagnosed his mind as lying, the last stanza should be a prayer for a
cleare and constant wit.

It is now possible for the speaker to reject outright the idea that
man can actually love God in the manner he has been attempting:

> Lord, cleare thy gift, that with a constant wit
>   I may but look towards thee:
> *Look* onely; for to *love* thee, who can be,
>   What angel fit?

The movement is through, not over, the flesh. Herbert's italics emphasize the final literal rejection of what the style had rejected earlier in its own terms; and the speaker's human identity is clarified.[54] The heavy metrical stress on *be* isolates the syntax of the whole line, and its suggestions are highly meaningful. No one—certainly not the speaker—exists simply to have his being in a love for God. The earthly lover may make over his beloved, but this process hardly lies within the divine poet's power. One does not love God in the way of *poesis*; and to avoid doing this, and realize it, is to clear the way for informing of the spirit.

It should be stressed that neither the style nor the explicit statement is speaking for any kind of settlement on minimal terms, what might be called the Rag-and-Bone-Shop aspect. Mitigating against such a conclusion is Herbert's disarming shift to the general point of view: "that *I* may . . . but *who* can be?" The speaker is not seeking to dissolve his own dilemma in a larger one; he is seeking to draw the larger dilemma into his own. Transcendence, perhaps, with a full consciousness of what has been transcended, but not self-annihilation.

Further, the poem has presented a problem and has resolved it: the poet who seeks to use poetry will, in turn, be used by poetry; determining how and when this can happen is one of the major concerns of the poem. The role of secular poetry in the poet's program is a strictly subsidiary issue, and I think it blurs the outline of the whole poem to conclude, as does one reader, that "Herbert never wavered in his resolution to devote his poetic gifts exclusively to the service of God."[55] Of course Herbert never does seem to be in immediate danger of dashing off a sonnet sequence to a cruel curly mistress. In "Dulnesse," the poetic techniques with which he introduces the thought of this possibility insure that it can only be discarded. The comparison itself is present only to backlight other more significant concerns. For Herbert in this poem, the problem at hand is not so much that of choosing between amatory and divine verse as recognizing a torpor of

[54] The import of this passage, and its considerable significance for the meaning of the whole of "Dulnesse," will sound familiar to readers of Rosemond Tuve's penetrating study, "George Herbert and *Caritas*," *JWCI*, 22 (1959): 303–31. Tuve emphasizes that Augustine's thought on God's image in man is important for an understanding of *The Temple* and "Dulnesse" in particular (pp. 325 ff.). However, her remarks on this poem seem rather general and in places oversimplified for the sake of polemic.

[55] Bennett, *Four Metaphysical Poets*, p. 149.

flesh and mind which, by an extended lie, can make poetry seem a process that can replace the giving of oneself.

Study of the poetic techniques of the last stanza can appropriately conclude these comments. I have already alluded to the suggestive breaks in the syntax. Coordinate with them as a factor in reducing the mellifluousness of the first half of the poem is the ordering of principal ideas, coinciding with the line divisions. In these respects the last stanza seems simple, even crude, by comparison with a stanza like the first. But the metric of the last stanza has some important contributions of its own to make:

> Lorde | cleare thy gift # that with a constant wit |
>
> I may but look | towards thee #
>
> Looke onely # for to love thee | who can be #
>
> What angel fit #

There are a number of small patterns of interest here. Rhythmically the phrases *for to love thee* and *what angel fit* are nearly the same; and the second repeats, in a slightly expanded form, the rhythm of *who can be?* There is a similar balance in *cleare thy gift, a constant wit,* and *look towards thee.* Here the balance in short phrases, however, without a corresponding balance in syntax, seems only to have a certain preventive power—the lines are not harsh but neither are they easily isolated for their lyricism, something usually rather easy to do with Herbert. The rhythmic patterns are not easily sorted out, given the shifts in syntax and logic: "do this, in order for that; that only, not this." (I note this not to imply that the lack of parallelism is a flaw, but only to point to some connections in meaning.)

The particular care that has gone into the making of the last stanza needs to be emphasized, for by this stanza, Herbert is into the poem past the point of retreat. The preceding stanzas have laid down a series of challenges on both religious and stylistic planes of meaning; there is a great deal of risk involved in such a plan, for the last stanza may fail to deliver the goods that have been invoiced in the preceding stanzas. Closing on a neatly worked out parallel or an expansive lyricism would be, in the terms the poem has worked out, a decided betrayal, a fraud. As a solution then, Herbert has chosen to give his stanza a kind of latent strength and avoid flaunting any conspicuous technical weaknesses. In its verse techniques the poem achieves the very sort of balance that Herbert has been explicitly treating as his subject. The orchestration of form and meaning is a process which, in this case, cannot be separated from the strength-out-of-weakness pattern of the poet's inner life. As "Dulnesse" combines the themes of both the secular lyric and the Psalms, so it combines the poetic techniques of elegance and bathos. In its consciousness and controlled energy, its sophistication and humility, it is the kind of poetry that Augustine would have written if he could, poetry that goes, like the Psalms, beyond one man and into universal history.

FOUR

Tentative Form

The way in which language signifies is mirrored in its use.
That the colours are not properties is shewn by the analysis of
physics, by the internal relations in which physics displays the
colours.
Apply this to sounds too.[1]

—Ludwig Wittgenstein

Studying Herbert's use of metrical psalm techniques will show that
there is sometimes a discrepancy between the way a Herbert poem
behaves and the way it says it behaves. Whether this is a matter of
Herbert's poetic instinct, or mere accident, I do not know, nor does
the difference seem important. What is important is that "the internal
relations" of the language, and study of "uses" rather than "properties," will tell us something about Herbert's mind and craft. This area
can be somewhat risky for criticism to enter, and I would notify the
reader at the outset that by "tentative form" I refer to the role of the
form in a poem and not necessarily to the ideas themselves, which
may or may not be tentative. The prose sense of a poem may be asser-
tive while the form is hesitant; or the sense may be uncertain and the
form suggest an answer. Or, if we should prefer to regard the dis-
parity from the standpoint of tone, the form may suggest some doubt
about a subject described confidently or some optimism about a subject described darkly. And there is finally a middle land in which the

[1] Wittgenstein, *Notebooks: 1914–1916*, ed. G. H. von Wright and G. E. M. Anscombe and trans. G. E. M. Anscombe (New York: Harper & Bros., 1961), p. 82.

194

poem may make an assertion of some sort and the form simply under-cut it without implying any alternative meaning.

Herbert has a deep certainty that his strengths come out of his weakness, in both the moral and poetic senses. His use of tentative forms is thus both natural and inevitable, given his themes, techniques, and lyric gifts. "The Crosse" passionately states the paradox:

> One ague dwelleth in my bones,
> Another in my soul (the memorie
> What I would do for thee, if once my grones
> Could be allow'd for harmonie):
> I am in all a weak disabled thing,
> Save in the sight thereof, where strength doth sting.
>
> (13–18)

The speaker starts to descend into self pity, but the last line makes a decisive recovery with the awareness that in his self-consciousness, *the sight thereof,* he has a mortification and a corrective. However, the stanza immediately following this recognizes that even poems themselves may duplicate the process:

> Besides, things sort not to my will,
> Ev'n when my will doth studie thy renown:
> Thou turnest th'edge of all things on me still,
> Taking me up to throw me down.
>
> (19–22)

Yet in Herbert's view the simultaneity of oppression and power, sickness and health, weakness and strength, are not simply the identifying marks of his own poetry and life; they are those of every Christian:

> A Christians state and case
> Is not a corpulent, but a thinne and spare,
> Yet active strength: whose long and bonie face
> Content and care
> Do seem to equally divide,
> Like a pretender, not a bride.
>
> ("The Size," 31–36)

The way in which Herbert's poems take him up to throw him down is nothing less than equal division, a Christian's lot.

There are no simple examples of tentative form, but we can at least begin with a poem that has an explicitly announced tentative subject. If asked which of Herbert's poems expresses the greatest uncertainty in subject and form, most readers would probably name "The Collar." But this view is usually qualified by directing attention to the poem's ending: God calls, and the speaker returns to rhyme. In this view, the poem is actually an expression of Herbert's orderly temperament. He cannot help writing a poem that is carefully patterned, and actually the poem "contains all the elements of order in violent disorder."[2] For all the apparent anarchy of form, so this argument goes, the poem really implies a definite order: "the disorder of the poem provides a constant implicit criticism, and with the final lines we realize that 'The Collar' is a narrative in the past tense: the message for the present concerns the necessity of order."[3] Order, like the present, is a product of the past, which is disorder. In this view, the poem is like an amateur movie title, in which a jumbled heap of letters magically assemble themselves to announce the "real" theme.

This view is perhaps somewhat oversimplified; "The Collar" has a discontinuity between style and subject that is functional and even essential. This discontinuity is obvious though ingenious, and thus the poem is a good place to start in the study of tentative form. Herbert's formal strategy in "The Collar" is to abuse lyric form and then return to it, and as a result the greater part of the poem skates close to parody. The poem's thoroughly scrambled but purposeful rhyming has often been noted; yet the scattered rhymes attack and affirm established order in style. This conclusion emerges from study of the syntax and metric. Lines 10 to 12, for example, show a conspicuously rearranged dimeter and trimeter stanza, in alternating half rhyme:

> Sure there was wine
> Before my sighs did drie it: there was corn
> Before my tears did drown it.

---

[2] Summers, *George Herbert*, p. 92.

[3] *Ibid.* In *The Metaphysical Poets* (New York: Macmillan, 1936), Helen White points to the "profound cogency" of the ending (p. 173), and her remarks accord with Summers' formal analysis. Depending from Summers's remarks is the essay by Larry Champion, "Body *versus* Soul in George Herbert's 'The Collar,'" *Style*, 1 (1967): 131–37. My analysis seems thoroughly opposed to Champion's, for he finds that "the body agitates for release" but in the face of the Master's admonition "can offer no opposition," as it is "totally unable to cope with the logic and power of the spiritual collar" (p. 136). On the contrary, God quite directly draws the body into the spiritual life.

Although the meters of the poem are predominantly iambic, on occasion they fall into an exaggerated lurching song and provide gathering points for the speaker's energies. His first surge of complaint closes in rhythms which are nearly dactylic:

Is the yeare onely lost to me?

Have I no bayes to crown it?

No flowers, no garlands gay?

(12–15)

Maybe the tone of this could be construed as the music of the speaker's missed spring, but the same tendency to doggerel falling meters returns as his temptor voice ends its reply to the complaint:

Forsake thy cage,

Thy rope of sands,

Which pettie thoughts have made, and made to thee

Good cable, to enforce and draw,

And be thy law,

While thou didst wink and wouldst not see.

(21–26)

And when the speaker finally resolves to go, he falls into a blunter version of the same swinging pattern:

He that forbears

To suit and serve his need,

Deserves his load.

(30–32)

The speaker's jouncing "numbers" and timing may be taken to indicate his frivolous state of mind, in the way that a graver music was commonly regarded as a necessary indication of worship. The meaning of Herbert's rhythms may be seen if we look at Wither's defense of versified scriptures:

> Whereas they say that *Verse* cannot retain that gravity, which
> becommeth the authority of holy scriptures, it is false: for how
> can that speech be denied to have in it gravity, wherein every
> word and syllable must be considered in quantity and number?
> or who can bee so ignorant, to think so, but such as are altogether
> strangers unto the *Muses?* [4]

Herbert's rhythms are "strangers unto the Muses," if by that term we
mean the muses of divine poetry. The lines lack the usual gravity of
devotional song; a decorum is being ignored. The cliché quality of
meter is instrumental in creating the sound of small authority in the
speaker's words.

It would be appropriate at this point to discuss that authority, in
particular its negative aspects. As an exercise in blasphemy and sacrilege, "The Collar" has few equals, even among the wilder poems of
Donne. No other English poem comes to mind in which there is such
a violent rejection of Christ, the Resurrection, and salvation. The
speaker begins by striking the communion table,[5] and as his hysteria
quickly rises, it has no goal except rejection; his "program" consists
simply of abdication and withdrawal. At the peak of his frenzy, as he
grows "more fierce and wild," he makes a brilliant and horrifying
projection of his own brand of freedom:

> Call in thy death's head there: tie up thy fears.
>   He that forbears
>   To suit and serve his need,
>   Deserves his load.
>
> (29–32)

Because the poem is set at the communion table, the first of these lines
quite probably concerns the poet's desire to remove Christ as his emblematic leader. The literal meaning of death's head is uncertain;
there is probably not a skull on the communion table. Given the argument on self-serving, the term very likely refers to Christ, who was
literally death's head: Donne had used similar terms in his poem
"Upon the Annuntiation and Passion," describing Christ as "the

---

[4] Wither, *Preparation to the Psalter*, p. 7. *False* may refer specifically to a defective metric; compare the usage in Touchstone's comment on Orlando's doggerel:
"This is the very false gallop of verses!" (*As You Like It*, III. ii. 119).

[5] *Board* (l. 1) refers to the communion table; see Martz, *Poetry of Meditation*,
p. 301, n. 6.

head/ Of life, at once, not yet alive, yet dead" (9–10). After the death's head line, Herbert's rejection becomes most corrosive, for he goes on to see Christ as an example of someone who failed to grasp the main chance, and as a result got only what he deserved. Surely it would be hard to find anyone who failed so completely as did Christ "to suit and serve his need" in the ordinary human terms; this is the point of the sustained irony of "The Sacrifice." The last line above is especially notable: if Christ's load is the accumulated sins of all men, then self-seeking, not *caritas*, becomes a cardinal virtue, and we are plunged into the world of Edmund's "Thou, Nature, art my goddess."

The final quatrain does not—and given Herbert's own interests, cannot—resolve the poem in terms of the hysteria and abuse that have preceded it. In spite of the abuse God accepts the poet; however, this does not throw the burden of abuse back onto the poet, as we might expect. Instead God is merciful. He does not strike the poet with lightning bolts, or pin him to a rock, or inflict any of the technicolor justice characteristically demanded by the romantic poet. The poet's overwhelming ridicule and rejection of charity is met only with more charity. In short, there is a difference between the way that the last stanza resolves the poem in terms of subject, and the way it resolves it in terms of style. As I shall show in a moment, the poem's conclusion is, stylistically, an inevitable and necessary evolution of what has preceded; but theologically, the conclusion is neither inevitable nor necessary.

Herbert's use of tentative form in this manner is also related to the speaker's own volition. Ernst Curtius has described a medieval folk belief which bears upon the psychology of the speaker:

The Devil too was a poet: he composed the oracles, which as everyone knows were in verse. For though through his fall he lost "the works of the will," yet "the works of the mind remained to him, as to the other angels." Though once, when he was present in the body of a man possessed, he was ordered by the exorcist to recite some verses and made a mistake in one stanza, as is well attested, "it was only because he wished to do so, not from ignorance."[6]

[6] *European Literature and the Latin Middle Ages*, trans. Willard R. Trask (New York: Pantheon, 1953), p. 557. Cf. *Outlandish Proverbs*: "When God will punish, he will first take away the understanding" (Herbert, *Works*, p. 344, no. 688). The lesson of this should be stressed. Paul M. Levitt and Kenneth G. Johnston have argued that "The Collar" is an extended and coherent metaphor for a sea voyage;

Herbert's speaker is full of the devil, and like the Devil he makes his mistakes because he wishes to do so. (We should notice that in Curtius's account the Devil did not unknowingly start speaking prose; verse with mistakes is still, or especially, verse.) If we see the speaker's positive desire to commit blunders, we understand better the commentary provided by the verse technique. If we view the poem as being essentially ordered, albeit rearranged, we lose the dramatic tension and the reason for the conclusion. By trying to take and reject at the same time, the speaker plays into God's hands. Having made the style and the subject of the poem work at cross-purposes, Herbert insures that this will be apparent.

Although there are many psalms in which the speaker laments his decay and chances missed, there is one in particular—Psalm 102—that contains some of the major images and situations of "The Collar." (Incidentally, Athanasius recommends the singing of this psalm "if for the imbecillity of thy nature thou art weary with the continuall miseries and griefes of this life, and wouldest comfort thy self.")[7] Like the Herbert of "The Collar," the speaker in the psalm says, "My heart is smitten, and withered like grass; so that I forget to eat my bread. By reason of the voice of my groaning my bones cleave to my skin . . . . For I have eaten ashes like bread, and mingled my drink with weeping" (verses 4, 5, 9). The psalmist is confident, however, that God "will regard the prayer of the destitute, and not despise their prayer . . . . For he hath looked down from the height of his sanctuary: from heaven did the Lord behold the earth; to hear the groaning of the prisoner; to loose those that are appointed to death to declare the name of the Lord in Zion, and his praise in Jerusalem" (17, 19–21). God can do this because, as the psalmist concludes, "thou *art* the same, and thy years shall have no end" (27).

There are a number of obvious parallels here, and the most interesting is found in the way Herbert finally asserts divine permanence by means of poetic form rather than literal statement. The technique

---

see "Herbert's 'The Collar': A Nautical Metaphor," *SP*, 66 (1966): 217–24. The authors overlook some possibilities in selecting their metaphors; if their argument is correct, Herbert is sailing about in a pirate ship under the "death's head" or Jolly Roger.

[7] "A Treatise made by Athanasius the Great. . . ," in the Old Version, sig. [A 7r]. The question of whether Herbert was familiar with the treatise is not directly pertinent. The treatise does suggest, however, psalms which the sixteenth- and seventeenth-century reader might have found relevant to the situations in the poem.

of Herbert's ending in "The Collar" acts out the statement at the
psalm's ending. As neat as this is, there is still one more step in the
poet's integration of mind, verse, and God, as we can see in the final
quatrain.

> But as I rav'd and grew more fierce and wilde
> At every word,
> Me thoughts I heard one calling, *Child!*
> And I reply'd, *My Lord.*

The poet points out that his frenzy has reached its height, in a pentameter line followed by a dimeter line. Then God calls, rhyming off
the pentameter line as if to show the poet how to learn his trade:
"wilde/*Child!*"[8] But Herbert gives the poet an even better rhyme,
which recognizes his own fealty, its interrelations with his verbal excess, and the nature of God as *logos*: "word/ *My Lord.*" When God
entered the poem, however, He dropped a foot off the long line that
could have yielded a symmetrical quatrain: His line was in tetrameter.
Now the poet responds with a final trimeter line, making half a Common Meter stanza. The end of the poem has a nexus of psalm meaning
and psalm technique: in the thought as in the verse itself, the poem
concludes in the plainest common denominator of contemporary
religious song. In the relation of this end to the thought and verse
technique that precede it, the poem most fully reveals its tentative
form.

It would be useful to contrast "The Collar" with a poem in which
there is a more subtle tension between form and meaning. In the
preceding chapter we saw how psalm effects in "Praise" (I) were used
to help complete the meaning of the poem. In "Praise" (II), on the
other hand, similar devices work in an opposite way. The stanza shape
greatly resembles that of Common Meter, and there is some appropriateness in this, given the subject of the poem. Within the stanza,
however, Herbert is employing the Sidneyan line with its odd syllable
count and falling rhythms:

---

[8] Jerome Mazzaro has some interesting comments on poems of this sort, in
Transformations in the Renaissance English Lyric (Ithaca: Cornell University
Press, 1970); he finds in "The Collar" a shift from a "sincere" to a "normative"
ego and concludes that dialogue and irony give tension to "the interplay of these
egos" (p. 168). However, I think that Herbert often attempts to cut away our faith
in any human ego by presenting tensions directly in his poetic style.

> King of Glorie, King of Peace,
>   I will love thee:
> And that love may never cease,
>   I will move thee.

(1–4)

The mechanical precision of the meter is evident in the regular placement of the caesura and the even stress levels; these continue through
the second stanza, describing the poet's *working breast*, then break up
in the third:

> Wherefore with my utmost art
>   I will sing thee,
> And the cream of all my heart
>   I will bring thee.

(9–12)

This time logic invites only a light pause at *with*, and the enjambment
with the second line furthers the sense of expansion. The third line
again places the caesura conventionally but has some of the expansiveness of the first two lines as it runs on into the fourth; the last two
lines of the quatrain make a bridge back to the dominant motion of
the poem.

Such criticism may seem fanatically minute; but I think it is important to point out how few formal variations Herbert makes in the
whole poem.[9] In the next three stanzas, as the speaker asserts Christ's
great mercy, he returns to the same unvaried pattern, every line end-
stopped, every caesura regularly placed, and the timing left quite even.
It should not be surprising, then, that as the poem reaches the final
stanza, the return to variation becomes almost irresistible:

> Small it is, in this poore sort
>   To enroll thee:
> Ev'n eternitie is too short
>   To extoll thee.

(25–28)

---

[9] T. S. Eliot has called attention to the "masterly simplicity" of the first stanza
(*George Herbert*, Writers and Their Work, no. 152 [London: Longmans Green,
1962], pp. 33–34); this is valid, but of course the judgment does not apply automatically to all the other stanzas.

The enjambed lines are only a part of the grace of this; particularly notable among other controls on timing is the long elided *eternitie* in the third line, which stretches the line out as far as possible. The form stretches before God just as time must stretch.

In many respects this ending is very strange. In the third stanza we were shown, in a quietly impressive manner, the extent of the poet's craft, and we were told, very directly, that he would exercise it. Yet he does not return to the form of this announcement until the end. Like few poets in the language, Herbert was highly conscious of his great lyric gifts, their power and their temptation. In this poem, however, he chooses not (or is unable) to employ his gifts, although he nonetheless invokes them. Thus if the first two lines of stanza 3 are intended to refer to the sort of praise the speaker has been offering, they verge on making the stanza a rather peculiar joke. The commentary provided by the form of the stanza is almost ironic; and it removes the poem to a level of speech that has not been in sight in the rest of the poem. The last stanza then shifts our attention. An interesting parallel might be the last line and a half of Keats's "Ode on a Grecian Urn," in which the assertion of all we need to know is as striking an attempt to rise to transcendent knowledge of time as Herbert's stanza is to sink to knowledge of humility. The difference is that Keats attempts his rise on the verbal level and Herbert attempts his on the technical level. There is little point in pressing this comparison further, for all I am attempting to show is that in "Praise" (II) the speaker reveals one form of his "utmost art" in praise, and then, as if to point out the poverty of his craft, does not use it again until the end of the poem. In short, there is some constriction in the poem; as an artist, Herbert is working very hard indeed to retrieve or discover his humility. In many ways the poem is an incorrigible statement.

It is of course true that a certain ceremonial stiffness is appropriate on some occasions, and there would not be much point in saying that the poem is not spontaneous or natural. The poem offers its own commentary, and the question of the goodness or badness of stiff meters *per se* is impertinent. But the place where Herbert varies his rhythms, and what he says when he varies them, suggests some tension in his mind. There is not much chance of clarifying this tension by referring it to the religion and art problem of the "Jordan" poems.

Unlike those poems, "Praise" (II) has a chilliness because of its simultaneous conventionality and sophistication.

Comparison of "Praise" (II) with "An Offering," discussed in the previous chapter, may clarify some secondary statements about tentative form. It should be apparent that the relations between form and structure, within the two poems, are somewhat different. Although "An Offering" has an unyielding and negative speaker, the form is still a realized extension of his character. The internal relations in "Praise" (II) are rather different, in that the form seems to argue with the literal meaning. The attitudes of the two speakers are similar in their general outlines, but this only reminds us that similar attitudes need not always express themselves in similar harmonies of form and meaning.

"Justice" (II) corroborates this generalization, for although it ends with an explicit statement of hope, the hopefulness is only vaguely realized when compared with the specific and stately pictures of torture. The poem is divided in half: two stanzas describe the torture awaiting the poet and two describe his hoped-for redemption. The first part is magisterial:

> O Dreadfull Justice, what a fright and terrour
> Wast thou of old,
> When sinne and errour
> Did show and shape thy looks to me,
> And through their glasse discolour thee!
> He that did but look up, was proud and bold.
>
> The dishes of thy ballance seem'd to gape,
> Like two great pits;
> The beam and scape
> Did like some torturing engine show;
> Thy hand above did burn and glow,
> Danting the stoutest hearts, the proudest wits.
>
> (1–12)

The imagery derives much of its strength from the combination of a broad field of view and a fine resolution of detail; it has the simultaneous breadth and minute clarity of a Piranesi prison etching. This effect of heightened detail is directly referred to in the fourth line: we are to see a "show" with some elements of artificial heightening. The speaker's imagining power is not at work only in the slow detail of his *pittura metafisica*,[10] for the meters and syntax also help draw out the terror. The slow syntactic movement one associates with the more somber passages of the Old Version is particularly effective here. In the first stanza, for example, the dangling *to me* helps draw attention to the speaker's pride and boldness; as the next stanza testifies, he was one of those who dared to look up. The general lack of active verbs, the emphasis on the intensives, and the slight suggestion of three feminine rhymes (*terrour/ errour/ discolour thee*) all slow the stanza and build the tension. However, the last line has some rather intricate footwork that is typically Herbertian:

He that did but look up, was proud and bold.

The sudden contraction in the middle gives the line its surprise and emphasizes the dead march of stanza 2. To remark that the imagery of that scene is solemn is only to identify God's *balance,* and for Christians there is only one *torturing engine.* It is reassuring nonetheless to have Tuve point out that medieval commentators on Scripture long identified the Cross with the balance used in judging men's souls: "The basic concept is the weighing by the just Father of man's sins in one dish against the sufferings of Christ as Man—so that when the Crucifixion took place the sufferings in their dish completely outweighed the sins, and the *just* verdict can be in favour of man's salvation."[11] However, much of the torturing engine is of Herbert's own make. The two significant details that Herbert has added are the *pits* at the ends of the balance arms and the red-hot hand that is holding the balance. It is hard to ignore the infernal tendencies of the imagery, and Herbert's picture of *both* sides of the balance as gaping pits is not indicative of a right-thinking Christian spirit: either way he faces a flaming deliverance. The scene is hardly the objective or ideal medieval picture of redemption that Tuve implied that it is but a vision of the proud and bold spirit who has heightened his perceptions in a controlled style. That the speaker takes the scene to have a very personal application is indicated in the last line of this stanza, "Danting the

[10] The psychology of the term is explained by Wolfgang Kayser in *The Grotesque in Art and Literature,* trans. Ulrich Weisstein (Bloomington: Indiana University Press, 1963), pp. 168–73.

[11] Tuve, *A Reading of George Herbert,* p. 165; the discussion of the sources continues to p. 168.

stoutest hearts, the proudest wits." As we have noticed, in stanza 1 he
also identified himself as proud and bold.

Much of the cumulative horror of the scene in stanza 2 comes from
its steady rhythms; again the intensive verbs slow the action, and
there is a predominance of falling rhythms in key phrases to insure
the stability of the metric: "The dishes of thy ballance," "some torturing engine," "the stoutest hearts, the proudest wits." These prevent
any ambiguity in stressing and give the vision its steadiness. The verb
structures themselves are broken up in the heavy, naive manner of
Hopkins, with the auxiliaries placed in the middle of the lines and
the verbs used for rhymes.

But we should not go so far as to say that the verse method of these
stanzas suggests a complete naiveté, a sense of relief and self-congratu-
lation at having passed a major crisis in faith. The terror has a considerable reality, especially when set off against the two stanzas that
follow and attempt to resolve the dilemma:

> But now that Christs pure vail presents the sight,
> I see no fears:
> Thy hand is white,
> Thy scales like buckets, which attend
> And interchangeably descend,
> Lifting to heaven from this well of tears.
>
> For where before thou still didst call on me,
> Now I still touch
> And harp on thee.
> Gods promises have made thee mine;
> Why should I justice now decline?
> Against me there is none, but for me much.

(13–24)

Our chief difficulty here is in deciding exactly what the speaker is
describing and how he views his own relations to divine justice. Even
Tuve was bothered by the conclusion, referring to it as "cloudy" and
"somewhat illogical."[12] At least the images themselves have some
history that holds out the promise of our understanding the poem:

---

[12] *Ibid.*, p. 164. The following explication of Christian imagery is drawn from
Tuve. One problem in "Justice" (II) is that the imagery is quite free, in the
sense that Herbert does not present it with *a priori* moral judgment. That
would considerably simplify iconographical interpretation. As an instance of dead
imagery, fairly smothered under moral tags, see the second stanza of "Vanitie" (I).

Christ's "veil, that is to say, his flesh" (Hebrews 10:20) removes the speaker's fears of divine justice, and the veil of Christ is itself traditionally a symbol of the New Dispensation. How all of this is poured into the image of the well, and what that is in itself, in this poem, neither Tuve nor anyone else has explained satisfactorily. Further, how all of this is related to the speaker's attitude toward justice is not immediately clear. Tuve said that "he can call for and be saved by the operation of that very justice he had feared."[13] But this is taking some small liberties with the next-to-last line, in which the speaker only asks why he should decline justice. In the face of Tuve's most ingenious typological analysis, the meaning of the poem still seems intensely personal.

Perhaps the style and form of the stanzas will tell us something about the speaker's attitudes toward the scene. The "Christs pure vail" stanza is rhythmically unlike those that have preceded it; it lacks the resonant and regular stresses of the previous lines and is considerably more hesitant and exploratory in its meters. The movement of the caesura is important in this, for it creates some effect of dissolving the fomerly rigid pattern, especially in the third stanza. The long and leisurely motion of the lines is appropriate to the subject and to the speaker's proclaimed relaxation. There is another element of fantasy, though, or perhaps fancy, in the transformation of the cross into the well. Hutchinson has pointed out (p. 527) the resemblance of the image to a similar passage in *Richard II*; and like Richard, the speaker is a poet, who is "making" or "presenting a sight," that is, making an imaginative object from his own humiliation. Accordingly, the images in the stanza reveal the poet's attitude toward the scene and toward himself.

The third stanza is graceful by comparison with the first two, and its more heightened theatrical quality owes much of its effect to the gliding rhythms. The run-on fourth line in particular and the long lightly stressed *interchangeably*, a resonant polysyllable worthy of Richard, create a sense of suspension before the final stanza. The fourth stanza then asserts God's mercy and the speaker's need of it,

[13] *Ibid.*, p. 167. As Tuve admits (pp. 165–66 and n. 25), much of her commentary is based on studies which have been generally refuted. One difficulty in reading poems of this sort in terms of earlier poems and prose "sources" is that Herbert's poetic often depends as much on what is left out as on what is said. As Ellrodt says, "ce qui est charactéristique chez ce poète, c'est la réticence de l'expression: il dit presque toujours moins qu'il ne pense ou qu'il ne sent, et *il en a a conscience*" (*L'Inspiration*, 1: 307, Ellrodt's italics).

but the rhythm and metric of the stanza have more in common with
the picture of torture than the picture of redemptive grace. Certainly
the speaker does not reject divine justice; his rhetorical question only
seems to imply the declarative statement lurking within it: "Why
should I justice now decline?" Why do I decline it, or what is there
to stop me: the latter may be intended but the former is unavoidable
because of the long syntax that wobbles out to place a stress on
decline. We have looked at structures of this kind in the Old Version;
usually they manage to suggest all the wrong things, by means of inverted syntax that stresses the improper word. Here, it is somewhat
harder to say what is intended. It is an oblique way to ask for justice,
if that is actually what the speaker is doing, and the vague last line
does not give us much leverage: "Against me there is none, but for me
much." The poet may not desire the wrath of God, but his imagination is much more fully aroused by it than by His mercy.

The fact that the speaker *still* touches and harps on justice is connected with a theological problem that the poem has sidestepped, and
it seems to be in this area that the speaker's irresolution is centered.
There is a similarity between the speaker's argument and Luther's
description of the discovery that was to change his—and Europe's—
life. In 1513 or 1514, while working on his lectures on the Psalms
(*ubique formidable*), Luther says that he "was absorbed by a passionate
desire to understand Paul in his epistle to the Romans."

> Nothing stood in my way but that one expression, "The justice
> of God is revealed in the Gospel" (Romans 1:17). For I hated
> those words, "the justice of God," because I had been taught to
> understand them in the scholastic sense as the formal or active
> justice whereby God, who is righteous, punishes unrighteous sin-
> ners . . . . Then I began to understand that this "justice of God"
> is the righteousness by which the just man lives through the free
> gift of God . . . . Thereupon I felt as if I had been born again
> and had entered Paradise through wide-open gates. Immediately
> the whole of Scripture took on a new meaning for me . . . .
> Whereas the expression "the justice of God" had filled me with
> hate before, I now exalted it as the sweetest of phrases with all
> the more love.[14]

[14] Quoted and translated by E. Harris Harbison, *The Christian Scholar in the
Age of the Reformation* (New York: Charles Scribner's Sons, 1956), p. 120.
Harbison has a helpful analysis of the passage on pp. 120 ff. Herbert had a con-
siderable respect for the thought of the German Reformation; see "The Church
Militant," ll. 79–88.

Of course I have omitted the description of what provided the key to Luther's understanding, and it is quite pertinent to "Justice" (II); in the middle of the passage quoted above, Luther says,

> after I had pondered the problem for days and nights, God took pity on me and I saw the inner connection between the two phrases, "The justice of God is revealed in the Gospel" and "The just shall live by faith." . . . The justice "revealed" in the Gospel is the passive justice of God by which He takes pity on us and justifies us by our faith, as it is written, "The just shall live by faith."

I should like to suggest that in "Justice" (II) the hesitation of the speaker, as it is revealed in his style, is the result of something like a missing middle term in his reasoning. A familiar passage in the Book of John has Herbert's metaphor of lifting and states the one condition of Christ's redemption that the speaker has avoided:

> No man can come to me, except the Father which hath sent me to draw him: and I will raise him up at the last day . . . Verily, verily, I say unto you, He that believeth on me hath everlasting life.
>
> (6: 44, 47)

Even more to the point is Herbert's own prose statement on the subject; in one of his notes on Valdesso, he remarks, quite as precisely as Luther, that

> it is Faith and Infidelity that shall judge us now since the Gospell, and that no other sin or vertue hath any thing to do with us; if we believe, no sinne shall hurt us; if we believe not, no vertue shall helpe us. Therefore [Valdesso] saith here, we shall not be punished (which word I like here better than chastizement, because even the godly are chastized but not punished) for evill doing nor rewarded for weldoing or living, for all the point lies in believing or not believing.
>
> (311, 22–30)

The magnificent dramatic tension of "Justice" (II) seems to me to result largely from the distance between the style and the whole logical necessity of belief, which is essential to the speaker's salvation. The elements of bathos in the syntax also carry the omissions in the idea. The ideas do not advance as far as the style; but the poem does show how very well Herbert could follow the curve of his own reflexes.

As modern readers we are disposed to feel that the artist who confidently proclaims a belief in some ordering principle is actually sunk in despair at the thought of the principle, or fears that his principle is collapsing. It might be well to point out that "Justice" (II) does not express any doubt about the ordering principle but only about its application. Notwithstanding the role of the tentative form, the poem still affirms its ordering principle; nothing has been "put in doubt," in Donne's phrase, except the speaker's immortality. This is quite enough to put in doubt, but there is little if any evidence in his work, that Herbert doubted the general assumptions of his faith. The bulk of the evidence indeed goes so far the other way that it may be no overstatement to say that Herbert's proclamations of despair are usually supported by a reasoned confidence in, if not a personal cure for, the despair itself. He nearly always intuits a larger controlling purpose within which his despair serves some coherent function. There is a kind of faith in his poetic form itself at its origin in the *logos*.

"Longing" is a convenient illustration of this, and the way in which it employs alternating bathetic and elegant styles says something about the poem's final intention. As in numerous Psalms, the speaker laments his being forgotten utterly, but this poet is longing for good rhyme and meter as well as God's love:

> My throat, my soul is hoarse;
> My heart is wither'd like a ground
> Which thou dost curse.
> My thoughts turn round,
> And make me giddie; Lord, I fall,
> Yet call.

> (7–12)

I shall have to limit my quotations because the poem is rather long. This example can show, however, how the rhetorical movement of the stanza, like that of each of the first three stanzas, is all toward self-dramatization. The motion of the lines is as openly pitiable as the idea. The regular meter is chopped up by the numerous pauses, and the rude bump of the final rhyme seems designed to emphasize the lack of poetic coordination attendant upon the speaker's state.

These may not seem to be important points until we move to the fourth stanza, in which we see the speaker adopting a different and

more graceful style for his address to God. The short, rhyming lines
now become run-on and energetic:

> Bowels of pitie, heare!
> Lord of my soul, love of my minde,
>   Bow down thine eare!
>   Let not the winde
> Scatter my words, and in the same
>   Thy name!
>
>   (19–24)

The method is generally quite similar to what we noticed in Sidney's
Psalm 6:

> Mercy, O Mercy lord, for Mercy's sake,
>   For death can kill the Witness of thy glory;
> Can of thy prayse the tongues entombed make
>   A heavnly story?
>
>   (13–16)

Herbert's speaker continues in this vein for two more stanzas, in a
series of extended parallelisms and sweeps across the line-ends:

> Look on my sorrows round!
> Mark well my furnace! O what flames,
>   What heats abound!
>   What griefs, what shames!
>
>   (25–28)

> Lord Jesu, thou didst bow
> Thy dying head upon the tree:
>   O be not now
>   More dead to me!
>
>   (31–34)

If Old Version style is characterized by its insistently regular meters
and forced rhymes, this devotional style is characterized by its lyric
flexibility-within-regularity of meter and by its pressure against the
stanza form through enjambment and varied placement of pauses
within the lines. The manner that Herbert's speaker now uses in his
direct appeal is quite different from his earlier manner in self-descrip-

tion, and he is not unaware of this, for he stresses that the performance is for the benefit of God-as-poet. The italics are Herbert's:

> Lord heare! *Shall he that made the eare,*
> > *Not heare?*
>
> > > (35–36)

Maybe this is an ultimatum, or maybe it is only a way of guiding, by
means of direct reference to the style, the speaker's attention toward
God. It might be a craftsman's equivalent of a formal meditation
upon God, in which the speaker, after composing the ground of his
relation to God, ultimately rises out of his state to a direct colloquy.
At this point in "Longing," the practice is elaborated only on the
level of style, perhaps another sign of Herbert's "dominance of sensibility over intellect."

After this appeal, however, Herbert changes his direction, breaking
the colloquy and returning to his abject state:

> Behold, thy dust doth stirre,
> It moves, it creeps, it aims at thee:
> > Wilt thou deferre
> > To succour me,
> Thy pile of dust, wherein each crumme
> > Sayes, Come?
>
> > > (37–42)

The depravity of this, or the weak diet upon which the stanza formally subsists, bears a resemblance to the lame negations of Sternhold
and Hopkins:

> They shall heape sorrowes on their heds,
> > which run as they were mad:
> To offer to the Idoll Gods,
> > alas it is to bad.
>
> > > (Ps. 16:3)

There is no particular similarity in content, but there is in rhythm,
and in the conjunction of lame, almost defective rhyme (*crumme/
come*) and bathetic idea (How long can you stand to look at me).
"Longing" continues to plod on in this flat manner for five stanzas,

almost as if Herbert's speaker were determined to wear down his Creator with the heavy resonance of his stanza. This sort of strategy is not without its intellectual limits, and it also creates a dramatic situation that is static.

Herbert may have realized this problem intuitively, or perhaps more consciously decided to make a dramatic shift in style at the end of the poem. In the closing two stanzas, the speaker's situation, arguments, and pleas remain the same, but are voiced with an eloquence which is unlike his formerly bathetic falterings:

> Lord JESU, heare my heart,
> Which hath been broken now so long,
>> That ev'ry part
>> Hath got a tongue!
> Thy beggars grow; rid them away
>>> To day.
>
> My love, my sweetnesse, heare!
> By these thy feet, at which my heart
>> Lies all the yeare,
>> Pluck out thy dart,
> And heal my troubled breast which cryes,
>>> Which dyes.
>
>>>> (73–84)

There are still some elements of confusion and disorder here: the image in the first of these stanzas is not one which a decorous or literal-minded reader would be likely to approve—one could imagine what Dr. Johnson would do with it; and in the second stanza the heart with tongues becomes a wounded animal (a hart). Nonetheless, there is a final organization to these stanzas which is able to control this sort of confusion and make it not irrelevant but meaningful. Earlier the poet had characterized his words as wind-scattered fragments, and their change to their present status, as a mob of Lilliputian tongues, is an accurate metaphor for the changes in the poem's style. Most of the bathos of image in these stanzas is subsumed under the Sidneyan exuberance of rhetoric. The relatively high number of lightly stressed syllables in the lines, along with the enjambment in the middle of the stanzas, create a final surge that achieves the coordination the speaker desires, even though he says he has not achieved it. Herbert has perhaps instinctively shown the direction his cure must take, by drawing together the two strands of his rhetoric. And for this, as far as I know, we may find no models in either the Old Version or Sidneyan psalms, even though they may have, on the simple level, some of the same themes.

The tentative form of "Longing" is by no means singular, and it might be helpful to show how Herbert can arrive at similar ends by both similar and different processes. The interplay between Sidneyan grace and rhetoric, and Old Version overstatement and fumbling, is one of Herbert's most consistent concerns. But it is necessary to stress that throughout *The Temple* there does not seem to be any consistency in the way that the grace and fumbling are deployed. That is, it is not possible to abstract a meaning from either of the styles considered singly. Each poem carries with it its own set of critical questions, and even though some of these sets of questions overlap, the style is always integrated with the images, for example, and their hieratic functions. It is still possible to generalize to some extent on the relations between poetic style and dramatic intention, for Herbert does tend to employ speakers whose situations are usually implied by their styles. We have seen that simpler assertions of faith often appear in the phrasing of the Old Version, and that the more complex outbursts or complaints often appear in Sidneyan phrasing. But even this formula is subject to modifications; Herbert never seems to attempt successive approximations to a theme, as did, say, Wordsworth. Even when he uses the same stylistic materials in two poems, their employment will usually be different.

An instructive case in point is "The Banquet." As in "Longing," Herbert plays short lines off against long, but now with very different motives. The stanza of "The Banquet," we have noted before, is the same as that of Sidney's Psalm Thirty-eight, and there are perhaps some verbal echoes of another of Sidney's psalms, the Thirteenth. As is frequently the case with Herbert's borrowings, the contexts of the two poems are reversed. Psalm 13 is a sustained assertion of the speaker's miseries, and its central point might be expressed as "Find me!" "The Banquet," one of Herbert's poems on Communion, is concerned on the contrary with the working out, here and now, of Christ's sacrifice: "I have been found (and found out)." The miseries of Herbert's speaker have been or are being relieved by the agency of the bread and wine. "The Banquet" properly comes after Psalm 13;

it is a sequel to the recitation of earthly miseries, and its style is
naturally different from that of the Psalm. As we have noticed before,
the querulousness and anguish of Sidney's speaker are conveyed by
his style of complaint; his hopes rise and fall with his rhymes.

> Behold me, lord, let to thy hearing creep
>> My crying:
> May give me eyes, and light, least that I sleep
>> In dying.

Herbert's speaker, on the other hand, is full of authority and grace:

> Doubtlesse, neither starre nor flower
>> Hath the power
> Such a sweetnesse to impart:
> Onely God, who gives perfumes,
>> Flesh assumes,
> And with it perfumes my heart.
>
> (19–24)

In each case, the tone is a direct function of the statement; the false
starts and stops in Sidney's syntax and the assured motion in Herbert's
are functions of their respective misery and happiness. Even though
both use short lines for contrast, they use them in different ways.
Sidney's short lines are rhythmic extensions of the longer lines and
make no unexpected associations; but the end of Herbert's stanza has
a quirky bathos in rhyme—"who gives perfumes,/Flesh assumes"—
which keeps the speaker firmly on the ground in spite of his acceptance of the Eucharist. Perhaps the ambiguity of *assumes*, which tele-
scopes God's assumption of flesh and the speaker's acquisition of
physical knowledge of the Presence, is what most distinguishes the
technique of Herbert's short line from Sidney's.

More interesting than this, however, are the different ways in which
the two poets handle their closes. Herbert seems to have appropriated
Sidney's rhyme, but it is a theft, and not a borrowing, for he has put
it straight to his own use:

> Let the wonder of his pitie
>> Be my dittie,
> And take up my lines and life:

> Hearken under pain of death,
>   Hands and breath;
> Strive in this, and love the strife.
>
>   (49–54)

Sidney's close has the same sense of committing oneself to God in song:

> No, no I trust on thee, and joy in Thy
>   Great Pity.
> Still therfore of Thy graces shall be my
>   Song's Ditty.

Pitie/dittie is not an inevitable rhyme, although at first it might seem so; Herbert uses *wittie/dittie* twice (in "The Sacrifice," 141–42, and in "The Forerunners," 11–12). The rhyme in "The Banquet" is not phonologically inevitable but logically fitting for a lyric poet preoccupied with the subject of divine mercy. The heavy rhythms of the last three lines of Herbert's stanza draw off some of the falling lightness of the feminine rhyme, and although the parallel structure at the end of the stanza is typical of the Psalms in its repetition, its conciseness owes more to the Sidneys than to the Old Version; Sternhold would have written, "Eke struggle so, and love thy strife."

The tightness and pressure of Herbert's lines represent one permutation of Sidney's grace. There never was any limit to the number of combinations available for an ear as fine as Herbert's: his ability to coordinate short lines with long in an almost endless number of ways can only be proposed, not demonstrated. Thus in the use of tentative patterns, Herbert never needs to rely on the same movement to prepare for a conclusion, even though he may not be handling new materials. "Affliction" (I), for example, follows a course generally similar to that of "Longing" but is quite different in many details. Our comments may be brief: after the first four stanzas, which move gracefully and elegantly as the poet traces the way he was "enticed unto thee" (10), the verse plunges into broken rhythms and clogged syntax, one of the most familiar examples of this conjunction being the following:

> When I got health, thou took'st away my life,
>   And more; for my friends die:
> My mirth and edge was lost; a blunted knife

> Was of more use then I.
> Thus thinne and lean without a fence or friend,
> I was blown through with ev'ry storm and winde.
>
> (31–36)

The first four lines of the stanza have a metric structure that is quite close to that of the hymn and Common Meter, but the divisions in the thought are not so firm, in spite of the heavy diction. This sort of broken movement continues to the end, where the speaker verges on resolution only to make his bizarre appeal:

> Yet, though thou troublest me, I must be meek;
>   In weakenesse must be stout.
> Well, I will change the service, and go seek
>   Some other master out.
> Ah my deare God! though I am clean forgot,
> Let me not love thee, if I love thee not.
>
> (61–66)

The speaker's agony seems at first projected into a final state of indecision. Although the last line seems paradoxical, it is actually a unified statement; the real paradox appears when it is played off against the second half of the preceding line. "Though I am clean forgot" contradicts the last line in its stand toward God, just as the first two lines in the stanza contradict the second two. If the poet feels that God has clean forgotten him, there would be no point in asking God anything. The quatrain has the balance of a couplet: after writing six broken and disordered stanzas, the speaker has finally worked into a balanced (or at least antithetical!) stanza. The balancing antitheses show that an order is evolving in the speaker's mind, and it is not the order of the first three stanzas. Many critics have cited the biographical relevance of much of the poem, particularly the opening,[15] but have failed to note that the development of the form has as much biographical relevance as the literal statements. The style begins with a courtly grace and sweep and after a period of disorder comes under the control of an order which attempts to state, in as radically simple a

---

[15] See, for example, L. C. Knights, *Explorations* (London and New York: George Stewart, 1947), pp. 141–44; Joan Bennett, *Four Metaphysical Poets*, 2d ed. (New York: Vintage Books, 1958), pp. 63 *et passim*; White, *The Metaphysical Poets*, p. 159.

fashion as possible, the contradiction that has been present all along in the speaker's mind. In circumstances such as these, the form of the poem, as it works out across the subject, may have some right to claim a biographical relevance. Certainly the poem's technique implies, in its development, the same sort of expansion through limitation that Herbert was to find in his life.

This method can be carried one step further, and must be, if we wish to see the full integrity of Herbert's faith and craftsmanship. If we recognize that the form of a poem can have truths to tell that the statement cannot, we shall find that even the downward side of Herbert's devotion is permeated with a faith and confidence. There is no finer example of this than "The Flower."

Most of the poem reflects a quietly amazed consciousness of renewal; the speaker feels the beneficent presence of God by using an extended metaphor that compares himself to a flower and God to the elements. The drama of the poem consists in its placement in time, within this metaphor: the still thawing of winter yields to the growth and storms of spring. Both the narrative and the verse itself create the speaker's character. Technically the stanza has that uniquely Herbertian quality of order and surprise: an alternately rhymed tetrameter-pentameter quatrain, followed by a dimeter couplet and a last tetrameter line rhyming with the pentameters above. One immediate advantage of the stanza is its ability to move from rigidity to looseness; there is also an appropriateness in the last long rhyming line, which formally has the same surprising restorative quality the speaker notes in himself.

The declines and restorations in the chronology of the poem are swift: in the first stanza the speaker marvels at his reawakening; in the second he recalls his dormancy; in the third he links the "killing and quickning" with God, implying that the process is humanly understandable, and in the fourth he desires to transcend the whole process; the fifth shows him in a drastic decline, and the sixth totally recovered; in the final stanza he appears to realize that the whole cycle is inevitable and a necessary part of entering God's "garden."[16] This zigzag course is mirrored in the stanza form and in the different ways in

---

[16] In "Time and *The Temple*," *SEL*, 6 (1966): 97–110, Stanley Stewart suggests that this poem reveals much of Herbert's attitude toward time in general and thus the three divisions of *The Temple*. Time in "The Flower" is also discussed by Earl Miner, in *The Metaphysical Mode from Donne to Cowley* (Princeton: Princeton University Press, 1969), pp. 231–46.

which that form is used. The stanzas describing the speaker's decline are close and contracted rhythmically, while those describing his restoration are expansive. When the speaker describes his dormant state, the verse has a compactness of thought and rhythm that is based on numerous parallel structures crossing over the stanza's divisions:

> Who would have thought my shrivel'd heart
> Could have recovered greennesse? It was gone
> Quite under ground; as flowers depart
> To see their mother-root, when they have blown;
> Where they together
> All the hard weather,
> Dead to the world, keep house unknown.
>
> (8–14)

The ideas in the quatrain, for example, cut across the line-ends and the middle of the quatrain, where, as we have seen, Herbert is often prone to set up divisions in his thought, at least when working toward some sort of logical synthesis. The last three lines show a similar cross-knitting. The two stringing adverbial modifiers

> . . . they together
> All the hard weather,
> Dead to the world . . .

demand that the last three lines be considered as a logical unit. The whole clause in the last three lines is also related grammatically to the quatrain above. Herbert's thought here is dense, compact, "quite underground." The rhythms assist in creating some of this contraction by combining a relatively high number of run-on lines and reversed initial feet:

> Whó would have thought my shrivel'd heart
>
> Cóuld have recovered greennesse? It was gone
>
> Quĭte únder ground; as flowers depart
>
> To see their mother-root, when they have blown;
>
> Whére they together

All the hard weather,

Dead to the world, keep house unknown.

Style of this sort has little to do with the popular metrical psalm; the
stress shifts are muscular and certain, and the symbol is used with a
fairly stern regard for its physical properties.

What constitutes the special interest of "The Flower" for our purposes is that after this stanza, Herbert begins to loosen all the rhythms
and tends to open the thought more along the clefts of the stanza:

And now in age I bud again,
After so many deaths I live and write;
I once more smell the dew and rain,
And relish versing: O my onely light,
It cannot be
That I am he
On whom thy tempests fell all night.

(36–42)

One is reluctant even to comment on this, one of the most widely
quoted and admired stanzas in all Herbert. Herbert has managed the
falling rhythms by placing them within a formally iambic line, and
the looseness of the metric allows the last three lines to depend from
the quatrain, just as the storms of the previous night seem very distant
from the poet's restoration the next day. The integrity of rhythm and
meaning in the stanza precludes any analysis that would concentrate
on either alone; Herbert's idea seems bodied forth directly in the
technique to a degree extraordinary even for him. It is not surprising
to hear one thoughtful critic simply resign himself to the stanza, saying that "this is, I suppose, the most perfect and most vivid stanza in
the whole of Herbert's work."[17]

But a preoccupation with its flow and grace may lead us away from
the larger truth of the poem and its style as a whole. There is, after
all, one stanza that comes after stanza 6, and a fine one it is. Its intent
is to transcend the whole cyclical movement, or more exactly, move
through it and beyond:

[17] A. Alvarez, *The School of Donne* (London: Chatto & Windus, 1961), p. 67.

These are thy wonders, Lord of love,
To make us see we are but flowers that glide:
Which when we once can finde and prove,
Thou hast a garden for us, where to bide.
Who would be more,
Swelling through store,
Forfeit their Paradise by their pride.

(43–49)

The speaker proposes a state reached only by knowledge of, and passage through, the processes of human change. Temporal change is the inevitable prelude to growth into eternity. On this subject the verse technique of the last stanza presents some material of its own. The thought of the lines is rhythmically regular, sober and steady, and there is a close observance of the breaks suggested by the stanza form. This is an order which is not common to the rest of the poem. However, the lines are still compressed and full of ironies: "Lord of love" contrasts with the burning anger that had withered the speaker one stanza before, and it also contrasts with the statement that we must "finde and prove" our identities. As the poem has shown, this is only possible experientially; we cannot avoid being drenched and scorched by the Lord of love.

When the final considered judgment of the poem is added in the last three lines, on top of these ironies, it seems curiously detached and negative:

Who would be more,
Swelling through store,
Forfeit their Paradise by their pride.

The subject, the "who" who would, is at first unclear, for the speaker himself has not been hoping or even thinking of harvest; he has been living hand-to-mouth through all the hard weather. What seems to have happened is that the reference of the poem has expanded to include the nature of all men and all life processes, while the style has drawn back to a more conventional and authoritative form. The ground seems to be shifting uncertainly beneath us, and the compression of the thought and heaviness of meter seem to carry us back more in the direction of the "dead of the world" stanzas than to the manner

of budding growth. Does this mean that Herbert visualizes his paradise
in the form of decay or dormancy?

Herbert's point here may be clarified by what is perhaps the most
widely quoted biblical text on flowers, verse 15 of Psalm 103: "As for
man, his days are as grass: as a flower of the field, so he flourisheth."
(Oddly enough, this is the only time the generic term *flower* appears
in the Psalms.) Both the Psalm and Herbert's poem deal with the
paradoxes of sin and love, death and regeneration. More important,
both are concerned with the central paradox of a God who heals and
gives life by killing. Psalm 103 in fact contains nothing that is not in
Herbert's poem, while Herbert's poem contains much that is not in
the Psalm.

The resemblances between "The Flower" and Psalm 103 are evident
enough that their exposition need not be lengthy. The psalmist blesses
the Lord for His mercies ("who forgiveth all thine iniquities; who
healeth all thy diseases," 3) and praises his gift of immortality ("thy
youth is renewed like the eagle's," 5). He notes that "the Lord is
merciful and gracious, slow to anger, and plenteous in mercy" (8), but
like Herbert he also realizes that "neither will he keep his anger for
ever" (9). However, the Lord "pitieth them that fear him" (13); and
remembering that we are dust and flourish only like a flower, He will
be merciful "to such as keep His covenant" (18). Therefore the Lord
should be blessed by his angels, his hosts and ministers, and the
psalmist's own soul.

In its broad outlines moving from praise to recognition of weakness
and divine anger, then back to praise, the psalm mirrors the movement of "The Flower," without its final stanza. Augustine emphasizes
that the Psalm ends as it begins,[18] and the observation is equally valid
when applied to Herbert's poem if, again, it is considered without its
final stanza. One curiosity of the printing of "The Flower" is pertinent
here: its final stanza is sometimes deleted by anthologists.[19] The
reasons for this are not far to seek. So modified, the poem is better
balanced formally, and without the dogmatism of the last stanza the
tone is more purely lyrical.

[18] *Expositions on the Book of Psalms*, ed. A. Cleveland Coxe, in Nicene and
Post-Nicene Fathers of the Christian Church, vol. 8 (Grand Rapids, Mich.: Eerdmans, 1956), p. 510a.

[19] As in *The English Galaxy of Shorter Poems*, ed. Gerald Bullett (London:
Everyman's Library, 1939), p. 254. Aldous Huxley does the same in *Texts and
Pretexts* (New York: Harper & Bros., 1933), p. 13.

I would now like to return to that stanza and consider its craft in the light of Augustine's commentary on the Psalm. The most evident contrast in the stanza is that between the collocation of "These are thy wonders, Lord of love," and the last three lines. The lyric clarity of the first four lines of the stanza has been amply discussed by Arnold Stein;[20] I would like to add that the break in syntax at the end of the fourth line is an especially important one. One could not have guessed that those particular last three lines would end the stanza and the poem; they are, by virtue of their flat assertion, out of character with the endings of the previous stanzas. And Herbert has gone to extraordinary pains to emphasize the final lurch of the stanza: in the last line alone, for example, the initial reversed foot, the alliteration, the heavy elision in *Paradise*, the repetition of *their*, and the internal rhymes in *di, pride*, and *by*, all interlock to give the line a weight and mass that resemble nothing else in the poem. These elements of style and the dogmatism of the sentiment point more to the Old Version than to the neo-Arcadian effusions of the preceding stanzas.

Clearly the last three lines are aimed at some big targets. They describe not merely the rejection of the life process or something of the sort but have implications more serious, more definitely satanic. The stages by which Herbert moves from the metaphor of the flower to the forfeiture of paradise through pride are made quite explicit by Augustine. In his reading of the flower passage in Psalm 103, Augustine becomes positively lyrical as he works up to what is actually the central point of Herbert's poem and the leading motive of its final stanza:

> "For he flourisheth as the flower of the field." The whole splendour of the human race; honour, power, riches, pride, threats, is the flower of the grass. . . . In how brief a season do flowers pass away, and these are the beauty of the herbs! This which is so very beautiful, this quickly falleth. Inasmuch then as He knoweth as a father of our forming, that we are but grass, and can only flourish for a time; He sent unto us His Word, and His Word, which abideth for evermore, He hath made a brother unto the grass which abideth not. . . . How great then is the hope of the grass, since the Word hath been made flesh? That which abideth for evermore, hath not disdained to assume grass, that the grass might not despair of itself. In thy reflections therefore on thyself, think

---

[20] See Stein, *George Herbert's Lyrics* (Baltimore: Johns Hopkins Press, 1968), pp. 200–201.

of thy low estate, think of thy dust: be not lifted up: if thou art anything better, thou wilt be so by His Grace, thou will be so by His Mercy.[21]

The desire to escape the process of the flower would be the desire to escape what is no less than the resurrection itself; to be more than the mere flower would be to be more than God. That both Herbert and Augustine give this particular and almost gratuitous turn to the exemplum of the flower would seem to argue strongly for some association between the two.

But while the rationale of the ending is clear, the role of the style remains at odds with it. Although Augustine's comments clarify what Herbert is doing in his final stanza, they do not explain why Herbert chooses to stress the consequences of rejecting the resurrection in a suddenly heavy style rather than the joy of being resurrected in the considerably more graceful style of the previous stanzas. It seems likely that Herbert's vision of the garden takes that form because of his own absolute faith; his decay and dormancy are certainties, sensuously experienced and intellectually felt. When he moves out to areas beyond this direct experience, his craft and his faith may press him toward experiences and modes of expression that are as deeply felt and beyond question as these. The poem seems to close on a downward curve, but the way that the statement is made carries us up against and beyond the literal statement. To judge from the style, we must say that in Herbert's mind the connections between death and life are completely natural.

We might conclude our study of tentative form by observing a group of five poems, all of which use forms from the bathetic popular psalms in order to obscure their meanings. All have a lack of clarity which seems almost deliberately induced, in every case, by the faulty or incomplete parallel structures of the Old Version, its simultaneous dogmatism and vagueness, and the usual assortment of forced rhymes and meters. Further, all of these poems describe the speaker's position and attitudes by means of negations, much as many psalms attempt to describe a speaker by his invective against his enemies. Discussion of the poems in this manner is obviously not intended to be pejorative; a poet chooses the best tools he can, and different jobs require different tools.

---

[21] Augustine, *Expositions*, p. 509a.

The simplest of the lot is "The Familie," in which the first two stanzas describe the "house" of the poet's disordered heart, the next three the house of the orderly heart ruled by the Lord, and the last the conflict between the two. As the description of the two houses develops it becomes increasingly abstract, extending its thought into the suprarational, and then jumps back into the real with surprising consequences in form and meaning. The poet's disordered heart is pictured somewhat generally in terms of its commotion:

> What doth this noise of thoughts within my heart,
>> As if they had a part?
> What do these loud complaints and puling fears,
>> As if there were no rule or eares?
>
> (1–4)

The house of the heart ruled by the Lord is more substantial, in spite of its allegory, and the description renders godly behavior in everyday terms:

> First Peace and Silence all disputes controll,
>> Then Order plaies the soul;
> And giving all things their set forms and houres,
>> Makes of wilde woods sweet walks and bowres.
>
> Humble Obedience near the doore doth stand,
>> Expecting a command . . . .
>
> (9–14)

This well-ordered and domestic form continues its quiet tread, and the speaker seems to be realizing, in the sense of gaining, his goal of order and harmony. But the fifth stanza diverts some of this. Although the heart can be ordered, it is still after all human and perhaps susceptible to human ailments:

> Joyes oft are there, and griefs as oft as joyes;
>> But griefs without a noise:
> Yet speak they louder then distemper'd fears.
>> What is so shrill as silent tears?
>
> (17–20)

Distemper'd and *shrill*, as Canon Hutchinson glosses them (p. 525), denote "mental derangement" and "poignant," although the latter clearly implies the punning sense of "piercing (noise)" as well. These definitions are helpful, for they call to mind the fact that up to this point the whole drama, with its *loud complaints*, the *puling*, and the soul that *plaies*, is purely intellectual. That is, Herbert has conceived of the mind's maladies and cures in terms of noise and music, and when he now shifts to acts that speak louder than this noise, he seems to be shifting the context to one more remove. Louder than even an imaginary noise, the joys and griefs would seem to take place on some spiritual stage of illumination. The order seems something like that in a well-run sanitarium, and the otherworldly turn to the whole stanza is accompanied by the rather strange music of the shifting meters, repetition, and internal rhymes. The first line of the stanza is particularly notable in all of these respects, but although all of the lines seem bizarre by contrast with what has gone before, they are natural as an accompaniment for the jumpy logic.

Form and meaning in the last stanza float down again to earth; the ordered meter and tone return and are used to make a conjunction of meaning that presumably implicates the speaker:

> This is thy house, with these it doth abound:
> > And where these are not found,
> Perhaps thou com'st sometimes, and for a day;
> > But not to make a constant stay.
>
> > > > > > > > (21–24)

This is perfectly serious. The sobriety is impossible to mistake, being indicated in the strictness of the parallel grammar; but there is a certain fuzziness of meaning beneath which a tautology seems to be operating. The previous catlog was, we now learn, trout for factitious bait; and although the steady tread of the meter seems to lead somewhere, exactly where is uncertain. Partly by virtue of the preceding stanza, and partly by style, the last stanza to some extent allows the initial concern of the poem to drain off. All the world of the speaker, including his "loud complaints," seems suspended in wait for God's return, and the shifts in style are largely responsible for this. Instead of a parallel at the end, we are offered instead an ingenious circle. The words fly down, the thoughts remain above.

Minor curiosities of this sort are not uncommon in *The Temple*; most of them center around the parallel structures used throughout the Psalms, or more exactly, the imperfect parallel structures employed so often in the Old Version and other bathetic psalms. The device is quite suggestive, and Herbert does not seem to have been unaware of its possibilities for holding open a meaning. One very familiar example occurs in "Vertue" and is partially responsible for generating the many varied interpretations of the poem. I do not wish to explicate the poem but to point to its central difficulty and name it. The speaker of the poem, after describing the mutability of the day, the rose, and the spring, concludes that

> Onely a sweet and vertuous soul,
> Like season'd timber, never gives;
> But though the whole world turn to coal,
>   Then chiefly lives.

(13–16)

The knot of criticism that has formed about "Vertue" concerns itself largely with the problems of syntactic parallels and rhythm in this last stanza.[22] Is "never gives" an act of the soul or must it be mediated through the symbol? The meaning turns about the separation of the verb from its grammatic subject, a topic we have discussed at some

---

[22] Virtually every full-length study of Herbert has some remarks on the poem; periodical studies are numerous though mostly of the "note or query" sort. The content of the poem has been regarded as everything from platitudinous (White, *The Metaphysical Poets*, p. 184) to Ovidian (A. Davenport, "George Herbert and Ovid," *N & Q*, N.S. 2 [1955]: 98). Most readers ignore the bathetic compactness of the stanza, and typical of the enthusiastic overshot is George Williamson's comment, in *The Donne Tradition* (Cambridge: Harvard University Press, 1930): "What a sudden influx of stupendous and chilling thought is in that last line but one!" (p. 106). Michael F. Moloney, in *N & Q*, N.S. 1 (1954): 434–35, has closely regarded the rhetorical structure of the last stanza, but I believe he errs in describing it as "deliberately antithetical" (p. 434), when the syntax is not parallel and leaves the comparison open. Probably the neatest reading is that by Stein (*George Herbert's Lyrics*, pp. 178 ff.), although there are problems here; specifically, Stein notes that the last stanza has a "reversal of the imagistic pattern that leads from life to death," and although he notes the formal deliberation with which the metaphor is tagged as an example, he does not seem to apply the same scrutiny to the lacuna in syntactic form later in the stanza. In fact, if we accept Stein's comments on pp. 194–95, we may find some reason to believe that the syntactic problems themselves are a functional part of the poet's insistence on the fine separateness of the soul.

length in the previous chapter, although there we were not so concerned with the effects of vagueness produced by the practice. The problems of "then chiefly lives" are similar: Is the soul glowing like a red hot coal after the final fire, or during the fire, or must *lives* too be turned back through the metaphor? Even the terms upon which the metaphor must be laid out seem unclear, again because of the grammar which, by virtue of its parenthetical rhyming, is deceptively offhand. *But though* and *then* are not syntactically coordinate; and it is by means of this break that Herbert is able to set up the final diminishing metaphor, tangent at one point of meaning and opposed at all others. The *season'd timber* is apt to seem an arbitrary symbol when set beside the sweet day, sweet rose, and sweet spring, and the stylistic context of the stanza operates to keep it that way. We assume that the virtuous soul lives in death, and this can tell us at least what the timber *ought* to be doing; but it brings us no closer to solving the chemistry of the process.

Difficulties of a similar nature have obstructed the understanding of our three final poems, although in the case of these we feel more confident that there are coherent answers to the questions posed by the relation of form and meaning. These last and most impressive examples of tentative form are all poems which concern the subject of poetry: "The Quidditie" and the two "Jordan" poems. The Jordans in particular have been muddied, diverted, and dammed in the debate over the supposed tension, in Herbert, between sacred and profane poetry, and we might begin with "The Quidditie," the least critically clouded of the three. The poem is short enough to be quoted in full:

> My God, a verse is not a crown,
> No point of honour, or gay suit,
> No hawk, or banquet, or renown,
> Nor a good sword, nor yet a lute:
>
> It cannot vault, or dance, or play;
> It never was in *France* or *Spain;*
> Nor can it entertain the day
> With my great stable or demain:
>
> It is no office, art, or news,
> Nor the Exchange or busie Hall;
> But it is that which while I use
> I am with thee, and *most take all.*

The poem is morally Eleatic: its basic concern is the variety and multiplicity of worldly attachments, and its logical method is indirect, consisting of a whole string of discards. The aim is to assert that, for the speaker at least, the trivial multiplicity of the world is an impossible basis for existence. There is little appeal to logic except through the use of connected symbols, and these cover only a narrow range of experience, the adventures and recreations of the courtier, and the daily activities of the businessman.

The form of the poem is as tightly circumscribed as its social world. Herbert's range on both levels is narrow, the technical conventionality of the *a-b-a-b* quatrain being an analog to the range of choice before the speaker, although one is reluctant to press this point, since most of the early poems are regular as well. Herbert shows a remarkable ease in the form, particularly in the first two stanzas. The relative strictness of the end-stopping is no deterrent to Herbert's management of timing, for the lines swing and shift rhythmically within the iambic paradigm:

> My God, a verse is not a crown,
>
> No point of honour, or gay suit,
>
> No hawk, or banquet, or renown,
>
> Nor a good sword, nor yet a lute:
>
> It cannot vault, or dance, or play;
>
> It never was in *France* or *Spain;*
>
> Nor can it entertain the day
>
> With my great stable or demain . . .

The tone is never dogmatic, partly because of the timing and partly because the syntax is quite flexible. In the first stanza Herbert shifts from a negated verb to a series of adjectival clauses, not all parallel, and in the second stanza he shifts the verbs to indicate the imagined future, the imagined past, and the imagined present. The multiple forms of the grammar and the jigging speed of the last two lines make the intelligence jump as well as the ear.

As he closes in the final stanza, the style begins to change. This has almost become too much fun; while rejecting the vaulting, dancing, and playing, the poem goes on assimilating them in technique. On a small scale it is like Spenser's rejection of, and obvious pleasure in writing, the scenes in the Bower of Bliss. In the first two lines of the last stanza the speaker begins to come down to earth. The negations continue but are not present merely to fill out the time; the "office, art [cunning] or news" of the Exchange is the sober side of the worldly activity, and the businessman will preferably not be seen pirouetting behind his desk:

> It is no office, art, or news,
>
> Nor the Exchange, or busie Hall . . . .

The economy of the second line is to the point, considering the subject and the stanza as a whole, for now the verse becomes more regular and concludes in a most unusual line:

> But it is that which while I use
>
> I am with thee, and *most take all.*

The initial flurry of connectives is extraordinary. Such an excess is not a thing in nature, although it is common enough in the bathetic psalm. This may be part of Herbert's tendency, as we have noted frequently before, to adopt the more naive forms of bathos to express his faith, but I think the poem also shows an attempt to achieve on the level of style what is left vague in logic. Let us direct our attention to the last line. The stressing determines and is determined by the contrast in dramatic action: the suggestion is very strong that the speaker exists only when he is with God and that great flurries of motion, as from the courtier, do not in themselves establish one's existence. (Speech rhythms might argue a stress on *I*, but the rhythmic and tonal context of the whole poem seems very far from ordinary speech.) The form comes to involve not "most take all" but "most take least"; the movement of form in the stanza has set up a cross-current.

The last line itself, as F. P. Wilson pointed out, uses a little known proverb similar to that in "Providence" (1.52): "The great (fish) prey on (eat up) the little."[23] Wilson also proposed that the phrase is under-lined in the manuscripts and early editions in order to show that it is actually a borrowed proverb. One cannot but be indebted to Wilson's resourcefulness in tracing the proverbial line, but it seems to me that this evidence cannot be stretched so far as to assign any corresponding positive values to counter the mundane pleasures listed in the first two stanzas of the poem. Herbert, or the speaker, is only rejecting, not proposing—hence the ambiguity of *most*. Most what? the divine spirit, or the poet, or perhaps even (ironically) the great men invoked in the previous stanzas? And, as I have suggested, the phrase also has a stylis-tic referent. In any case, whatever specific values one assigns to the common symbols in the first two stanzas, they suggest no spiritual equivalents; the poem is not dedicated to God so much as to merely mundane activity. This may be why Herbert changed the title of the poem from "Poetry," in the Williams manuscript, to "The Quidditie." The word has two levels of meaning, and Herbert may have seen, when going over the poem some time after its composition, that he was looking at the quintessence of his being but also that in the colloquial sense he was being oversubtle and captious. Although the statement of the poem is not an assertion of the speaker's faith, the form presses on, to endow the poem with at least a stylistic authority.

Although the "Jordan" poems use different methods—different from those of "The Quidditie" and different from each other—they too have forms that gesture beyond literal statement. There is no need to dwell on the significance of the title, for the understanding of which previous criticism has defined two critical options. One uses the sym-bolism of the river Jordan to study Herbert's life, then takes that freshened biography back to the study of the poem.[24] The other some-what more plausibly explores Christian ideas of moral cleansing, particularly in the writing of sacred poetry.[25] I shall approach the

[23] "A Note on George Herbert's 'The Quidditie,'" *RES*, 9 (1943): 398.

[24] See, for example, Knights, *Explorations*, pp. 130 ff.; Summers, *George Herbert*, pp. 108 ff.; Margaret Bottrall, *George Herbert* (London: John Murray, 1954), pp. 121–22.

[25] See Tuve, *A Reading of George Herbert*, pp. 183–84, and Martz, *Poetry of Meditation*, pp. 259–60. Pertinent here is the suggestion by Valerie Carnes that, for Herbert, aesthetic experience as a whole is a trope for the Redemption; see "The Unity of George Herbert's *The Temple*: A Reconsideration," *ELH*, 35 (1968): 505–26. It is also true, however, that in some of its manifestations the aesthetic experience *per se* may be a means to a fall.

poems in a manner complementary to this second view. On the
literal and discursive level, both Jordan poems employ polemical
strategies similar to those we have already seen; on the level of style
and technique, however, they both resemble and differ from Herbert's
other poems on poetry.

On the surface "Jordan" (II) proceeds as does "The Quidditie," by
laying out a series of negations, but the connections between the negations and the assertions are much firmer logically:

> When first my lines of heav'nly joyes made mention,
> Such was their lustre, they did so excell,
> That I sought out quaint words, and trim invention;
> My thoughts began to burnish, sprout, and swell,
> Curling with metaphors a plain intention,
> Decking the sense, as if it were to sell.
>
> Thousands of notions in my brain did runne,
> Off'ring their service, if I were not sped:
> I often blotted what I had begunne;
> This was not quick enough, and that was dead.
> Nothing could seem too rich to clothe the sunne,
> Much lesse those joyes which trample on his head.
>
> As flames do worke and winde, when they ascend,
> So did I weave myself into the sense.
> But while I bustled, I might heare a friend
> Whisper, *How wide is all this long pretence!*
> *There is in love a sweetnesse readie penn'd:*
> *Copie out onely that, and save expense.*

As polemic this is more successful than "The Quidditie" because the
methods of secular verse are rejected on their own terms, if not *in*
them. In style, Herbert has almost precisely reversed the manner of
"The Quidditie," for here the rhythmic performance is regular and
steady in all but the last three lines. Even the description of the winding flames shows the calm of tranquil recollection. The rhythmic shift
that takes place in the last three lines seems natural and inevitable.
The effect is carefully plotted to produce a rise into ease that still
fits the context:

> As flames do worke and winde, when they ascend,
>
> So did I weave myself into the sense.

But while I bustled, I might heare a friend

Whisper, *How wide is all this long pretence!*

There is in love a sweetnesse readie penn'd:

Copie out onely that, and save expense.

If we listen to the poem's music, particularly in this passage, we may conclude that the "sweetnesse readie penn'd" has lyrically flexible lines, and the "quaint invention" has rhythmically workaday lines.[26] Louis Martz has pointed out that the poem has some thematic resemblances to Sidney's opening sonnet in *Astrophil and Stella*;[27] and indeed even the rhythms of the closing lines show a Sidneyan grace, when set over against the methodical and labored style in the lines above. The force of Herbert's poem derives from the interplay between the shift in style and the shift in content. In a way, the poem has something like an hourglass plot, in which lavish and ersatz-graceful ideas are set forth in a plain style and then are contrasted with plain ideas stated in a genuinely graceful style.

Granting that Herbert himself was capable of noticing this change, we shall not have to accept the conclusion that is sometimes reached, that Herbert did not really want to write poems like this. The position is state concisely by H. R. Swardson: "If the sweetness consists in what is 'readie penn'd' then the poet's skill and care as a 'maker' of the poem is just a "long pretense."[28] This is true if we assume that

---

[26] For this reason I find it difficult to agree with George Williamson's comment in *Six Metaphysical Poets: A Reader's Guide* (New York: Farrar, Straus & Giroux, 1967), p. 105: ". . . No invention or expression seems equal to his feeling of heavenly joy, and so he is lavish in poetic fictions, until the climax." The fictions may or may not be lavish; we do not know. We do know that the description of them is lavish, and we also know that the rhythms are as heavily labored as the speaker says the fictions are. The feeling of heavenly joy cannot exist apart from its description; and by that count the very joy that Herbert has to express is laborious and forced.

[27] Martz, *Poetry of Meditation*, pp. 261–62.

[28] Swardson, *Poetry and the Fountain of Light* (Columbia, Mo.: University of Missouri Press, 1962), p. 71. At this point it is quite easy to tie ourselves in knots; see, for example, Alicia Ostriker ("Song and Speech in the Metrics of George Herbert," *PMLA*, 80 [March 1965]: 65): "One finds, with lyrics like 'Complaining,' that while the words cause the mind quite properly to register despair, the sound and cadence of the words cause the ear to register delight." The truth of the matter is that despair may *be* delightful; this, a major component of the tragic emotion, is not peculiar to *The Temple*, nor do I see that Herbert has the slightest desire to keep us from feeling it.

"readie penn'd" implied for Herbert what it implies for us, as post-Romantics, that is, a completely spontaneous composition, or if we assume that the writer rather than the love is the source of what comes from the pen. These do not seem to be truths or inevitabilities at all, at least to judge from the poem's style, although I grant that they make some sense if we approach the poems, as does Swardson, expecting to find a conflict between Horatian and Platonic attitudes toward art. As I have suggested, the speaker's sprouting invention is a forced thing, in intellect as well as sound. For example, the lines describing the working and winding of the flames are not only rhythmically heavy, with a flat coincidence of metrical stress, rhythm, and idea, but have as well a stock filling of intensives to complete the form. The bustle of the poet's love does not create the sweetness of making but only a lot of machinery that is not easily kept in repair.

But when Swardson says that Herbert has "a deeper distrust . . . a suspicion of poetic craftsmanship that extends to the wit and the rhetoric, usually called baroque, stimulated by the Roman church itself in the Counter-Reformation,"[29] I believe he may lead us to the back door of something very important. Swardson's definition of poetic craftsmanship, as he elaborates this theme, seems only half the picture and a distorted half at that. Let us just say that if there is, somewhere in the poet's mind, a core of "associative rhythms" out of which lyric verse begins, it might be separate from, but pass through, the screening of conscious wit and rhetoric.[30] The "distrust" that Herbert feels is, I believe, largely unconscious, and is apprehended on the level of craftsmanship. Swardson—and other critics of the poem—do not bring this point under analysis. Although Herbert rejects mellifluous wit, he uses its style to promote his plain, no-pretence doctrine. This is possible for him because the section of the poem that articulates the doctrine of wit and pretense approaches the flat style of the popular devotional tradition. The triumph over wit is almost a Pyrrhic one,

[29] Swardson, *Poetry and the Fountain of Light*, pp. 261–62. Michael P. Gallagher, S.J., has described a much fuller view of Herbert's attitude toward the deceptions and beauties of rhetoric; see "Rhetoric, Style, and George Herbert," *ELH*, 37 (1970): 475–516. As Gallagher points out, there are occasions when the moral demands of the plain style may call for the rhetoric of a more elaborate style.

[30] I am thinking here of the sort of outline elaborated by Northrop Frye in his *Anatomy of Criticism* (Princeton: Princeton University Press, 1957), pp. 270–81, or more fully by Jacques Maritain, in *Creative Intuition in Art and Poetry* (New York: Pantheon, 1955), esp. chap. 8, "The Internalization of Music," pp. 202–32.

and rhetorically persuasive as the poem is, it still creates a self-closing form; the speaker's desire is working against the reality of the form, and the conflict is not very susceptible to resolution, in spite of the biographical materials we may bring to the poem.

The other "Jordan" is apt at first to seem fairly much of a set-up-knock-down argument, but upon closer reading the thought is far from simplistic and the development in form is quite subtle. The poem has the tentative relationship of form and meaning that we have noticed in other poems, but here Herbert is able to establish a context in which the inner tensions are deliberately planned and realized. The structure itself is simple: two stanzas set up the narrator's objections to secular verse and his criteria for judging it, and a third offers a short manifesto. The style seems mixed and more or less spasmodic throughout, but it is particularly jerky at the start:

> Who sayes that fictions onely and false hair
> Become a verse? Is there in truth no beautie?
> Is all good structure in a winding stair?
> May no lines passe, except they do their dutie
> Not to a true, but painted chair?
>
> (1-5)

The bucking meter, the mixture of short and long phrases, and the varied tempi all contribute to the outrageous tone; the snort of the opening line,

Who says that fictions onely and false hair,

helps enforce the suggestion that *no one* says that "fictions onely," etc. I can imagine no contemporary poet rising to the defense of these charges; they are too insinuating to elicit a serious answer. Far from engaging the issues themselves, the speaker is actually avoiding them. If Herbert came into the poem expecting a fight, he is not likely to get it this way: his statements are so extreme as to undercut his own position. The poem starts as a catechism in divine poetry, but it is not effective. As Herbert advises the country parson in catechizing, "the Questions must be propounded loosely and wildely [that is, neither in set form nor sequence], and then the Answerer will discover what hee is" (p. 259); this is an injunction more to spontaneity than to frenzy. Herbert may refer to the catechizing of children, and indeed the subject of his address in the first stanza of the poem is openly assumed to be naive. The opening of the poem will not elicit proper responses, and responses, as Herbert says, "are to be done not in a hudling, or slubbering fashion, gaping, or scratching the head, or spitting even in the midst of their answer, but gently and pausably, thinking what they say" (p. 231). No gentle and pausable answer is likely for the questions that the speaker of the poem has asked.

He changes his tactics in the second stanza, and the questions become more restrained, more connected with the experiencing of poetry. Again the important thing to notice is the point of view: the speaker is implicitly condemning not only the paraphernalia of pastoral but also the use of costume melodrama to hide bad craft:

> It is no verse, except enchanted groves
> And sudden arbours shadow course-spunne lines?
> Must purling streams refresh a lovers loves?
>
> (6–8)

The speaker also has some ideas on the ultimate source of such poetry. Joseph Summers has observed that the lines are full of clichés, and "the partisans of the pastoral love-poems . . . are expected to recognize the meanings (as well as the absurdities) of their own conventions."[31] But the meanings are not merely absurd. "Sudden arbours shadow course-spunne lines" has funereal implications; poorly crafted lines must meet their shades in the cardboard scenery. In this context, the "purling streams (that) refresh a lovers loves" invite comparison with another stream familiar to a reader of Herbert's generation, especially to any Cambridge alumnus. Equally a stage-prop is the "fountain like a girlond made;/ Whose bubbling waue did euer freshly well,/ Ne euer would through feruent sommer fade," in the first book of *The Faerie Queene.* "All that drunk thereof, did faint and feeble grow" (I. 7.5), and when the Redcross Knight refreshes himself in it, "poured out in loosenesse on the grassy ground" (I. 7.7) beside Duessa, "Eftsoones his manly forces gan to faile,/ And mighty strong was turned to feeble fraile" (I. 7.6). If, as Grierson specifically suggests, the poem is "a protest . . . against the pastoral allegorical poetry of

---

[31] Summers, *George Herbert,* p. 108.

the Cambridge Spenserians,"[32] the protest is made with a full awareness of Spenserian themes. Herbert is no longer making an idle rejection out of hand, as he was in the overstatement of the first stanza.

The control of thought in stanza 2 is evident in the imagery and
its associations, but the verse itself is still straining against the bounds
of the form. The ideas have darkened, but the somewhat colloquial
rhythms still predominate; the stanza even concludes with a line of
minor animation:

> Must all be vail'd while he that reads, divines,
>
> Catching the sense at two removes?
>
> (9–10)

One virtue of the rhetorical question, as a tool of argument in general, is that it allows the speaker to relish his material while rejecting
it. This happens with the negative structures in "The Quidditie" but
not here, where there is no self-indulgence in the relation between
form and meaning. "Purling streams" in sound as well as metaphor
hold little fascination for Herbert, and the larger motion of style in
the poem is going to plow them under.

The disturbed rhythms provide a link with the third and final
stanza, which, on the level of form and meaning, makes a profound
statement of the poet's attitude toward his job:

> Shepherds are honest people; let them sing:
> Riddle who list, for me, and pull for Prime:
> I envie no mans nightingale or spring;
> Nor let them punish me with losse of rime,
> Who plainly sing, *My God, My King.*
>
> (11–15)

The rhythms become more regular as the ideas begin to lighten. It
makes little difference whether the first line is read literally or ironically; either way it conveys a permissive attitude toward the writing
of pastoral verse (although Herbert could hardly be thinking about
real shepherds singing). "Riddle who list" implies a similar permis-

---

[32] *Metaphysical Lyrics and Poems of the Seventeenth Century* (Oxford: Clarendon
Press, 1921), p. 230. The poem's allusion to a familiar Platonic problem in l. 5
strengthens this judgment.

siveness toward the writing of allegorical verse. *Riddle* refers to the unraveling of the allegory, "vail'd . . . at two removes";[33] *pull for prime* apparently refers to the chancy card game of primero; and thus the line would seem to refer metaphorically to the hit-or-miss game that the reader plays in detecting the point of the allegory. Naturally this poet would never envy anyone his trite nightingales or springtime, and the pun in *spring* concludes the gambling metaphor while also suggesting the unnatural way that pastoral allegory has to work, by trapping and confining its symbols.

The last two lines maintain this density and press the conclusions out to their limits, as they apply to the speaker. Certainly, for the formal lyric poet, the loss of rhyme would be punishment and would be tantamount to losing the whole gift of making. (Compare Milton's "he knew/Himself to sing, and build the lofty rhyme.") But to whom does Herbert refer when he says "Nor let them punish me with loss of rime"? And why should the poet be punished? There is a possibility that the poet is being punished by someone else who has lost his own rhyme. The poet has not lost *his* rhyme; *punish*, then, seems to be used in its obsolete sense of "to exact from a person" (*OED*, B, 2), and the metaphor thus implies a contrast between the idle poet and the plain sensible poet. The metaphor further implies that the speaker's devotional verse has more claim to the title of "real poetry," symbolized here by the synecdoche of *rime*, than the pastoral allegory of his contemporaries. If we take the lines in this sense, the other poets are the ones who have lost their rhyme, speaking symbolically, for the poet has in the preceding stanza managed to condemn them in their own terms. Thus in the last line, when the poet finally characterizes

---

[33] The *OED* gives no reference for this specific sense of *riddle*, but the usage was not uncommon, and for an example we need go no farther than the Countess of Pembroke's Psalm 49. She is introducing not an enigma or puzzle, but a small morality on man's decay and vanity:

> Knowledg the subject is my hart conceaves,
> Wisdome the wordes shall from my mouth proceed:
> Which I will measure by melodious eare,
> And ridled speech to tuned harp accord.

(Rathmell, *The Psalms*, p. 115.) Walter King has called my attention to an amusingly ambiguous use of the term in *I Henry VI*, in which Talbot proclaims himself, before the Countess of Auvergne, to be "but the shadow of myself," to which the Countess replies, "This is a riddling merchant for the nonce!" (II. iii. 50–57). If Talbot were not so flat-footed, we could take the lines ironically and say that with an army behind his back, he actually *is* an allegorical character.

his own verse as plain song, he is doing so with a full consciousness
of his alternatives.

The progress of the argument has been defensive in an extraordinary way, for in the course of his defense the speaker has managed to
indict the alternative sort of poetry. The force of the indictment lies
in the developing relations between meaning and poetic style. We
recall that the speaker of the first stanza is obnoxiously defensive; in
fact, his attitude is like that of Herbert's forebears, one of whom in a
defensive battle "is said to have passed twice through the 'battail of
his adversaries,' armed with a poleaxe, and 'without any mortal wound
returned.' "[34]

If the first stanza works with an axe, the second works with a razor.
The movement is deft and the tone much lower. As we have noted,
the last stanza seems an apparently amicable settlement, but the
damage has been done. Even the speaker's conciliatory theme, "let
others write as they please," makes a firm judgment and leaves other
poets out herding in their honest fields or playing parlor games or
cleaving unto clichés. The poet's own attitude of high seriousness
toward his work has not vanished; the belligerence of the first stanza
became, in the second, a controlled and civilized counterattack. In the
third stanza the poet completes the rejection of profane poetry, not
by the bull-like headlong assault, but by employing its methods and
figures to establish his own style.

That final stanza is a culmination in style as well as thought. The
meters have lost their colloquial looseness; the metric, lightly disturbed for the first two lines, quickly settles into a more regular
pattern, as the lines become end-stopped and the syntax strictly
parallel. The tendency toward a gathering control and unity is evident
even in the rhymes, the first two of which are almost of the echo type
used by Sidney and also by Herbert in "Paradise": *sing/spring*, and
better, *Prime/rime*. Technically the whole poem aligns itself for an
assertion of faith, in the psalm-related manner typical of Herbert.[35]

---

[34] Leslie Stephen, in *DNB*, s.v. "Herbert, William." Sir William Herbert was the
brother of George Herbert's great-great-grandfather; the battle was at Hedgecote in
1469. Presumably it is irrelevant here that this Herbert was later taken prisoner
and executed.

[35] Herbert's integration of form and meaning in this poem has been noted
before, as by T. R. Barnes, in *English Verse: Voice and Movement from Wyatt to
Yeats* (Cambridge: Cambridge University Press, 1967). Barnes mentions Herbert's
"control of tone and melody" (p. 76) but says nothing specific on either. Superior

Yet we can even go so far as to say that the poem represents a
triumph for plain song, as the seventeenth-century devotional poet
would have understood the term, even while it uses the very tools the
poem rejects. The general situation of the speaker, his attitude toward
his situation, and the words he chooses with which to state his faith,
all seem to be based on Psalm 59, particularly the version by the
Countess of Pembroke. In all versions, the speaker of the psalm is
surrounded by enemies, whom he does not wish to see destroyed but
"put down," as the Prayer Book version has it. Further, the precise
nature of their sin is verbal:

> For the sin of their mouth, and for the words of
> their lips, they shall be taken in their pride:
> and why? their preaching is of cursing and lies.

The Countess's version uniquely stresses the speaker's dependency
upon God for his *own* strength in order to face his adversaries. Her
speaker, like Herbert's, is one in whom God's strength takes an appropriate and individual form. Neither in her psalm nor in Herbert's
poem is the singer simply a medium of God's strength. As her last
stanza has it,

> My strength doth of thy strength depend:
>   To thee I sing
> Thou art my fort, me to defend.
>   My god, My King,
> To thee I owe, and thy free grace,
> That free I rest in fearless place.

The phrase *"My God, My King"* may be underlined in Herbert's
poem because it is a quotation from the Countess's psalm—as F. P.
Wilson proposed that "most take all" is underlined in "The Quid-

---

in closeness of argument and historical sense is Douglas Peterson's study of plain
style; although Peterson does not touch on the problems I raise, his comments on
Herbert's use of plain style coincide with my conclusions on this group of poems:
it is "the medium of expression for those who for one reason or another are
opposed to the social, ethical, and literary norms represented by the Court as the
cultural center of London" (*The English Lyric from Wyatt to Donne* [Princeton:
Princeton University Press, 1967], p. 119).

ditie" to indicate its derivation—although the phrase is hardly extra-ordinary enough to assert this with absolute confidence. What is more to the point is the parallel in dramatic situation. The speaker of Herbert's poem conceives of his own strength in the same terms of independence and has the same dark attitude toward the words of his adversaries. Finally, the psalm provides a coherent framework for the study of the poem and points up the apparently permissive "let them sing."

One difficulty in the rhetoric of the poem is that the speaker's own devotion consists of only one line; the rest is all attack and counter-attack, using the ideas and images of the profane pastoral convention. But by building his argument upon the psalm, or at least developing the argument along similar lines, the speaker is able to work these ideas and images to their own defeat. The elaborate descriptions of other verse have all been in the service of devotion, just as the hasty and colloquial movement of the verse beats against the form in order to make the sober, regular ending possible. The victory is absolute, and here, perhaps more than in any other of the tentative forms we have discussed, the methods come entirely under the direct control of the poet.

FIVE

Epilogue

It is well to recall that Johnson's chief complaint against the metaphysical poets was not that their conceits were outrageous but that

> they never inquired what, on any occasion, they should have said or done, but wrote rather as beholders than partakers of human nature; as beings looking upon good and evil, impassive and at leisure; as Epicurean deities, making remarks on the actions of men, and the vicissitudes of life, without interest and without emotion.[1]

It is also well to recall that Johnson does not mention Herbert in his "Life of Cowley," and it is difficult to see exactly how his objections to what he considered this greater defect could have applied to Herbert.[2] Although Herbert is more concerned with the actions of Man rather than men, there is a general compassion in his work that one does not find so easily in Donne, Marvell, or even Vaughan, imitator as the latter is, and certainly not in the Clevelands or Cowleys with whom Johnson is most severe. One source of Herbert's compassion is his ability to find "himself in an humble way" in his life as well as in his poetry. Just as ministering to the needs of his rural congregation enabled Herbert to find his "perfect freedom," so the bathetic and homely elements of his style help locate the aristo-

[1] "Life of Cowley," in *Lives of the English Poets* (London: J. M. Dent, 1925), 1: 12.

[2] Johnson's objections to homely or indecorous similes, or to the *discordia concors*, would more than likely stand.

crat of high temper. Herbert's use of the psalms thus would argue a considerable integrity and it is not an integrity that is remote from "the vicissitudes of life." Psalm style is not an ornamental trim with Herbert, much less a glue or adhesive; it is a part of his character, his "real" character and his poetic character.

His earlier poetry and orations did not seem to be heading in this direction, and they must bear the weight of some of Johnson's criticism. But it would be wrong to expect studies in morality from a Cambridge Orator; they would be as unexpected and out of place for Herbert as they would for his modern counterpart, the Chamber of Commerce Greeter.[3] All of which makes it seem to some readers almost inevitable that there must have been, at some point in Herbert's career, a turning away from "all that worldlings prize" to the more practical concerns of Christian charity. L. C. Knights has proposed, in this regard, that Herbert actually had a "more ingrained self-distrust" all along and that his awakened sense of human responsibilities came late, after his translation to Bemerton, where he was truly able to find himself as he had not been able to before: "It was an even greater achievement to rid himself of the torturing sense of frustration and impotence and to accept the validity of his own experience."[4] As far as Herbert's psychology goes, I do not see how we shall ever be able to prove this, but it is a suggestion we should not wish to discard.

However, Knights's idea of an experiential sequence in Herbert's awakening (and the idea is not uncommon)[5] may involve some unnecessary assumptions about Herbert's character. To judge from the poems, Herbert's struggle was continuous; but there is a very human desire on the part of most readers to see some point of renunciation beyond which the struggle itself, while perhaps not ended, begins nonetheless to assume a different character. Here is a classic illustration of this desire, from Walton: Herbert is said to have told Woodnoth, on the night of his induction to Bemerton, that he could

> behold the Court with an impartial Eye, and see plainly, that it
> is made up of *Fraud,* and *Titles,* and *Flattery,* and many other such

[3] Thus the surprise of Herbert's oration on the return of Prince Charles and Buckingham from Spain (1623); under the circumstances, Herbert's absolute condemnation of war shows great earnestness and something like courage.

[4] Knights, *Explorations* (London and New York: George W. Stewart, 1947), p. 140.

[5] See also A. Alvarez, *The School of Donne* (London: Chatto and Windus, 1961), pp. 58 ff.

empty, imaginary painted Pleasures; Pleasures, that are so empty, as not to satisfy when they are enjoy'd.[6]

These are hard words, and the circumstances would call them out of anyone. Yet Herbert's later judgments would not always be so sure. Walton's picture is very like the now discredited one of Jack Donne versus Doctor Donne, and for a number of reasons—not the least of them Walton's factual inaccuracy—we have come less and less to accept this sort of easy reversal. In Herbert's case, and if we accept implicitly Knight's hypothesis and the dating of the poems, the usual view seems to be that Herbert's battle was one that *did* change its character after his decision to go to Bemerton.

Yet if we can draw upon our study of psalmody and Herbert's use of it, we may regard the poems of Herbert's ministry, that is, the bulk of *The Temple*, as representing a submerged continuation of the mentality that had preceded them. Let us back up for a moment. As we have seen, the popular metrical psalm had emphasized by its crude verse technique, and was notorious for its emphasis upon, the violent passages in the Psalms themselves. The more elegant psalms which came later were notable for their restraint and their emphasis upon intellectual relationships and lyric style, and their style acted to keep the violence at a distance. (These characteristics, at least the second set, are not necessarily those which early seventeenth-century poets might have noticed, but this is not to discredit their existence or operation.)

It is here, I believe, that we may observe a connection of form and idea on the most profound level. We have noted before that by Herbert's time there was a convention in the metrical psalms by which stylistic homeliness in devotion had come to be identified with the more violent moods of the Psalms, that is to say, aggression or repentance, while stylistic elegance was taken as indicative of more controlled emotions. Other poets, contemporaries of Herbert, seem to have noticed conventions of this sort, as we remarked in the historical chapter, but only Herbert was to realize the full significance of them in poetry. In this respect, Herbert uses psalm form in a highly personal way. For it may be that the metrical psalms, regarded collectively, provided a model for Herbert of a way to maintain both one's pride and humility. Herbert's fusion of elegant and bathetic styles,

---

[6] Walton, *Lives*, p. 289. This is quoted (with some light editing) in *Explorations*, pp. 140–41, where Knights offers a sustained analysis of the sort I am discussing.

represented by two strains of psalmody, may be a way for his pride and aggression to be employed in a manner acceptable to his consciousness and his vision of God. It is a part of the whole process of weakness becoming strength.

If this process is to satisfy a temperament as restless as Herbert's, it must be constant, and for a temperament as meticulous as Herbert's, it must apply to every aspect of the poet's existence. Thus the great diversity of forms in which the strands appear: "Except thou make us dayly, we shall spurn/ Our own salvation." The effect and the effort are like those in the Psalms themselves, and what Augustine said of the Psalms may apply both to Herbert's poems and to his character: "The rational and well-ordered concord of diverse sounds in harmonious variety suggests the well ordered City of God."[7] It is not necessary to say anything beyond this. Herbert's use of his poetic materials is such that he is finally able to commit even his own proud and rebellious instincts to the service of God.

[7] *The City of God,* trans. Marcus Dods (New York: Modern Library, 1960), p. 595.

Index